*Silent Exodus—
Parents' Silent Suffering*

Silent Exodus—
Parents' Silent Suffering

Empowering Chinese Canadian Parents in Ethno-Religious Communities Impacted by Generational Assimilation and Dechurching

Matthew Richard Sheldon Todd

WIPF & STOCK • Eugene, Oregon

SILENT EXODUS—PARENTS' SILENT SUFFERING
Empowering Chinese Canadian Parents in Ethno-Religious Communities Impacted by Generational Assimilation and Dechurching

Copyright © 2025 Matthew Richard Sheldon Todd. All rights reserved. Except for brief quotations in critical publications or reviews, no part of this book may be reproduced in any manner without prior written permission from the publisher. Write: Permissions, Wipf and Stock Publishers, 199 W. 8th Ave., Suite 3, Eugene, OR 97401.

Wipf & Stock
An Imprint of Wipf and Stock Publishers
199 W. 8th Ave., Suite 3
Eugene, OR 97401

www.wipfandstock.com

PAPERBACK ISBN: 979-8-3852-4452-2
HARDCOVER ISBN: 979-8-3852-4453-9
EBOOK ISBN: 979-8-3852-4454-6

VERSION NUMBER 05/07/25

All Scripture quotations, unless otherwise indicated, are taken from the Holy Bible, New International Version®, NIV®. Copyright ©1973, 1978, 1984, 2011 by Biblica, Inc.™ Used by permission of Zondervan. All rights reserved worldwide. www.zondervan.com. The "NIV" and "New International Version" are trademarks registered in the United States Patent and Trademark Office by Biblica, Inc.™

Scripture quotations marked "NASB" taken from the (NASB®) New American Standard Bible®, Copyright © 1960, 1971, 1977, 1995, 2020 by The Lockman Foundation. Used by permission. All rights reserved. lockman.org.

> It is the glory of God to conceal a matter;
> to search out the matter is the glory of kings.
>
> PROVERBS 25:2, NIV

Contents

Preface | ix
Acknowledgments | xiii
Abbreviations | xiv
Illustrations | xv

1 Purposeful Pathways for Parenting | 1
2 Impact of Dechurching on Parents | 10
3 Probability of Handing On the Faith | 23
4 Wrestling with Cultural Assimilation | 32
5 A Theology of Family | 53
6 A Social Sciences Framework for Family | 84
7 Breaking Research on Parents' Silent Suffering | 114
8 Supporting Impacted Parents | 132

Appendix | 145
Bibliography | 163
Index | 175

Preface

MANY ARE AWARE OF the broad cultural issue and trends of youth and emerging young adults leaving the church. One pastoral observation is identifying parents who get stuck in a rut over the dechurching of their children. The challenge cannot be overstated: many immigrant church parents are coping with a Silent Exodus. The attachment disruption and, in many cases, deculturalization of their youth away from their ethno-religious communities can be stressful, creating high levels of unresolved anxiety, guilt, regret and frustration. Often the deep wounding and hidden burden on parents is covered in a shroud of silence which also contributes to impeding healthy family and cultural development. Leaders (clergy) need to gain some skills on intergenerational impact of dechurching and learn to diagnose symptoms in parents for the sake of building healthy families and churches. This book identifies parents' silent suffering when parents' kids leave their immigrant (ethnic, bicultural, Asian) church. In particular, it reflects on a study done with Chinese Canadian churches. The book aims at identifying ways Chinese Canadian immigrant Christian parents are impacted by the generational assimilation of their second-generation children when youth abandon the faith and ethno-religious communities. The original contribution to knowledge is substantiating that Chinese Canadian Christian parents are variably impacted emotionally, spiritually, socially, and psychologically by the exit of their youth from ethno-religious communities, and the book proposes supportive recommendations. The book involved interdenominational participants either formerly from or currently in Chinese churches. Qualitative research was utilized to elicit findings on the impact of the Silent Exodus on parents. The significance of the discussion in the book is that it provides solutions for parents facing family complications during generational assimilation. A discovery was the connection between the Silent Exodus and five differentiated high-to-low

Preface

intensity impacts on parents. I draw insights from sociology of religion; developmental psychology; emerging adulthood theory; life cycle and social learning theory; and cultural anthropology interfacing with a theology of the family. Families experiencing generational disconnect and difficult parenting transitions in ethno-religious communities during acculturation will find ideas here to build healthier families. My journey into writing this book was an extension of a former book titled *Crisis of English Ministries in Chinese Canadian Churches* (Wipf & Stock). At that time, I saw a need to find ways to promote Canadian-born Chinese[1] remain-in cohesion with Chinese churches. I was told by a conference leader, who published a review on that book, that there was a missing voice: the parents', whose hearts' desire is that the family faith circle not be broken. I was finding that the blame for the Silent Exodus was being targeted primarily at clergy and parents. Given my experience serving in the clergy and as a parent who has gone through the full cycle of parenting (and I am still parenting), I intuitively felt that laying all the blame for the youth's leaving the church on parents and clergy wasn't entirely accurate. I believed there were other dynamics at play in the developmental process and forces of culture, which I describe in this book. Because of my former writing on the Silent Exodus, I became aware that next to nothing was being reported about the impact of the Silent Exodus on the parents and the church. My question for this book began to take shape in separate discussions with various counselors, theologians, and clergy. I was glad to have completed my book's data collection for phases one to two of the study prior to the pandemic. It allowed me to capture a snapshot of the impact of the Silent Exodus on parents without confusing it with the closing of churches during the epidemic or confusing it with the losses of youth post-pandemic. The pandemic escalated the Silent Exodus and it heightens the need to be supportive to parents in these transitions. My hope is that the recommended supportive strategies will empower leaders and assist parents in the challenging transitions they find themselves in when impacted by the Silent Exodus of their youth from their churches. During part of the writing of this book, the world was struggling with the COVID-19 pandemic, and many realized church is not all about buildings. I have thought about the irony of writing about the impact of the Silent Exodus (youth leaving the church) on parents when, during this period, families could not attend worship in a church building. It was a reminder there are those *not* in the church who have faith in Christ. In *The*

---

1. CBC = Canadian Born Chinese

Preface

City of God, Augustine highlighted that there are people who have faith in Christ but do not attend church.[2] How strange it was writing about the impact of the Silent Exodus[3] on Chinese parents when my country was closing churches. The biblical term for "the church" is "ecclesia," meaning "the called-out ones." The idea is that of being called to a Person, that Person being God. I especially want to dedicate this volume to the memory of my former "called" ministry colleague who had a passion to serve amongst Chinese parents and Chinese families, Rev. Tom Cheung. We had discussed a meeting to talk about this venture and his participation in one of the clergy surveys, but before we could meet, his bright light was abruptly taken out of this life in 2019. I also want to dedicate this book to the many Chinese parents who have wrestled with generational assimilation in their families and churches in the struggle to keep their families in the faith community. To the Chinese church leaders, clergy, and denominational workers, this study resonates with your labor and hope for a future for generations to come. It echoes and resonates also with the indigenous seventh-generation principle that the decisions made today might result in a sustainable ethno-religious community seven generations later.

Chapter 1, "Purposeful Pathways for Parenting," presents a baseline and foundation for godly parenting with biblical purpose. Those of you just looking to understand the impact of dechurching on parents can turn to chapter 2, which discusses a summary of the problem, the current situation, and the significance of the impact on parents. Chapter 3 explores the probability risks and opportunities of handing on the faith. It reviews the broad cultural phenomenon of youth leaving the church, generational assimilation in ethno-religious communities, the current cultural delays of adulthood, and how parents with high religious commitment tend to be more intensely impacted by youth leaving the church. Chapter 4 explores the issue of parents wrestling with the cultural assimilation of their locally born children and the impact of generational acculturation. Chapter 5 provides a theological framework for understanding the family and why youth leave churches. The section moves towards a biblical mandate and goal for the family of God. Chapter 6 explores a social-sciences framework to understand the attrition of youth from ethnic churches, but the findings are broadly applicable to all churches. Chapter 7 introduces my breaking

---

2. Augustine, *City of God*, xi.

3. Emerging young adults *leaving* from the Asian church they grew up in is labeled the "Silent Exodus."

Preface

qualitative research on parents' silent suffering. Details on the methods used in this study are briefly provided. Chapter 8 outlines the findings of all three phases of the study on how to concretely support parents who are impacted by their dechurched youth and young adults. This chapter cites the significance, implications, insights, and recommendations of the study. Chapters 2, 7, and 8 are the heart of the study, and some readers may just want to focus on those sections. For those interested in reading the 799-page raw version of the study refer to this footnote.[4]

---

4. Todd, "Empowering."

Acknowledgments

I WANT TO ACKNOWLEDGE my wife for the time she gave me during the thousands of hours invested in writing this book. For the support that went behind this work, I want to thank Dr. Martine Audeoud, Dr. David Chan, Dr. Les Hirst, Dr. Eddie Kwok, research consultant Willie Kwong, Rev. Larry Anderson, and Nick Suen. You all provided reflection, referrals, feedback, encouragement, resources, advice, assistance, suggestions, and a listening ear. Willie, you have shared my soul on this topic; thank you for all the effort you shared in conversations and assisting me in the focus group coding. I also want to thank former conference minister David Leung, who served with the British Columbia Mennonite Brethren Churches for the Chinese congregations. He was looking for my previous book to include comparative perceptions of OBC[1] parents on the Silent Exodus. There was identified a need to include OBC's general reasons for CBC's changing or leaving churches. Because of his previous review of my former book, my surveys behind this book capture that perspective and takes it into account for the purposes of being able to strategize "an optimal model of vision for change."[2] Lastly, I want to express thanks to the Chinese clergy and parents interviewed in the data collections of phases one to three and the additional Chinese parachurch consultants. Thank you for being generous in sharing a personal and important side of your family and life with me for this book.

1. OBC = Overseas Born Chinese; first generation immigrant Chinese.
2. See Leung, "Research."

Abbreviations

ABC	American-Born Chinese
BCP	Broad Cultural Phenomenon
CBC	Canadian-Born Chinese
CFG	Clergy Focus Group
CM	Cantonese Ministries
CRC	Canadian-Raised Chinese
DGR	Dutch, German, Russian
DO	Drop Out
EA	Emerging Adulthood
EM	English Ministries
GA	Generational Assimilation
LBC	Locally Born Chinese
LRC	Locally Raised Chinese
MB	Mennonite Brethren
MBCCA	Mennonite Brethren Chinese Churches Association
MO	Move On
NACC	North American Chinese Churches
OBC	Overseas-Born Chinese / First Generation Immigrant Chinese
PFG1	Parent Focus Group 1
PFG2	Parent Focus Group 2
PGMBC	Pacific Grace Mennonite Brethren Church
PMPGMBC	Port Moody Pacific Grace Mennonite Brethren Church
PRC	Parent Religious Commitment

Illustrations

Figures

1. Strategies and solutions recommended on how to support parents
A2 Phase 1: Clergy survey invitation to participate
A3 Phase 2: Parent Questionnaire

Tables

1. Overview of the Three Phases of Research
2. Demographics
3. Top Eight Clergy Observations of Impacts on Parents
4. Phase 2 Parents' Self-Report on How Long the Exodus Impact Took to Settle
5. Mean Perceived Impacts of CBC Exodus on Exodus Parents as Reported by Phase 3 Participants
6. Major Themes in Focus Group Discussion
7. Interventions, Strategies, and Solutions from Recommendations to Help Impacted Parents
A 8. Phase 2 Question Types and Topics
A 9. Phase 2 Parents' Rating of 33 Emotional Reactions and Comparison with Clergy Observations

A 10. Emotional Reactions to the Impact of the Silent Exodus: Comparison of Top 8 Phase 1 Clergy Observations and Top 8 Phase 2 Parents' Self-Rating

A 11. Guide for Moderators of Phase 3 Focus Groups

A 12. Phase 2 OBC Parents' Experience of Interaction with People at Church About CBC Exodus

A 13. Shows the Age and Stage of Life the Child Left the Church

A 14. Shows the Comparisons Between OBC's and CBC's Top Reasons to Exodus the Church

A 15. Main Reason Parents Thought Child Left the Church

Resource

An Example of a Parent Workshop for Impacted Parents

1

Purposeful Pathways for Parenting

THESE DAYS, PEOPLE ARE curious about their ancestry. They will spend thousands of hours searching through ancestry.com or 23andMe, hoping to better understand their identity, their inherited traits, or the reasons their families turned out the way they did. It is even more important to pay attention to one's spiritual heritage and identity because godly influence can be intergenerational and have eternal implications. We don't begin Christian parenting in a vacuum. I want to start painting with broad strokes a general sketch of Christian teaching on parenting. For parents with young kids, this provides a foundational baseline and general road map. For parents with older youth and young adults who have dechurched, this chapter may affirm that you were properly engaged or that there were a few things missing. The hope is that you will see grace or find grace for your journey. If you are new to the Christian faith, you will want to integrate your Christian faith into your parenting. If the Christian faith has been handed down to you from your families, you will want to grab hold of a Christian biblical vision for your family because you know that your parenting influence matters forever. If you are an intergenerational Christian, have you given any thought to the history of past believers in your family who intentionally bridged the gospel to you? I have memories of my maternal grandparents telling me about the missionaries and an itinerant country preacher in my family line. I remember the faith of my great-grandmother and great-aunt, both saying grace at the same time (because they were deaf) during the Christmas dinner. My great-aunt's husband was an influential minister in the family. By the grace of God, both of my grandparents died in the faith, and both my parents and my wife's parents embrace faith in Christ. We know that our parents prayed for us. Our parents had a measure of influence on us in placing our faith in Christ. I remember my dad making special Sunday night arrangements for me to be baptized at age twelve. My wife's father studied in Italy to be a priest and later became an Italian Protestant in Canada and a faithful leader in the church. The family were all baptized at the same service when my wife was fifteen. When my wife and I married, our maxim was, "We are going to fear God and work hard." We weren't thinking about children yet, but when they did come, the "work hard" part really kicked in. Then it was time for us to ask ourselves: "Why did God give us this family?" Part of the answer is the opportunity and responsibility to participate in God's redemptive and missional plan of salvation. It was our turn to recognize the historical interval we were living in and to bridge the gospel to our children and grandchildren. It was our turn to recognize that we would leave a legacy that has not yet been fully actualized. Since the day my first child was born, I began learning what it means to parent through a variety of developmental life stages. I thought I had a good handle on my job description as a new parent, as I had psychology and theology undergraduate degrees and experience as a youth pastor. I had seen a wide range of issues with Christian youth and different parenting styles, and I thought those experiences gave me an advantage. I didn't know it at the time, but I was in for a truckload of adjustment, new learning, and recalibration. As my parenting experiences unfolded, I found that there is what you know but also what you know you don't know and what you don't know about what you don't know. I had inherited ideas on parenting that I would default to but that would need to be deconstructed and adjusted in order to align with biblical values and interdisciplinary insights. I came to realize that I am not a "superparent," that I am broken and a sinner saved by grace, and that I have stumbled to parent well. I have had joys and challenges in every stage of my children's growth. Some of my experiences with my children have been precious, especially when they were babies, toddlers, and elementary and middle school students. And then the teen years hit, and the emerging young adult stage. I recall the many things that we as parents did (and are still doing) to be intentional in helping our children and pointing them towards Christ.

One of my hobbies is gardening, which offers an analogy for what we encounter in our parenting journey. Gardening has its seasons. It starts with a vision of what I hope my garden will look like. In the spring, I need to bring in good soil and turn the old soil. My focus is on creating a good environment for the growth that I envision taking place. Initially, this is labor-intensive. Then I proceed with planting seeds, germinated seedlings, and small plants and organizing them into sections and rows. I won't be able to control the weather (that's in God's hands), although I hope for plenty of sunshine, but I will need to be diligent with watering, staking, weeding, and pruning. I always look forward to enjoying the fruit of my labors by midsummer and early fall, putting food from my garden on my table. Some years are great, and some years have been challenging. My harvests have been negatively affected by a heat wave, an ant infestation, and an occasional rat, skunk, or squirrel stealing from my garden. One year, a bear dug up and stole my carrots. But every year, there's been some kind of harvest, whether some of the produce is big, small, or even deformed.

Some of us got into parenting with careful planning, and others of us didn't. One of our children was planned like a scientific experiment—but we didn't anticipate his handicaps. The other child came to us by adoption. In both cases, we felt the sovereign hand of God in it: "Children are a heritage from the LORD" (Ps 127:3). Part of parenting looks like this: we seek to root our family in strong churches, God's spiritual family, where the gospel is faithfully taught, where there are safe places for our families to be loved and cared for, and where spiritual connections and godly friendships can be made. We were intentional in having our children regularly be a part of the church with ministries relevant to them, such as children's church, Sunday school, youth groups, youth camps, and being a part of our family groups. We worked hard to get our hands on resources that could nurture the spiritual growth of our children in our home. When our son was a little guy, I have great memories of reading through C. S. Lewis's *Narnia* stories and telling him dramatic Bible stories. I discovered with our girl that when we played board games or when I took her for walks around the lake or along the river near our home, it was easier then to communicate values. At such times, she would be "a chatty Sally" and often open up about what she thought about God and faith. I looked for lots of opportunities to strike up a conversation or a teaching moment to talk about God and influence my children. We have not been perfect parents, but we have been intentional to influence our children's spiritual formation. I have also discovered that our children reexamined the beliefs that they learned in our families to form their own views.

That is why everything we do in the family life cycle counts. My guess is that you have picked up this book because you are interested in finding preventative and proactive things that you can do to increase the probability of influencing your minor or adult children or grandchildren in the faith. I commend you because Scripture conveys God's intention for the faith community and the family. God has generations in view, that one generation would pass on the faith about God's faithfulness to the next generations (Gen 12:3; 17:4, 7; Exod 10:2; 13:8,14; Deut 4:8–9; Ps 78:1–4; Gal 3:8). We have an example in the Bible of Paul recognizing that Timothy's family had done just that. Paul said in 2 Tim 3:15, "From infancy you have known the Holy Scriptures, which are able to make you wise for salvation through faith in Christ Jesus." Paul commented in 2 Tim 1:5, "I am reminded of your sincere faith, which first lived in your grandmother Lois and your mother Eunice and, I am persuaded, now lives in you also." This wasn't a second-hand faith—Timothy had now professed his own personal faith in Jesus Christ. What does it look like for you to live your faith in your home? In 1 Tim 1:5, Paul described a faith "which first lived in" Timothy's older family members—it was an alive faith that shaped a way of living and was modeled in the home. Acts 16:1 tells us that Timothy was born of a Greek father and a Jewish mother who became a Christian. We might be getting a sense that Timothy didn't come from a picture-perfect Jewish home. It's possible it was a household with two belief systems (Judeo-Christian and pagan); this can be one way of reading Acts 16:1: "But whose father was a Greek." In the twenty-first century, we would have said that Timothy grew up in an interfaith home, similar to having a father who was a Buddhist or Muslim. Researchers call marriages where each spouse identifies with a different spiritual faith as "religious heterogamy." Acts 16:3 tells us that Timothy was not circumcised, so we get a clearer indication that the father wasn't observant of Judaism or first-century Christianity either. Given this, there is every indication that Timothy's mother and grandmother had to be intentional in handing on the faith to him. Mission accomplished! Timothy is later mentioned in seven of Paul's letters to churches. There was a good amount of time and energy devoted to instilling faith in Timothy.

The Bible advocates for a multigenerational transmission of the faith (through parents, grandparents, aunts, and uncles), and we are seeing this backed up in research. Psalm 145:4 tells us, "One generation commends your works to another." Training is parents' first obligation in raising children, and this includes spiritual formation. Parents, enroll your children in the ministries of the church, but don't look to the church to raise your children—the church is to supplement what parents are doing at home. Parents, you must teach your children first because the secular culture will communicate its ideological worldview and ethos to them. In the secular culture, your children will be exposed to secular teachings on morality, the origin of the world, and many other topics. A key goal of parental training is the socializing function. God has designed families as a means to teach children and direct them on a path to responsible maturity. Parents are to give a vision to their children, tied to gifts and eternal purposes. Psalm 127:1–5 states, "Unless the Lord builds the house, the builders labor in vain. . . . Children are a heritage from the Lord . . . like arrows in the hands of a warrior." Parents are to point their children, like arrows, towards a purposeful, godly life and help them build deep roots and cultivate a love for God. Parents, you should want to intentionally be the first to tell your next generation about God's care. Deuteronomy 6:5–9 advocates that parents be deliberate every day, in every space, and in every room to communicate to their children: "Love the Lord your God with all your heart and with all your soul and with all your strength. These commandments . . . are to be upon your hearts. Impress them on your children. *Talk* about them when you *sit* at home and when you *walk* along the road, when you *lie down* and when you *get up*" (emphasis mine). There are things we can do to point our children to experience God, but it is not so much about "doing devotions" as about you, the parent, "being devoted." Our children watch us carefully. They watch how we love God. They watch our prayer life. They witness how we live in hope, when we forgive, when we are generous (when we give of our funds, time, and talents), and how we practically help and love others. They watch to see if we prioritize participation in the faith community or a small group. They observe how we behave on a mission trip with them. They watch to see how we include faith in Christ in their bedtime stories, when we are in the car together, and when we are in conversation at the dinner table. We are encouraged as parents in Deut 11:19 to "fix these words of mine in your hearts and minds; tie them as symbols on your hands and bind them on your foreheads. Teach them to your children." Parents, be inspired by Joshua's words in Josh 24:15 when he said, "As for me and my household, we will serve the Lord." We are called to predispose our children to the faith and to increase the probability of handing on the faith. It's about being faithful in our duty as parents as we invite our children into a walk with Jesus. We should also remind our children that God looks at the heart, and we should encourage them to "guard your heart, for everything you do flows from it" (Prov 4:23). As parents, we should want to reflect the heart of God, connect with our children, and incline our children to have a heart for God. Parents, we should be intentional in sharing and living the good news with our children. Psalm 78:3–4 describes "things we have heard and known, things our ancestors have told us. We will not hide them from their descendants; we will tell the next generation the praiseworthy deeds of the Lord, his power, and the wonders he has done." At each stage throughout the various stages of our children's lives—infant, toddler, preschooler, elementary student, teenager, emerging young adult, adult—we should be adjusting our approach to encourage them to internalize the gospel for themselves. God wants "godly offspring" (Mal 2:15). Knowing that God intended the family to flourish and develop into the purposes of God should move parents to regularly pray for each child. If you have spent any time in the church, you will have become aware of families with multigenerational legacies of influence. Longitudinal studies have captured some of this in the literature.[1] One fascinating historical study is the comparative analysis of Max Jukes's and Jonathan Edwards's family trees. This study revealed some interesting data about the legacies of influence on successive generations. Max Jukes's family legacy was studied by sociologist A. E. Winship[2] in the late 1800s. His legacy came to the attention of Winship because forty-two different men in the New York prison system were traced back to Max Jukes. Of Jukes's 887 descendants, 7 were murders, 60 were thieves, 190 were prostitutes, 150 were career criminals, 310 were paupers, and over 100 were physically wrecked by alcoholism. Of the 887 descendants that were studied, 300 died prematurely. The cost to New York was in the millions. By comparison, the study also looked at the family legacy of Jonathan Edwards, who lived during the same period.[3] Jonathan Edwards is best known for being a college president and a popular Puritan minister, theologian, and missionary in the 1700s. Jonathan Edwards was raised by godly parents, Rev. Timothy Edwards and Esther Stoddard (the daughter of Rev. Solomon Stoddard). He enrolled at Yale University at the age of thirteen and later became one of the early presidents of Princeton. He and his wife Sara had eleven children. Every evening, Edwards would spend an hour in conversation with his family, and the two

---

1. See Bengston et al., *Families*.
2. Richard L. Dugdale conducted the study.
3. Albert Edward Winship conducted the study.

parents would pray over each child. They passed on a godly legacy. Winship traced the descendants of Jonathan Edwards for almost 150 years after his death.[4] Jonathan Edwards's descendants include thirteen college presidents, sixty-five professors, seventy-five military officers, eighty public servants, sixty authors, sixty doctors, thirty judges, one hundred pastors, one hundred lawyers, three United States senators, and one vice president (Aaron Burr Jr., vice president during President Thomas Jefferson's first term). This study on the multigenerational legacies of two families is fascinating and has received plenty of critique. I want to state the obvious at the outset, that not all godly families have the same legacy of handing on the faith to all of their children. I am not saying that Edwards had a perfect family. He had a grandmother who was certifiably insane and an uncle who murdered an aunt, and Edwards himself did own slaves in his time. There are no perfect families. We all have fallen natures, and we all have free will. Nevertheless, Edwards led a complicated life of faith in his generation and passed that on to his family. Also, it is true that some ungodly family lines have godly descendants; God's grace shows up in unexpected places; Winship's study has received plenty of critique; and some of the differences with the family legacies can justifiably be attributed to socioeconomic status. Nevertheless, it is generally true that the life you live can determine the legacy you leave. Godly influence and legacy are important. The Bible's genealogies reveal the ongoing influence of a godly legacy. The influence we bring to bear can make a big difference in people's lives. We are called to be salt and light, and this includes in our families. Traits of faithful parenting are cited throughout the Old and New Testaments. Ephesians 5:22–33 and Col 3:18–21 elaborate on how family relationships are to be God-honoring. One of the most important traits of faithful parenting is love. Love is put into action by attending to basic needs, offering affection, listening and watching, affirming, giving opportunities for play, giving comfort, giving advice, and directing your child's giftings. Another trait of faithful parenting is respect, which means encouraging your child to obtain wisdom (Prov 4:20–21). Another trait of faithful parenting is establishing boundaries and limits. This includes teaching our children to avoid evil (Prov 4:14; 15:9, 26) and advising them on the choice of friends. It also involves discipline; no one likes to discipline, but it is necessary since it "gives wisdom" (Prov 29:15). Proverbs 29:17 says, "Discipline your children, and they will give you peace." Hebrews 12:1 discusses the issue of creating moral boundaries to control what

---

4. See Winship, *Jukes-Edwards*.

you let in and what you keep out. Parents, don't neglect this. Children are like a garden: if you neglect a garden, it quickly becomes problematic, overrun with weeds and unproductive. Ephesians 6:4 and Col 3:21 instruct parents in another trait: not to be overly forceful or picky, exasperating their children in the process. Parents, we are teaching our children how to live under authority, and this is transferable to every authority. We should be helping our children understand why they do the things they do and to reflect on motivational issues such as pride, fear, selfishness, and insecurity. Another positive trait of faithful parenting is modeling grace and forgiveness: our parenting should be grace-based rather than shame-based; we need to be quick to forgive and not be pharisaical. We should be modeling thankfulness (Phil 1:3–4), modeling adaptability (Phil 4:11: "I have learned to be content whatever the circumstances"), and giving our children quality time.

If your shoulders are feeling a bit heavier after reading this far, remember that we should be learning to trust the grace of God in our parenting. Parenting can expose our sinfulness, for example, by being impatient or indulging our tendency to yell—how easily we can be that way! We need to live in constant readiness to ask forgiveness and rest in God's grace. Christ's work in our family is not based on us being perfect parents. We all fail in some ways. I confess that there were times in the ministry when I was a workaholic. I needed to ask my older child to forgive me for that.[5] And there have been times I put more emphasis on Christian behavior than on having a right heart with God: I was more concerned about how my child's behavior made me feel or look than the state of my child's heart with God. It can be hard to admit we want our kids to be good so we can be proud of them and our neighbors be proud of us. At times, I was trying to live my dreams through my children. I have asked God more than once to forgive me and help me do it right—and God is gracious. Being a Christian parent is not about the parent; it's about God and trusting in his grace where we need it. After my older child went prodigal for nine years and later came back to the faith, I asked him, "Where did we as parents get it right, and where did we get it wrong?" He expressed appreciation for the fact that we cared for him and introduced him to Jesus, but he also said that we were overprotective on things that he was curious about. If we were perfect parents, our children wouldn't need Jesus. We need Jesus just as much as

---

5. Research identifies how the gospel is helpful in intergenerational reconciliation. See Lu et al., "Chinese Immigrant Families."

our children do. The things that increase the probability of our youth remaining in the faith start at home. Here are two true things that you need to remember: parental influence is real, and God has given you your child. In transmitting the faith to our children, there are longitudinal studies that show what will improve the outcomes for our children years later. Studies of young adults show that there is a higher probability of handing on the faith when both parents are committed to their faith in the home and church, when both parents are committed to the same faith in a healthy marriage, and when parents practice reasonable and authoritative parenting.[6] Our children are watching our testimony (see Exod 13:8) in our marriage, our faith, our parenting, and our hardships. The health of our marriage and parenting will influence the spiritual trajectory of our children. That is why it's important to think about the home environment we are creating. Parents, you are the primary source of socialization for your children,[7] and handing on the faith is highly dependent on how much your children are exposed to faith by you.[8] Lower levels of handing on the faith are seen in longitudinal studies where one or both parents are not committed to the faith and where there are unhealthy marriages and unhealthy parenting styles. This is empowering information because it shows a way forward. In a former study I conducted,[9] I discovered that CBCs were more likely to stay in their family churches if their parents positively modeled Christian faith. When parents spoke positively about the church in front of their children and were constructive role models, the young adults tended to have a more positive outlook on the church; they often used the word "fulfilling" to express their growing-up experience. Parents, if you want to increase the probability of handing on the faith to your children, get serious about having a committed relationship to Christ yourself. Be in Scripture, prayer, church, and adult discipleship groups (small groups). Keep growing. Be a real Christian. Regularly invite Christ into your marriage and parenting. Be intentional in working on your relationship with your child. The research is clear: passing on the faith begins at home and in the family. I would like you to think about this question as you read through this book: where do you see your challenge in parenting? That will be the starting place to take up the shield of faith, pray, and engage in your calling as a parent.

6. Gunnoe and Moore, "Predictors," 614.
7. Petts, "Parental Religiosity," 19.
8. Petts, "Parental Religiosity," 2.
9. Todd, *English Ministry Crisis*.

2

Impact of Dechurching on Parents

MOST PARENTS WANT TO provide their children with a better future and greater opportunities than they grew up with. Many parents join a church of other like-minded parents with this goal in mind. I think it is easy for parents to dream about their children having positive and fun developmental experiences, moving successfully through the educational system, going off to college, and landing a good job. This is fine, but the call on the Christian parent is broader and more holistic, tied into God's eternal spiritual purposes. We all have dreams for our family and children. Maybe one of your dreams has been that your children would remain in the faith, or that they would remain with you, worshiping together in the same church, serving and taking up leadership. What is your dream for your family and children? Do you have a clear sense of calling? Intentional parenting means having a carefully thought-out plan. In anything you do, if you don't have an anchor (principles, a purpose, a goal) or a vision (the long picture, where you are casting your "fishing line," so to speak), then you will get bogged down or sidetracked in your calling as a parent. The old saying goes, "Aim at nothing, and you will hit nothing."

If I had a nickel for every time I had a conversation with parents who had raised their children in the church and had then seen the children leave the church, I might be rich. Every time I mentioned that I was doing research on the impact of dechurching youth on parents, fathers and mothers would often tell me about their adult children who no longer attended church. You probably know of many godly Christian parents whose children left the church or went prodigal. Hurting parents can be the forgotten people in the story of a prodigal child. In the past, when I was called on to officiate a wedding, frequently, one of the parents would quietly reveal deep discouragement that, after raising their children in the church, their adult child had left the church or the faith or had married a spouse with no faith or from a different religion. Parents can feel like failures when their young adult children give themselves over to prodigal living and engage in a range of embarrassing lifestyle choices that might include leaving the church, cohabitating, abusing substances, brushes with the law, or other sinful practices. Parents in these situations have disclosed to me deep confusion, making statements such as, "We loved them, and we did our best to raise them—how did it get so far off the rails?" Parents often go through this alone, and yet, statistically, every church has both prodigals and parents who walk a lonely road of defeat. Davis and Graham's 2023 national study noted, "We know of almost no parents over the age of fifty who don't have at least one adult child who is dechurched." They also state that "no . . . ethnicity has escaped the dechurching" phenomenon."[1] Smith and Adamczyk's 2021 national study on handing down the faith stated that "there are many parents who have so many sorrows over their adult kids, it's ridiculous."[2] Why is it important to know how parents are impacted by dechurched children? Because if we don't know how parents are affected or what the identifiers are, we won't know how to help them. Are parents navigating these impacts in a healthy, biblical way? If not, what's missing for parents to be able to process their impact experiences? There appears to be plenty of anecdotal evidence that parents are impacted by their youth leaving the church and faith, but the question is: in what ways are they impacted? I am going to talk about the gap that occurs in a transitional period of the life cycle of parenting and also address the need the gap represents. Preparing for this transitional period is often not carefully thought through by parents.

In the field of immigration and the intergenerational transmission of religion and culture, Chinese North American churches have been identified as leading church growth statistics. However, one challenge is that they have also been identified as having a high level of second-generation Exodus.[3]

1. Davis and Graham, *Great Dechurching*, 9.
2. Smith and Adamczyk, *Handing Down the Faith*, 25.
3. There does not seem to be precise statistics on second-generation attrition; many of the studies have been classified as informal, anecdotal, or surveys in specific regions. Sohn, "Attitudes of Asian American Christians," 1–3, 17–29. For the interested reader, see Chuang, "Silent Exodus."

There is a gap in the research regarding *how* parents are impacted by this Exodus. The purpose of this book is to identify *how* Chinese Canadian Christian immigrant parents are impacted by the Exodus of their second generation from their ethno-religious communities in order to strategize leadership and propose ways to address those findings. This book addresses the problem of the impact from generational assimilation on Canadian Chinese immigrant Christian parents when their children separate from the faith and Chinese family church. I want to emphasize early that this book is not focusing on the multiple factors that are behind the emerging adult leaving, nor is this book focused on the outcome of emerging adults after they leave. Emerging adults *leaving* the Chinese church they grew up in is labeled the Silent Exodus, which is in essence defined as the *leaving and exiting* from their churches. This book does an assessment of the impact of the *leaving*, recognizing that the *impact* may be variably positive or negative on the parent depending on timing, the parent's expectations, the current spiritual choices of the emerging adult, and the parent's belief system.

After immigration, and during acculturation, Chinese parents experience new tensions and challenges with their children, and many exit ethno-religious communities.[4] The phenomenon of the development of intergenerational tension[5] and the abandonment of faith of second-generation Chinese youth from ethno-religious contexts during generational assimilation is well documented.[6] The leaving of CBC emerging young adults impacts a Chinese Christian perspective of the Chinese church being an extension of the Chinese family.[7] It is anecdotally reported that the impact over the losses

---

4. The problem of next-generation CBC English-speaking adults leaving their congregations is deemed a problem termed the "Silent Exodus." See Lee, "Silent Exodus." For the interested reader, see Ong's blog post titled "7 Issues in the Chinese American Church," where he comments that amidst the cultural diversity, "The greatest site of tension is usually between the older OBCs and the younger local born."

5. ChenFeng et al., "Intergenerational Tension," 143–64.

6. Wong. "How Am I."

7. Tse, "Making a Cantonese Christian Family," 761.

to parents in a shame culture[8] is hurt, guilt,[9] discouragement, withdrawal, and the undermining of ministry and shalom in the church.

Previous studies on why youth leave their parents' ethnic community context have focused on value polarization and parenting styles that provide a push factor out of the ethno-religious community. Parenting styles have been identified as contributing to "intergenerational strains related to acculturation differences."[10] The acculturation of CBC youth into a Canadian value system creates a deep challenge to the immigrant church over values. The second generation experiences "conflict with their parents' expectations" for "their choices," and "both generations describe" feelings of "tension and disconnection."[11] Value polarization and parenting styles are anecdotally considered factors in youth leaving churches and impacting parents.[12] Previous studies have identified that many Chinese immigrant parents encounter a host of difficulties as their children progress through the various stages of acculturation and integration in the North American context.[13] A challenging tension is that their children acculturate differently. Such stressful life events on parents include their child leaving home or changing churches, which can be difficult events to navigate. The Silent Exodus of youth generally transpires during the most challenging life stage

---

8. I will explain shame culture more later but provide a brief definition here: Chinese culture is a collectivist, honor-and-shame culture, making "shame a group concern." Chinese immigrants ". . . belong to a closely integrated group on which their honor or shame is reflected. . . . When people achieve well, the entire community shares the honor. Likewise, when people fail . . . they shame all those around them." A measure of "shame in Chinese culture" is rooted in Confucian thought and can cause one to "fear losing face" to try to avoid feelings of "guilt," "disgrace," "condemnation," and "embarrassment." Zhang, "Understanding," 1–2.

9. Bedford, "Guilt," 127–44. The author finds that "in Chinese culture . . . the sense of duty and obligation to family and group is . . . strongly experienced so guilt may be aroused over lack of capability" (47), feeling "inadequate" (45), or that "one has failed or is deficient in some way" (46), or that "one's personal ideals" (46) have not been achieved. Sohn comments that the "leaving" of the second generation "continues to be a heartache and concern among first generation parents and pastors"; Sohn, "Attitudes of Asian American Christians," 24.

10. ChenFeng et al., "Intergenerational Tension," 154. For the interested reader, see Tsai-Chae and Nagata, "Asian Values," 205–14.

11. ChenFeng et al., "Intergenerational Tension," 155, 157.

12. Balswick and Balswick, *Family*, 104–23. The authors review parenting styles that empower youth and provide a biblical model of parenting to empower youth toward maturity.

13. Qin, "Our Child," 162–79.

for parents.[14] The decision of a CBC youth to leave their faith community or their faith entirely can collide with a Chinese theological and cultural understanding of the faith, the church family,[15] and expectations for their children. While it is known in research that value polarization, cultural parenting style, acculturation, and life stage transition stressors all may be converging factors with youth leaving ethno-religious communities, how parents are impacted by the leaving lacks documentation.

Anecdotal reporting suggests that parents are impacted[16] with the loss of their next generations leaving the Chinese church. Notably, the "numerous stories of second-generation Exodus" are also accompanied by "first generation heart-brokenness."[17] Anecdotal reporting suggests that after youth leave churches, impacted parents manifest withdrawal in church attendance, decline in expressions of faith, decline in volunteerism and engagement, decline in confidence in the mission of the church, and a decline in confidence in preaching, along with manifesting a generational disconnect. There is an opportunity for churches to address this gap and contribute to efforts in the integration of immigrant families into

---

14. Garland identifies "movement from one stage to another creates stress or adds to any stress the family is already experiencing" (Garland, *Family*, 188), and furthermore, "families also experience stress when stages of development are disrupted in some way or family events occur out of what the culture considers the normal sequence of individual development" (188–89).

15. The Chinese theological and cultural understanding of the church is that of being an "extended family" (Lu et al., "Chinese Immigrant Families," 123), "one family" (124), church as a "Big Family" (123–25), church as a second home (125). ChenFeng notes that the Chinese immigrant Christian community generally sees the Chinese church "as a place of safety and connection." In a North American context where they have often "experience[d] discrimination" (ChenFeng, "Lived Experience," 18), the Chinese church is seen as a place that provides "healing," "positive outcomes," "social belonging," (18–19), "support" for "parenting efforts" (20), and support for "the identity of the Chinese [Christian] family" in "reinforcing cultural values . . . in a Chinese Christian way" (20). Six of those core cultural values include, "collectivism," "conformity to norms," "emotional self-control," "family recognition through achievement," "filial piety," and "humility,"—"these values are modeled and reinforced in the Chinese church context" (21).

16. Chen notes the struggle for trying to keep youth in the ethnic and moral environment of the Chinese church, but "we just can't use our OBC ways on our [local born Chinese] children." Chen, *Getting Saved*, 49.

17. Leung, *Looking Back*, xiii.

the Canadian context.[18] Chen and Park identify that immigrants look to churches "as bridges" to adapt socially and culturally.[19]

The Significance of This Book in View of Previous Studies

Despite all the previous studies mentioned, there is an absence of qualitative studies on *how* Chinese Canadian Christian parents are impacted by their youth leaving the church. There are gaps in the research in the following areas:

- how parents are impacted emotionally, socially, psychologically and spiritually;
- how parents are impacted if the leaving is compounded by multiple children leaving the church;
- how Chinese parents are impacted depending on the degree of their religious commitment; and
- what support systems the church is using to support and care for these parents.

The consequences of not addressing the problem leaves immigrant parents struggling and ill-equipped without interdisciplinary knowledge and skills to integrate faith and parenting during generational assimilation. Understanding how parents are impacted might do the following:

1. assist leaders with diagnostics for caring ministry;
2. create strategies for support and equipping parents; and/or
3. contribute to empowering parents.

These gaps have been factored into the development of my book inquiry.

---

18. Janzen et al., "Integrating," 441–70. Hirschman notes that ethnic churches can help bolster "religious values [that] . . . provide support for . . . intergenerational obligations . . . and customary familial practices—that are threatened with adaptation" into the North American context. Hirschman, "Role of Religion," 1211.

19. Chen and Park, "Pathways of Religious Assimilation," 666.

Who Are the People to Benefit from This Book?

I envision that the audience and stakeholders for this book include parents; denominational leaders; Asian church pastors and leaders; second-generation CBC, CRC, and ABC young adults; and social agencies in the fields of spiritual and family counseling. This book would be of interest to leaders in other ethnic, intercultural, or mainstream church models as the issue of parents experiencing emerging young adults leaving their faith community is common.

Participants mentioned in this book are Canadian immigrants. For part of this study, I interviewed former and current clergy and parents from Chinese churches predominantly in the Metro Vancouver region who presently or formerly worked or attended a Mennonite Brethren Chinese church from the MBCCA Chinese churches. In another part of this book, focus group recommendations came from interdenominational Chinese participants. The most significant numbers of stakeholders, volunteers, and power base in the Chinese Canadian Christian church has, to date, been found in the adult-parent demographic. There is a potential future benefit of this book to those immigrant families in gaining insight on navigating generational assimilation. There is an opportunity in assisting immigrant ethno-religious communities facing acculturation issues. As Chow has identified:

> Immigrants typically face a bewildering array of needs and challenges. . . . Immigration itself is often a "theologizing experience" because religion offers an ethical slant and valuable resources that nourish the immigrants' outlook as they react to the confusion, disorientation, and alienation that result from their uprooting experiences. . . . Religious institutions have always been a vital dynamic in the lives of immigrants as they provide an anchor for individuals undergoing the process of resettlement in a foreign land.[20]

Chinese churches are contexts where "identities and ethnic languages [can be] maintained [and] where individual and social services [can be] provided."[21] It is well documented that Chinese immigrants seek out support, community, and relationships, which contributes to the growth of Chinese churches.[22] Xu notes that "church communities draw people to-

---

20. Chow, "Religion," 99.
21. Chow, "Religion," 99.
22. Xu, "Immigrants."

gether. Belief comes later."²³ The findings of this book can benefit Canadian Chinese church leadership in the discipleship, spiritual formation, and mentoring of new immigrant Christians in a powerful way in dealing with generational assimilation.

Worldviews, Values, and Beliefs of Canadian Chinese Christians

Participants in the interviews were *Chinese* Christians (with one clergy member being the exception) who hold a spectrum of integrated Christian, Confucian, Eastern, and Western worldviews.²⁴ Chow observes that a Chinese immigrant's worldview depends on whether they have been trained to discern competing worldviews with a biblical worldview.²⁵ Tse notes Confucian values come through on topics of parenting, education, family, church as extended family,²⁶ and obedience.²⁷ Difficulties between parents and immigrant children are thought to be related to the parental Confucian perspective "that produce[s] hierarchical, collective, obligation driven and

---

23. Xu, "Immigrants."

24. Ten Elshof argues that just as Western Christians' thinking is influenced by a Western philosophical tradition, so too Christians in or from Eastern (Asian) family backgrounds have also been influenced by Eastern philosophical tradition. For Ten Elshof, this ranges from cultural perspectives on family (Ten Elshof, *Confucius*, 8–28) to learning (29–45) to ethics (46–65) to ritual (habits that shape our moral thinking; 66–82). Amongst Chinese Christians, some would argue it is debatable as to the extent of conscious or unconscious cultural perspectives they hold that stem from an integrated Eastern Christian, Confucian, or Western worldview. The Chinese ethical system, shaped by the wisdom tradition of Confucian thought, and many Chinese cultural ideas transfer easily into a Christian perspective, such as following wise and moral behavior and right ways to live life and govern.

25. The author notes that "assimilation challenges . . . identity (Chow, "Survey of Worldview Understanding," 203)," and inadvertently "Chinese churches become facilities for the preservation of Chinese traditions" and "values" (204) which are "derived from Confucian concept[s] of humanity and . . . emphasis on goodness." The ability to discern competing worldviews comes with intentional training regarding how the "Bible frames and orders human life" and the difference between a Confucian and biblical worldview (202). Chow, "Survey of Worldview Understanding," 1–257.

26. Tse, "Making a Cantonese Christian Family," 758, 761.

27. One can see how conservative Protestantism can feed into the perspective on obedience. Ellison and Sherkat argue that "conservative Protestants are prone to endorse authoritarian parenting orientations . . . and [are] especially supportive of obedience [and] intellectual autonomy." Ellison and Sherkat, "Obedience and Autonomy," 313.

emotionally restraining characteristics in contrast to [the second generation] . . . equalitarian, individualistic, rights-driven and emotionally expressive characteristics."[28] Confucian-based ideas on filial piety are identified with expectations "to submit to the wishes [advice] of parents . . . well into adulthood."[29] It is believed a polarity of values and beliefs develop during generational assimilation. Chinese culture is a "group-oriented culture" that emphasizes an honor-and-shame worldview.[30] Shame is felt in a culture that has shame as a value, and parents may feel shame when certain events trigger it like when a parent cannot keep the family together in the Chinese church and a youth leaves the church. Parents can feel they have failed and shame culture can be experienced with the "loss of face [and] feeling shame that occurs with loss of reputation or standing in the eyes [or opinions] of other[s]."[31] The community tends to avoid focusing on the impact of the Exodus on parents to buffer the sense of shame parents may feel. It is a Chinese cultural practice to not disclose such family information so that the parents can save face.

Two-thirds of the participants mentioned in the study in this book have had a *history* in the context of Mennonite Brethren Chinese churches. These churches are a young movement going through immigrant assimilation. Their history interfaces with a historical narrative of Chinese immigration. The mother tongue of the Mennonite Brethren Chinese churches' initial groups and congregations was Cantonese, which would later prove to be a challenge for these congregations when the Chinese immigration into Canada shifted to large numbers of Mandarin-speaking peoples. Cantonese congregations do missions by establishing English- and Mandarin-speaking congregations.[32] Canadian Chinese MB church plants have been largely a Metro Vancouver phenomenon, with the exception of Chinese MB congregations in Winnipeg, Regina, and Calgary.

A goal in this book is to use concepts and apply elements of developmental theory on social forces found in life cycle theory, social learning theory, emerging adulthood theory, and parents' religious commitment

28. Wang, "Moving Beyond," 146. For the interested reader, see also Shin and Silzer, *Tapestry*, 138–50.

29. Elshof, *Confucius*, 14.

30. Li et al., "Organization," 769.

31. Frank et al., "American Responses," 888.

32. The churches have separate congregation services and ministries in the Cantonese, Mandarin, and English languages, along with leaders that service these language groups.

research to help explain why youth leave churches, resulting in parents being impacted. Concepts from these various theories help to address the question as to how parents are impacted by the Exodus of their children and shed light in the following ways:

1. Developmental theory—Elements in this theory help describe moral development, which factors into why youth change in their spiritual interest and faith, thus impacting parents.

2. Life cycle theory—This theory provides an explanation as to why youth tend to drop out of the church, which impacts parents.

3. Social learning theory—Elements of this theory provide insight and clues into social, familial, cultural, and institutional dynamics that contribute to shaping a youth's perspective on whether they have a sense of belonging to the church or not and how parents are impacted by their youth leaving.

4. Dynamics of emerging adulthood theory[33]—Explains multiple religious[34] and nonreligious trajectories that impact parents.

5. Parents' religious commitment research—Elements of this research on the intergenerational transmission of religion is meaningful to demonstrate the probability that a higher religious commitment of parents does correlate with a higher religious commitment of children, along with a higher level of stress for such parents if or when a child abandons the church or faith.

6. Assimilation theory—Concepts and theories taken from Will Herberg's[35] and Milton Gordon's[36] classical theories on phases of immigrant assimilation which provide plausible explanations for why the needs of various emerging young adults outgrow the ethnic church. Current theories address Asian families in the present era of immigration[37] and help explain why the acculturation strategies some youth use may lead them to leaving their faith communities and thus impact their parents.

33. Arnett and Jensen, "Congregation of One," 451–67.
34. Drovdahl and Keuss, "Emerging," 130–44.
35. Herberg, *Protestant Catholic Jew*.
36. Gordon, "Nature of Assimilation," 95–110; see also Gordon, *Assimilation*.
37. Brown and Bean, "Assimilation," 826–74; Williams Jr. and Ortega, "Dimensions," 697–710.

Ideas in these theories do converge and factor into describing the phenomenon of youth leaving the Chinese church and therefore provide insights on how and why parents are impacted. These ideas helped shape the study and informed the analysis, including recommendations as to how impacts on parents can be minimized and the phenomena of youth leaving improved.

Ideas were especially drawn from the four fields of research on the causes of youth leaving the church. The four fields include the broad cultural phenomenon of youth leaving the church,[38] generational assimilation research,[39] emerging adulthood stage development theory,[40] and parents' religious commitment research.[41] There are interrelationships between these four fields of study that account for and explain certain causes of youth leaving the church and thus impacting parents. The study confirmed that the interface of elements in the life cycle phenomenon of youth leaving churches, the impact of generational assimilation, the social forces impinging on emerging adulthood, and the expectations behind the religious commitments of parents intersect and compound the impact on parents depending on the trajectory of their child.

The Phenomenon of Leaving the Church in the Broader Western Culture

Dropping out and leaving the church is widespread, and that disengagement tends to be the greatest between the teen years and the early twenties.[42] There is a measure of agreement that "social learning theory" is a dynamic in both apostasy and remaining religiously engaged.[43] Several studies positively identify early religious upbringing and training as impacting an adult

---

38. Pew Research Center, "Young Adults"; Osei-Owusu, *African Elephant*.
39. Chen and Park, "Pathways of Religious Assimilation," 666–88.
40. Arnett, "Emerging Adulthood," 469–80.
41. Petts, "Parental Religiosity"; helpful are Petts's findings on "observation" (3) and "imitating role models" (3, 4).
42. See Wong et al., *Listening to Their Voices*, 11–15; Roozen, "Church Dropouts," 429, 433–34. For the interested reader, see Hoge et al., "Determinants," 245; O'Conner et al., "Relative Influence," 723.
43. See Hunsberger, "Apostasy," 3, 22–23; Hoge et al., "Determinants," 242; Packard and Ferguson, "Being Done," 511–12.

trajectory of religious engagement,[44] which is important with lasting implications.[45] There is some agreement that through socialization, parents have a significant influence in "shaping" their youths in a way that "continue[s] into adulthood."[46] Classic social learning theory and studies on leaving the church have evolved into emerging adult theory in focusing on a specific stage in the life cycle.[47] With the development of the discussion on youth leaving the church expanding into emerging adulthood theory, multiple religious and nonreligious trajectories have been identified in mixed-method studies.[48] Insights from this field of research partly explain why youth leave the church and parents are subsequently impacted.

The Phenomenon of Generational Assimilation

There is a deficit of research studies on the impact on parents of Asian youth leaving church. In order to capture the demographic of youth leaving the church, this book looks into studies regarding the impact of generational assimilation[49] on Chinese North American Christian parents and youth exiting ethno-religious communities. New Canadian research has emerged that focuses on studying the phenomenon in Chinese Canadian churches on the various trajectories of leaving the faith and the ethnic church and living out the faith in an ethno-religious context.[50] Insights from this field of research help specifically address the process of acculturation that happens with immigrant children in ethnic churches and how parents are impacted.

The Phenomenon of Emerging Adulthood

This field of research provides insights into the puzzle as to why young emerging adults are less involved in religious organizations and leaving

---

44. See Roozen, "Church Dropouts," 440, 443; Hoge et al., "Determinants," 242–43; Myers, "Interactive Model," 864 ("parents' religiosity" and "quality of family relationship"); Smith and Adamczyk, *Handing Down the Faith*, 2.

45. Myers, "Interactive Model," 865.

46. Smith and Snell, *Souls*, 180–81.

47. See Smith and Snell, *Souls*; Clydesdale and Garces-Foley, *Twenty-Something*.

48. Smith and Snell, *Souls*, 166–79; Clydesdale and Garces-Foley, *Twenty-Something*, 20–50, 140–62.

49. Chung, "Gender," 376–86. A key impact identified was intergenerational conflict.

50. Wong et al., *Listening to Their Voices*, 16–22, 50–54.

the church for longer periods (or permanently) on account of an emerging developmental life stage that impacts identity, faith, spirituality, participation, commitment, religious trajectories, and involvement with the church. This field of research has elements that help to explain developmental trends pertaining to why youth leave the church that subsequently impacts parents.

The Religious Commitment of Parents

A survey of the literature was done to identify whether parents who register high in the domain of religious commitment also factored high in experiencing stress or failure in sense of duty, responsibility, or obligation if the children they raise abandon the faith and/or ethnic churches they were raised in. Insights from this field of research were helpful in highlighting differences of impact on parents depending on their religious commitment and provide insight into the impact on highly religious parents.

We will explore the ways Chinese Canadian immigrant Christian parents are impacted by the Silent Exodus of their children. Some of the supporting questions in this exploration will be:

1. How are parents impacted in their spiritual journey once their child leaves the Chinese church?
2. What support systems does the church have to come alongside parents?
3. What strategies could be proposed to empower parents whose children have abandoned the church and left the faith?

Determining the impact of generational assimilation on Chinese parents is crucial in identifying key impact factors in how parents are affected by the experience of loss of their children from their ethno-religious faith communities. The Silent Exodus can be an unintended consequence of generational assimilation impacting parents. However, there are other factors to be considered, like the broad cultural phenomenon of youth leaving the church and family practices in intergenerational transmission of religion. Qualitative findings are needed to help discern theological and interdisciplinary recommendations.

3

Probability of Handing On the Faith

IF YOU HAD ASKED me twenty years ago about *how* I would hand on the faith to my children, I would have told you about all the activities and programs I would be bringing them to. I really thought that if I just brought my kids to church and to children's and youth ministries, supplemented by camps and retreats, they would pick up the faith contagiously like a common cold. Part of my problem from the start was that I was bequeathed a deterministic, behaviorist approach to parenting. The idea was that raising Christian children was like baking a cake: just do A, B, and C, and add water and the Betty Crocker cake mix, and voila, out would come the finished cake. Somehow, I felt I could determine the spiritual outcome of my children (social conditioning) despite their free will. Shockingly, I began to discover that parenting can feel more like walking through a labyrinth, as I discovered that each of my children had dispositional differences. I needed to revise my thinking on parenting because some of my ideas were shallow, unbiblical, and ineffective.

Parents could greatly benefit from reviewing the teaching and ideas that they have inherited and embraced from their family and church. Do those teachings reflect a deterministic or a free-will perspective on a child's spiritual trajectory and outcome? Some parents experience heartbreak and anxiety when they discover that raising their children in the church did not guarantee the desired outcome of handing on the faith. The history of some churches has been marred by badly interpreted biblical proof texts such as Prov 22:6 ("Train a child in the way he should go, and when he is old he will not turn from it") and Acts 16:31 ("Believe in the Lord Jesus, and you will be saved—you and your household."). Acts 2:39 points out that forgiveness is available to all the family, but it doesn't teach family or household salvation; each person must make their own faith decision. These texts are not a guarantee but merely a reminder that the influence of parents can produce lasting good. Proverbs 22:6 refers to helping to shape children's will and cultivating an appetite for what is right. It is about adapting our training to a child's disposition (inclinations, interests, bents, gifts, etc.). It refers to helping children in the process of discovering how God made them, something Ps 139:13–18 refers to as well. Parents can study, talk about, and listen to what is of interest to their children, observe what they are good at, and help them develop their gifts. These things are God-given. Parents also need to address, correct, and confront sinful bents in their children. But the bottom line is to look for ways that God is already at work in your children's lives and help them understand and cultivate their giftings and inclinations as they make life choices. Many parents think the biblical texts mentioned above offer a promise or guarantee of conversion. In fact, such deterministic outcomes are not supported theologically (consider Josh 24:15; Matt 23:37; Rom 10:9–10; Mark. 8:34), nor are they supported in the research on the dechurching of youth. The research consistently indicates that youth dropping out of the church is an ongoing trend and a broad cultural issue. As you will discover in this book, dechurching is a culturally sensitive issue because of the emotional, social, and spiritual implications it carries for struggling parents. We want to see healthy families and healthy churches. The health of families impacts the health of churches and affects the mission of the church. One of the key findings of the research detailed in this book is that 62 percent of impacted parents were still not over the impact of their youth dechurching ten years later. I think there are a number of cultural myths about parenting that are active in the broader culture and in the church. For example, when they see youth doing well, people can assume they must have had good parents; conversely, when they see youth acting badly, people can assume they must have come from bad parents. How often do we hear parents taking the full credit for the successful educational, athletic, moral, and spiritual outcomes of their children? Conversely, spouses often blame each other for the negative character traits of their children. I am not discounting the parents' influence, but we must recognize that youth have free will.

Busting Parenting Cultural Myths

I would like to explode a cultural myth about parenting that exists in the church related to the topic of dechurching youth. What I am about to tell you is a true story. Some time ago I attended a Father's Day Sunday service at a large local church in my city. Four fathers were picked to sit on four chairs on the stage. The pastor said, "I want to interview four successful Christian parents of young adults who serve the Lord and are in the church." I gasped because I had been researching statistics that revealed 60–66 percent of youth leave the church in high school or after. I suspected that 60 percent of the parents sitting in the pews hearing this introduction and presentation would have recognized that they were not being represented on the platform. This could well have induced a guilt trip, and my guess is that some parents probably didn't feel great leaving the church that day. Perhaps the pastor didn't intentionally try to present an unrealistic message, but he was either ignoring or oblivious to the phenomenon of dechurching youth. In research, we would call this an improper sample. When a sample used in a presentation or study doesn't represent the people, it is considered a research error. The other 60–66 percent of the parents should also have been represented on that stage. The presentation that morning misrepresented the long-range outcomes of godly parenting. This pastor lost an opportunity to instruct parents on the biblical mandate of parenting in the life cycle and equip them to deal with the risks and probable outcomes of parenting. That Father's Day, the dads onstage spoke of what they did in parenting and what their young adults were studying in various universities and colleges or working at in various professions. I could almost visualize these dads patting themselves on the back. I want us to pause for a second to reflect on what this pastor had done. He had inadvertently supplied a defective (or incomplete) theological definition of a "successful Christian parent." That is, the pastor was implying that if a child had stayed in the faith and the church, and if the child had been successful as a student and in a vocation, then that was an indication of a successful Christian parent. The pastor appeared to be oblivious of the fact that he was stigmatizing the parents of dechurched children, giving the impression that they were failures because they had not succeeded in handing on the faith. Let us consider this question: is handing on the faith *the* biblical definition of a successful parent? What does that say to the 60–66 percent of parents, many of whom did their best to be an intentional, godly parent? Another question: is the definition of what makes successful parents determined by whether their youth or young adult children stay in the faith or the church? Can God never say to such parents, "Well done, you good and faithful parent?" One last question: can parents be blamed for the rebellion and sin of a youth or young adult? I want to introduce a correction to the definition of success in parenting and what it means to be a faithful parent (see Gen 18:19; Deut 4:8–9; 6:1–2). The outcome is based on the free will of the young adult. Yes, parenting influence is real, but good, godly parenting is not a guaranteed loyalty program. Let me make this case by looking at families in the Scriptures.

We can find examples in Scripture of godly parents who had godly children:

- Jesse's son David was useful in Saul's service (2 Sam 7:8) and was said to have served God's purpose (Acts 13:36).
- Abraham conducted himself faithfully with the goal of seeing God's will happen in Isaac's life.
- Hannah was persistent in her faith and was willing to surrender everything to God and seek his will for her son Samuel.
- Lemuel's mother provided him with godly teaching, warning him against fornication and drunkenness, encouraging him to stand for social justice (for the needy, destitute, and poor), and instructing him on how to find a virtuous wife (Prov 31).
- The Recabites obeyed their ancestor Jehonadab in regard to abstaining from wine (Jer 35:12–14, 18–19).

We can also find in Scripture portrayals of godly parents who attempted to hand on the faith but in the end had ungodly children:

- The father of the prodigal son (Luke 15:11–32).
- Noah's son Ham was judged for sexual sin and dishonoring his father.
- Abraham's son Ishmael was a rebel and likely an unbeliever (Gen 16:12; 25:18; Gal 4:22–31).
- Samuel's sons were not like him—they cheated, took bribes, and judged unfairly (1 Sam 8:1–9).
- Jotham was a good king, but his son Ahaz was wicked.
- Job's ten children worried him with their partying.
- Hezekiah was a great and godly king, but his son Manasseh was extremely evil.

We can also find scriptural portrayals of the outcomes of inconsistent parenting:

- Lot's children are portrayed as being foolish.
- Isaac and Rebecca played favorites. Jacob was a follower of God, but Esau was a fool and disregarded God.
- Jacob showed favoritism with Joseph.
- Eli's parenting fault was not addressing his sons' immoral practices, and he had two sinful sons.
- David was a neglectful parent. Only Solomon showed promise, but he drifted later in life.
- Solomon had no known good children.
- In the time of the Judges, the Israelites who entered the promised land knew God, but the third generation knew only rumors about God and had an inconsistent relational experience with him—they "did as they saw fit" (Judg 21:25).

We can also find in Scripture portrayals of sinful parents whose children, by the grace of God, learned from what happened to their parents and became godly children. A prime example of this is the sinful Exodus parents at Sinai, who were followed by the godly generations which entered the promised land under Joshua.

The point of this biblical review is this: parents do have firm direction from Scripture to direct their children in the ways of the Lord, and God tells them to do this, regardless of what the outcome will be, but we should be cautious of being judgmental on the basis of whether a youth stays or leaves the faith. A very important point here is that God won't assess your parenting based on the outcome and the choices of your children, but he will assess whether you tried to consistently and faithfully influence your children to follow him. In my conversations with leaders and parents in ethno-religious communities, several have expressed that they think the attrition of their second-generation youth is connected to forces which are also impacting the majority culture churches. Many studies over the past several decades have focused on the broader cultural phenomenon of youth leaving the church, yet very little has been written on the resulting impact on parents in ethno-religious communities. I want to help provide an understanding of the reasons immigrant parents experience such a devastating impact because of the exit of their youth from the Chinese church.

Four theoretical fields of research in the literature that help explain the phenomenon include the broad cultural phenomenon of youth leaving the church, generational assimilation in ethno-religious communities, emerging adulthood, and parents' religious commitment. Themes that run through these four fields of research include the social forces of disengagement and reentry.[1] Religious attitudes and behavior can be transmitted and learned.[2] Themes in generational assimilation tend to look at the conflict, process, and strategies.[3] An important theme in emerging adulthood is that youth "reexamine beliefs they have learned in their families"[4] and "explore worldviews"[5] that can have various trajectories. An important theme that runs through the field of parent religious commitment is that longitudinal studies do provide findings that can be used to broadly predict general probability of religious influence and later religious outcomes of youth.[6] Life cycle theory identifies a couple of important insights with the broad cultural phenomenon of youth leaving the church. First, dropping out is widespread, and second, it is the greatest between the teen years and the early twenties.[7] It is agreed that "social learning theory" helps explain apostasy and remaining religiously engaged.[8] Early religious upbringing and training is identified as impacting an adult trajectory of religious engagement[9] with lasting implications.[10] The theoretical field of inquiry has

---

1. Roozen, "Church Dropouts," 427–50.

2. Hunsberger, "Apostasy," 23.

3. See Kwak and Berry, "Generational Differences," 152–62; Chung, "Gender;" Cavalcanti and Schleef, "Case for Secular Assimilation?," 473–83.

4. Arnett, "Emerging Adulthood," 474.

5. Arnett, "Emerging Adulthood," 474.

6. The research is mixed; parents get viewed as both "socializing agents" and "the religiosity" does get "related to the religiosity of their parents" (314), but there are conflicting "longitudinal studies that report little connection" (314). Barry et al., "Religiosity," 311–24.

7. See Roozen, "Church Dropouts," 429, 433–34 ; Hoge et al., "Determinants," 245 ; O'Conner et al., "Relative Influence," 723; Wong et al., *Listening to Their Voices*, 11–15.

8. See Hunsberger, "Apostasy," 3, 22–23; Hoge et al., "Determinants," 242; Packard and Ferguson, "Being Done," 511–12 ("social basis for religious practice").

9. See Roozen, "Church Dropouts," 440, 443; Hoge et al., "Determinants," 242–43; Myers, "Interactive Model," 864 ("parents' religiosity" and "quality of family relationship").

10. See Myers, "Interactive Model," 865; Smith and Snell, *Souls*, 180–81; Clydesdale and Garces-Foley, *Twenty-Something*, 153, 154.

expanded between 1980 and 2025 from classic social learning theory[11] on leaving the church and has evolved into emerging adult theory, focusing on a specific stage in the life cycle.[12] Most of these studies have been done with Caucasian youth, and to a lesser extent African American youth. Lacking are research studies with Pan-Asian youth and families. Some of the positive directions in the research are that reentry back into the church is common,[13] often associated with marriage and having children.[14] With the development of emerging adulthood theory, multiple religious and nonreligious trajectories have been identified in mixed-method studies.[15] Important concepts and theories regarding generational assimilation in ethno-religious communities reveals that conflict between the first and second generation is often about retaining the next generation in the heritage culture. Herberg's[16] and Gordon's[17] theories on phases of immigrant assimilation provide plausible explanations for why the needs of emerging young adults outgrow the ethnic church. Ethnic churches go through life cycles, and assimilation is a challenge to the retention of the second generation. If the church "resists adaptations" over "cultural" and "linguistic preservation,"[18] research identifies that youth may leave, which is a "problem of organizational adaptation."[19] Berry and Hou's research (2016, 2017) identifies that acculturation strategies are about advancing wellbeing. Youth follow multiple trajectories in assimilation, including leaving the ethnic church, which in turn impacts the parents. Important concepts and theories in emerging adulthood include the fact that this field is an outgrowth of developmental theory and social forces. The implications of emerging adults being hindered in reaching full adulthood (career,

---

11. Bandura, "Social Learning Theory," 1–46.

12. See Penner et al., *Hemorrhaging Faith*, 1–138; Smith and Snell, *Souls*; Clysdale and Garces-Foley, *Twenty-Something*; Bulger, "Bridging the Gap."

13. See Roozen, "Church Dropouts," 444, 445; O'Conner et al., "Relative Influence," 731.

14. See O'Conner et al., "Relative Influence," 723; Uecker et al., "Losing My Religion," 1681; Clydesdale and Garces-Foley, *Twenty-Something*, 46.

15. See Smith and Snell, *Souls*, 166–79; Clydesdale and Garces-Foley, *Twenty-Something*, 20–50, 140–62.

16. Herberg, *Protestant Catholic Jew*.

17. Gordon, "Nature of Assimilation" ("stages of assimilation"), 102.

18. Gordon, "Nature of Assimilation," 325.

19. Gordon, "Nature of Assimilation," 326.

marriage, parenthood)[20] consequently delays religious participation and attendance, and with the absence of youth, parents are impacted.

Social learning theory provides a plausible explanation for studies on parents' religious commitment and the intergenerational transmission of religion. The field has expanded to recognize that there are worldview and cultural differences and emerging trends that enlarge intergenerational influence. The field has expanded to recognize differences of influence in family structures and practices. The field has shifted to accommodate change in the family through immigration, the longevity of grandparents and social change, and the changes in family structure. Social learning theory identifies that there are several predictors linked to parents' religious commitment that influence youth religiosity.[21] "Parents are among the strongest influences on religiosity," especially in the context of a "happy marriage," combined with "reasonable" and "authoritative parenting."[22] "Parents . . . are the primary source of socialization"[23] and "youth religiosity is highly dependent on how much they are exposed to religion by their parents."[24] A finding that resonates with common sense is that "youth raised in religious families are more likely to be religious than those raised in nonreligious families."[25] All four theoretical fields of study identify that the Asian North American families have been understudied. What the four theoretical fields of study have in common is identifying push-and-pull factors to leave faith communities. Much of the research done on youth leaving the church points to social, developmental, and cultural forces that combine and either contribute for or against choices that youth make to leave or stay with the church. Depending on parents' religious commitment, the probability may be higher or lower that youth will leave. It is assumed that the four fundamental theoretical fields I have mentioned could be combined explanations for why youth leave ethno-religious communities and impact parents. Those four theories are (1) developmental life cycle theory, (2) social learning theory, (3) assimilation theory, and (4) emerging adulthood theory. Each of these theories have elements that could be predictors of probability outcomes of the phenomenon and thus predictors of

---

20. Arnett, "Emerging Adulthood," 470.
21. Gunnoe and Moore, "Predictors," 620. For a list of other predictors, see 615.
22. Gunnoe and Moore, "Predictors," 614.
23. Petts, "Parental Religiosity," 19.
24. Petts, "Parental Religiosity," 2.
25. Petts, "Parental Religiosity," 2.

impact on parents. When the elements, factors, and concepts are aligned in particular directions, the probability trajectories of Exodus can range, and theoretically, so could the impacts on parents' range. These four fields of research converge on findings that factor into the phenomenon of youth leaving the Chinese church and therefore provide insights on how the impact of the phenomena of youth leaving can be mitigated.

4

Wrestling with Cultural Assimilation

IT IS COMMON IN immigrant churches to speak of the first generation as retaining their country-of-origin culture and language and to speak of subsequent generations as being an ethnic hybrid because of experiencing cultural assimilation.[1] When I was working in an Italian church in Canada, a visitor from Italy commented that the first-generation immigrant Italians were culturally "stuck in the time they left Italy," and the next generation in the church were neither culturally Italian (as per Italy) nor culturally Canadian—they were something else. My wife's family was from an Italian church that in three generations became assimilated into mainstream majority churches. Getting there is messy, and the struggle happens in the center of the immigrant family and church. It can be stressful for immigrant parents, after sacrificing much and moving to a new country, only to discover that the relationships with the children in their family are becoming polarized, partly because the children are acculturating to the local culture. Conflicts can flare up in the family over identity formation. The parents speak to their children in their native language, and the children reply in English. The parents can insist to their locally born children, "We are Chinese, and nothing can be changed," while the children shout, "We are Canadian!" The parents may not really understand their children's struggles, feelings, and language problems while they are studying in this new culture. A different generational interpretation of autonomy and making choices evolves and results in conflicts over asking permission and who gets the final say. Asian parents give their best to their children and expect the children will behave

1. A version of this chapter was published as Todd, "Impact of Assimilation," 65–88.

the way they think is right and will bring honor to them. But the local born generation is straddling expectations in two cultures, which impacts rules, choices, and family priorities. Some of this has to do with the Asian honor and shame culture. Individualism can be very hard to accept by Asian parents, and yet local born Chinese are growing up in a majority North American society that encourages independence and free thinking. There are expectations rooted in filial piety and hierarchical perspectives that touch on the local born child's educational, social, church, vocational, and marriage choices. Parents can begin to feel frustration, anxiety, and fear of losing control over their children because of the Confucian ethic of obedience, which is often taught in Chinese churches as a Christian core value. Parents can begin to feel a sense of failure and shame and blame themselves because they feel they are not raising their children well. The issue of control can be a constant issue projected onto an English ministry in the Chinese church. The next generation wants to experience God on their own terms. Chinese congregations have their own experiences, but such experiences cannot be superimposed on the second generation. If the next generation (English ministry) does not perform as well as the Chinese congregation, the parents can lose face and feel shame. A generalized expectation of many traditional immigrant parents is that their children will stay and form the leadership of their church and that their grandchildren will be raised in the same church, thus passing on the language and culture. Therefore, the impact of an Exodus is significant in terms of cultural heritage, leadership development, and faith transference. The immigrant Christian identity is tied to the structure of the church, and thus exiting from the immigrant church can be seen as a rejection of not only the faith but of culture and tradition as well. In short, it can be construed as a disrespectful rejection of the immigrant parents, their faith, and their way of doing things in order to form a new identity in the host country. Of course, there are some immigrant parents who may view the Exodus as a way for the youth to seek to understand the Christian faith for themselves. They realize that the current ministry approach in their immigrant church may be only relevant to the parents and that to force their local born youth to fit into that might stifle their Christian spiritual formation. Such parents are more open to pushing for real change in the approach to English ministries. If the youth leave, the joy for the parents of attending the same church is gone. Furthermore, the church is weakened because it has lost people from the English ministries who contributed talents, finances, and services to help accomplish the mission of the local church. We are talking about wrestling with the impacts of cultural assimilation during generational acculturation. Prior to immigrating to the North American context, most immigrant parents don't anticipate that the process of acculturation on their next generation can distance the youth from the faith and family church. Anecdotal reporting indicates that there is an impact from generational assimilation on Chinese Christian parents when their children separate from the faith and Chinese church. This chapter contributes to the solution of the problem by helping the reader understand the cultural background and context in which the Silent Exodus occurs, which subsequently impacts parents. The history and context of Chinese churches has been shaped through the immigration experience. The background of two-thirds of the participants in the background study behind this book can be better understood by providing a historical framework and context of the MBCCA English and Chinese ministries. Because the MBCCA churches are a young movement, there is a need to very briefly report on the earlier historical Chinese church growth and movement in British Columbia and Canada as the development of Chinese churches in Canada has more historical depth and scope in other denominations like the Alliance, Presbyterian, or Anglican denominations. One-third of the participants in my study are part of this interdenominational background. There is also a need to briefly discuss immigrant assimilation into Canadian society and how it interfaces with the Chinese church English ministries. Recognizing assimilation is still ongoing would help the reader with a framework to understand the evolving development stages of English ministries connected to parents in the Chinese churches who later are impacted by the Exodus of many of these youth. The historical framework of a people navigating immigrant experience helps the reader understand a denominational context and cluster of Chinese churches in which the Silent Exodus and impact on parents is occurring on a spectrum with interdenominational parallels. Chinese churches in particular have been founded and launched through a specific theological lens on mission, evangelism, and church planting. This missional DNA has had implications for the development, growth, and trajectory of their churches. The following chapter is a historical review of foundational personalities who capitalized on Chinese immigration, resulting in rapid church growth. It explores in part the life cycle of the Chinese church and the sociological dynamics that set the stage for the acculturation of the second generation, challenges of retaining the second generation, and the subsequent impact on parents that have implications for focusing on mission. Following is a brief history of interdenominational Protestant Chinese churches in Canada and the development of Chinese churches, from whom many participants in this study find a present context.

Canadian Chinese Interdenominational Church History and Context

It takes ten years to build a tree and 100 years to build a people.
—CHINESE PROVERB

This section helps understand a background of beliefs and practices that have guided attitudes, values, meanings, customs, language, norms, and behaviors. This chapter recognizes that the formation and development of Canadian Chinese churches interfaces with the historical narrative of Chinese immigration—an experience all immigrant Chinese Canadian Christians share regardless of denomination. One aspect of the development of the Chinese church is the utility of faith and a utilitarian approach to joining ethnic faith communities; looking for community is a "characteristic path of adaptation of immigrants" to the North American context,[2] "[where] . . . one of the first acts of [many] new immigrants is to found [or join a] . . . church."[3] Yaxin Lu et al. have noted how "the Chinese Christian church plays an important role in coping, acculturation, and assimilation processes for many Chinese immigrant families."[4] They are able to find "material, social, and emotional support," relationships, and communities that "correlate with positive outcomes in marriage and family life."[5] Cavalcanti and Schleef noted that some immigrants turn to religion to aid in the process of acculturation to the host country, while others use religion to maintain ethnic and cultural ties.[6] Herberg recognized that ethnic churches

---

2. Hirschman, "Role of Religion," 1207.
3. Hirschman, "Role of Religion," 1208.
4. Lu et al., "Chinese Immigrant Families," 118.
5. Lu et al., "Chinese Immigrant Families," 118–19.
6. Cavalcanti and Schleef, "Case for Secular Assimilation?," 480. For the interested reader, see Dawson, "Religious Connections." Dawson identifies that immigrants tend to see "religious communities as a place of social integration (transitional institutions), especially in the first years after arriving in the country." Dawson, "Religious Connections."

frequently are an outgrowth of ethnic immigration,[7] as they help provide support for a sense of identity[8] and "continuity and security" through the disorienting period of "migration and resettlement."[9] They create communities where initially the "primary expression of . . . unity [is] language" and a shared culture.[10] Immigrant churches "represent a fusion of religion and culture that [is] of the very texture of immigrant life . . . more a racial and cultural than a religious institution . . .," a place where they can "learn the mother-tongue, and with it the attitudes and social ideals of the old homeland."[11] Hirschman concedes with Herberg's analysis that ethnic churches provide immigrants "cultural continuity and . . . psychological benefits of religious faith following the trauma of immigration."[12] Hirschman argues, "The centrality of religion to immigrant communities can be summarized as the search for refuge, respectability, and resources,"[13] and "the creation of an immigrant church . . . often provide[s] ethnic communities with refuge from hostility and discrimination from the broader society as well as opportunities for economic and social recognition."[14] The value of religious affiliation and communities to new immigrants is that they "provide . . . spiritual . . . social . . . [and] economic benefits (community service) and opportunities."[15] Herberg's and Hirshman's sociological theory on the role of religion in the origins and adaptation of immigrant groups applies to the planting and growth of the Chinese churches.

Li Yu focused some of his work on Chinese Christians in British Columbia. Yu discusses "the status of Christianity in British Columbia's Christian community and examine[s] the driving forces behind its growth"; furthermore, Yu provides a historical review of the past 150 years, "a period during which Christianity in this community changed from a Western religion into a Chinese belief."[16] Yu sums up a brief history of Chinese churches

---

7. Herberg, *Protestant, Catholic, Jew*, 14.
8. Herberg, *Protestant, Catholic, Jew*, 12.
9. Herberg, *Protestant, Catholic, Jew*, 16.
10. Herberg, *Protestant, Catholic, Jew*, 11, 13.
11. Herberg, *Protestant, Catholic, Jew*,110.
12. Hirschman, "Role of Religion," 1206.
13. Hirschman, "Role of Religion," 1228.
14. Hirschman, "Role of Religion," 1206.
15. Hirschman, "Role of Religion," 1224. See also 1208.
16. Yu, "Christianity," 245.

as having a history that dates back to 1858[17] and did not begin to flourish in numbers until after the Second World War when "the assimilating role of the churches gradually weakened as the mainstream denominational churches withdrew from the community and self-managed Chinese churches came into being."[18] Self-managed Chinese churches combined with the history of Chinese immigration since the 1980s[19] has contributed to the growth of the Chinese Christian community because Chinese churches have "adjusted their mission strategies to meet the needs of Chinese immigrants"[20] and provided a context to "solidify the Chinese identity of their members."[21]

Mennonite Brethren Chinese Churches (MBCCA) History and Context

This section takes a close look at one denomination's cluster of Chinese churches. This section helps with an understanding of participants' geographical and historical content, cultural conventions, social expectations, attitudes, motivations, and emotions shaped by the cultural context and considered normal. Historical and cultural conventions help understand how the Silent Exodus evolves and contributes to the problem of impacting parents. Two-thirds of the participants in my study came from this denominational demographic. The narrative on their development, attrition, struggle with generational assimilation, and impacted parents has interdenominational similarities. The intention here is to outline the Mennonite Brethren Chinese churches' start and subsequent development of their English ministries while acknowledging that interdenominational Chinese churches share many features of this growing narrative. A few prefacing comments here are necessary to set the stage for the discussion in this section. Kwan has noted that "most Chinese MB members were [from] . . . immigrant famil[ies] from Hong Kong."[22] Although the growth of the Chinese MB churches is rooted in evangelization and church planting, there were many Cantonese-speaking Christians who joined a Chinese MB church

17. Yu, "Christianity," 237.
18. Yu, "Christianity," 245.
19. Yu, "Christianity," 240.
20. Yu, "Christianity," 234.
21. Yu, "Christianity," 245. ("Chinese churches in BC play an important role in strengthening their members' Chinese identity," 242).
22. Kwan, "Building People," 11–12.

either because their original denomination in Hong Kong did not have a branch church in the Greater Vancouver area or because of invitations from friends.[23] The mother tongue of the Mennonite Brethren Chinese churches' initial groups and congregations was Cantonese. New immigration from China would later prove to be a challenge for these congregations when Chinese immigration into British Columbia and Alberta shifted to large numbers of Mandarin-speaking peoples. Once the Cantonese congregations were planted, they pragmatically discerned doing missions by establishing English- and Mandarin-language congregations. Canadian social trends indicate that the larger concentrations of Chinese populations are found in both the Vancouver and Toronto area;[24] however, the Chinese MB church plants have been largely a Metro Vancouver phenomenon, with the exception of a Chinese MB congregation in Winnipeg, Regina, and Calgary, and two Chinese MB church mission plants in Venezuela. Furthermore, although the "first Chinese church in Canada was established in 1892"[25] and the "first Mennonite Brethren congregation in Canada founded in . . . 1888[26] (the Mennonite Brethren traces its church growth in Canada back to large "Mennonite migrations . . . dating from the 1870s and the 1920s,"[27] later incorporated in Canada under the name Mennonite Brethren in 1946),[28] the first MBCCA church was only established just over fifty years ago. Contrary to Yu's documentation that "in the 1920s . . . a number of Protestant denominations, such as . . . Mennonite Brethren Churches, joined in the mission to the Chinese community,"[29] there is no historical documentation of the establishment of a Chinese Mennonite Brethren church until the early 1970s.[30] It has been noted that the "Canadian Mennonite Brethren movement was birthed in mission" that dates back to 1888.[31]

23. Kwan, "Building People," 11.
24. Calgary and Montreal are nearly tied for the third-highest Chinese populations.
25. Guenther, "Ethnicity," 379.
26. Ediger, *Crossing the Divide*, 13.
27. Ediger, *Crossing the Divide*, 11.
28. Kraybill, *Concise Encyclopedia*, 132.
29. Yu, "Christianity," 237. For the interested reader, see Guenther, "Ethnicity," 380.
30. Guenther, "Ethnicity," 380.
31. Reimer, "Executive Director," 4. "Rooted in our historic priorities, the Canadian Mennonite Brethren movement was birthed in mission. In 1883, at the USMB conference in Hamilton County, Nebraska, delegates expressed concern about the spiritual condition of the Mennonite church in Manitoba and wondered whether they had a responsibility to help. A motion was put forward that they send Heinrich Voth of Minnesota and David

The reason why the establishment of a Chinese MB church plant comes so late in the MB missions initiative is explained by that fact that it was not until the period between the 1940s and 1970s that the Canadian Mennonite Brethren Church "exchanged German for English as their primary language of religious usage ... [a] first step in the transformation of a unilingual German religious community in 1910 into a multilingual, multiethnic denomination by century's end."[32] The MB denomination began removing its "protective boundaries" used to "conserve their historic identity" and develop "a theology of missional activism."[33] George Peters was one MB leader who helped contribute to changing "the way Canadian Mennonite Brethren related their witness to people of other ethnic origins."[34] Peters is credited for influencing, inspiring, and helping "shape modern missions for the Mennonite Brethren"[35] and emphasized "keeping church and missions together."[36] Peters expressed that "missions were a part of Mennonite Brethren thinking from their beginning in Russia [and it has been evolving] over the years" and identified in various "entrepreneurial approach[es] to new starts [like] Henry Bartels going to China."[37] It would be a long road in changing the way MB people related their witness to people of other ethnic origins, but that journey also paved a road to think differently about local home missions with newer immigrants to Canada and a Mennonite Brethren response like supporting ethnic church planting. Guenther has "explored ... MBs who were culturally Dutch, German, Russian (DGR) and concluded [the MB] denomination had an underdeveloped theology of culture from the very beginning."[38] For those who don't have the DGR ethnicity, MBs had to learn to seize the opportunity to explore denominational multiculturalism.[39] Isaac Chang (a retired MBCCA clergyman) has noted that it could be very important for non-DGR Mennonites to be

---

Dyck of Kansas to Manitoba to investigate the possibility of beginning a missionary work there. The result of this action was the birth of Winkler MB Church in 1888. From there, mission efforts were launched in Gretna and eventually Winnipeg" (4).

32. Ediger, *Crossing the Divide*, 3.
33. Ediger, *Crossing the Divide*, 1.
34. Jantz, "Created," 112.
35. Jantz, "Created," 118.
36. Jantz, "Created," 119.
37. Jantz, "Created," 119.
38. Study Conference Reports, 16.
39. Study Conference Reports, 16.

familiar with DGR culture to learn from the degree of assimilation DGR Mennonites have had to Canadian culture: "It may help the Chinese MB churches increase their ability to assess cultural change [and be cautious of] holding to traditions only."[40] One parallel experience between the German- and Chinese-speaking MB churches has been the impact of acculturation on their English-speaking youth and the need to change.[41] The MB church would first have to deal with the "basic contradiction between the emphasis on ethnicity and the missionary nature of the church."[42] Mullins noted this challenge that comes with cultural assimilation for parents in Japanese, Norwegian, Swedish, Ukrainian, and Polish churches.[43] Di Giacomo noted the Protestant Italian churches struggles with cultural assimilation for nearly 100 years in Canada.[44] It would take a MB pastor in proximity to the Chinese community to exercise a less ethnocentric theology in outreach mission to the Chinese.

A. The Roots: Foundations

The Chinese MB church history and beginnings of the Pacific Grace Chinese and English ministries can be traced to the deference of Rev. Henry G. Classen and Mrs. Sara Classen in responding to the BC MB conference request for Henry to come to Vancouver as a city missionary in November

40. Study Conference Reports,16.

41. For the interested reader, the history of intergenerational tension over acculturation, language, and cultural issues in the German MB churches and the need to make changes to eclipse the youth leaving is well documented in the following: Plett, "Hindrances to Growth" (Plett cites acculturating youth leaving over "cultural narrowness" in the MB ethnic churches [332]); Redekop, "Ethnicity," 131–39; Toews, "Facing Cultural Change" (Toews cites thirty-two congregations in Canada concerned about losing youth if the churches don't change from German to English in next generation ministries—a painful process for the parent generation [329]), 323–41; Ediger, "Canadian Mennonite Brethren" (Ediger cites the "tension and pain" [249] and "strain" [253] over the cultural assimilation [259], language, and cultural issues with the youth [250]); Ediger, *Crossing the Divide*, 1–37, 192–94.

42. Ediger, "Canadian Mennonite Brethren," 132. It has been noted that "non-ethnic Mennonites, at times, seem to perceive what many traditional Mennonites miss. Speaking as a 'non-Mennonite' Mennonite, David Chiu challenged a large gathering of Canadian Mennonite leaders to take seriously the desire of his Chinese Mennonite church, 'We just want to be a church with Anabaptist essentials'" (Redekop, "Mennonites and Ethnicity," 132).

43. Mullins, "Life Cycle," 321–34.

44. Di Giacomo, "Identity and Change," 83–130.

1949 to 1950.⁴⁵ At that time, Rev. Classen focused on visitation, street meetings, and Sunday school work. On July 22, 1956, a new chapel was built and called Pacific Grace Mission Chapel of the Mennonite Brethren. The Pacific Grace Mission was founded to reach all the residents of the area surrounding the mission, including the Chinese from Chinatown. Initially, only one out of seven attending the Pacific Grace Mission was of Chinese descent. With the increase in Chinese immigration and movement into this sector of the city, the ratio began to adjust. The population of the area gradually changed as it became predominantly a Chinese community. Eventually, Rev. Henry Classen and Sara began taking Chinese language lessons to use in the ministry. A key focus concentrated on home visitation accompanied by their Chinese helper Rose Wong. The attendance of the church grew in the 1960s with increased Chinese immigration. Bremner has noted that "by the late 1960s the majority of the children in Sunday school were of Chinese origin, reflecting the changing composition of the surrounding neighborhood."⁴⁶ It was becoming apparent that a Chinese worker was needed. In efforts to reach the parents of the Chinese children attending Sunday school, Sara Classen and coworker Sue Neufeld started taking lessons in Cantonese, and a short-term Chinese worker was hired to assist with home visitations. By the autumn of 1972, there were twenty-two Chinese attendees.⁴⁷ The response was positive, and in 1972, Henry asked Paul Li (Li Him-Wor), a student of Northwest Baptist Bible College, to fill the position upon graduation. In May 1972, Paul and Great Li were appointed by the MB conference as workers in the Chinese section of Pacific Grace. The Chinese fellowship grew from a small group to a large fellowship, sharing the Sunday school and sanctuary space by 1973. "In 1974 a Chinese department was established with meetings conducted in Cantonese."⁴⁸ It had been noted that no major tensions ever developed between the Chinese and Caucasian believers in the mission; it was absolutely peaceful. "Paul's ministry grew to include forty-five people attending the Chinese speaking congregation, but his ministry was cut short due to cancer and his sudden death in 1975. Eddie Chu (Chu Yu-Man) assumed leadership for the Chinese congregation,"⁴⁹ but would leave shortly after to continue his studies;

45. Todd, "Port Moody."
46. Bremner, "Henry G. Classen."
47. Kwan, "We Are In."
48. Kwan, "We Are In."
49. Bremner, "Henry G. Classen."

the church would be without a pastor for two years.[50] Pacific Grace Mission Chapel celebrated their twenty-fifth anniversary September 28, 1975. Their motto was "Twenty-five years of Grace at Pacific." Their theme Scripture was Lam 3:23b: "Great is Thy faithfulness." The Chinese work continued to grow while the English Caucasian membership decreased, and on April 30, 1977, Pacific Grace dissolved as an organized church. In its place emerged a blossoming Pacific Grace Chinese church;[51] English-speaking Christians stayed behind until 1983 to help the church develop and teach children in Sunday school.[52] Mr. Classen's fruitful and visionary ministry would be handed over to the Chinese Christians to carry on the gospel work. Mr. Classen would "retire from full-time service in 1977 due to failing eyesight."[53] Rev. Henry Classen was the denomination's first Chinese group's English ministries worker. Mr. Classen's legacy was the foundation upon which the honorable Rev. Enoch Wong and Grace Wong would build upon when taking over the Pacific Grace Chinese church on August 1, 1980.[54]

Pacific Grace MB Church. Rev. Enoch Wong would eventually become a key figure (patriarch) in leading, advising, and promoting the future nurturing of multiple young Chinese MB churches in BC, including two in Venezuela. His influence over the leadership, direction, church planting, and strategizing of the Cantonese, Mandarin, and English ministries of these churches reverberates across several generations. Enoch had a deep love for the Chinese MB church and for church planting, which would further influence the missional DNA and development of the MBCCA's growth. Some MB denominational leaders outside the Chinese MB circle affectionately referred to Enoch as the "pope of the Chinese MB churches."[55]

Converted to the Christian faith in 1945,[56] Rev. Enoch Wong (Chinese name Cheung Ho)[57] became full-time pastor of the first Chinese MB church in Vancouver, established by the late Henry Classen. In 2010, Enoch was asked to describe a bit about the history of the Chinese MB churches

50. Kwan, "We Are In."
51. Fast, "Apostle to the City," 347–70.
52. Kwan, "We Are In."
53. Fast, "Apostle to the City," 350.
54. Wong, *Ripples*, 32, 36.
55. Todd, translated notes, 26–27.
56. Todd, Port Moody congregational members discussion with Rev. Enoch and Grace Wong, May 15, 2010.
57. Wong, *Ripples*, 25, 26.

planted during his years of ministry. Enoch had immigrated to Canada in August of 1976 and had been doing itinerant work for Scripture Union Canada.[58] Enoch noted, "I was in Toronto Canada with the Scripture Reading Society (Scripture Union Canada); I was to fly back via Vancouver to Hong Kong [however] when I arrived in Vancouver, I was invited to preach—there was no [Chinese] pastor, only thirty people; God gave us the burden to stay."[59] Grace Wong notes that "the deacons from Pacific Grace MB Church . . . invited him to preach" at this church that had not had a "pastor for eighteen months [and] attendance dropped drastically. . . . We accepted the invitation . . . and set to work on August 1, 1980."[60] Pacific Grace MB Church "was officially registered in 1981 and the membership grew from thirty to 105 in 1983, and 240 in 1989."[61] Grace Wong notes that

> there were not many young people [referring to teenagers and young adults] in our church, yet they were eager to start a fellowship. Enoch challenged them to bring more friends and he would lead this fellowship if there were at least eight people. In the end nine were committed. The first meeting was a BBQ at Burnaby Centennial Park on the first Saturday of September 1980.[62]

During 1989, Valerie Yiu would begin an "English worship service for English speaking Chinese youth."[63] Keynes Kan and Miller Zhuang would join the pastoral staff, with Zhuang eventually "sent to Venezuela where two Chinese MB churches were established."[64] Under the leadership of Rev. Enoch at Pacific Grace MB, during a period when "many Hong Kong peoples were immigrating to British Columbia on account of fears over the takeover of Hong Kong by China and the Tiananmen Square massacre in 1989,"[65] the Pacific Grace MB Church grew rapidly to the point that they would seek to initiate a church plant in 1990 with a congregation of approximately fifty. Yu cites Pacific Grace Chinese Church as being an example of the rapid growth of Chinese Canadian Protestant churches that

58. Wong, *Ripples*, 29–30.

59. Todd, Port Moody congregational members discussion with Rev Enoch and Grace Wong, May 15, 2010.

60. Wong, *Ripples*, 32.

61. Kwan, "We Are In."

62. Wong, *Ripples*, 37.

63. Kwan, "We Are In."

64. Kwan, "We Are In."

65. Kwan, "We Are In."

became "capable of producing several generations of descendent churches in a short period."[66]

Bethel Chinese MB Church. Kwan notes that

> although Pacific Grace MB was the first Chinese church to be established, the first Chinese MB church that was registered with the government was Bethel Chinese Christian MB Church, established in 1978 by the BC MB Conference Board of Church Extension under the leadership of David Poon.... It officially joined the BC MB Conference in 1980, becoming the first registered Chinese MB church in North America.[67]

Rev. Poon formerly had pastored an Alliance church in Hong Kong and at Christ Church of China in Vancouver.[68] In 1978, Poon was formally accepted as a church planter and pastor of Richmond Chinese MB Church (subsequently known as Bethel Chinese Christian MB Church), where he would pastor until 2007.[69] After several relocations, the church settled in Vancouver,[70] and by 1997, Poon and Bethel planted another church called North Shore Bethel Christian MB Church. Poon has also had an advisory role to the MBCCA.[71] The church has had multiple English ministry pastors.[72]

B. The Branches

A new church plant of PGMBC was called Burnaby Pacific Grace. This new congregation also grew rapidly, so Burnaby Pacific Grace congregants planted another congregation, and by February of 1995, the Port Moody Pacific Grace Chinese Church began their first services.[73] As a charter English ministry pastor with PMPGMBC, the development of that English

---

66. Yu, "Christianity," 235. Much of this new growth was fueled by immigration (236).
67. Kwan, "We Are In."
68. Leung, "Not I," 274.
69. Leung, "Not I, 278.
70. Leung, "Not I," 282.
71. Leung, "Not I," 281.
72. Notably, Ping On Cheng, Philip Yung, Kam Foon Tang, Nick Suen, Justin Yap, Derek Tou, and Tim Tse. Currently, in 2025, Peter Chong is the EM pastor. Esther Poon, email discussion with the author, October 11, 2018. Esther Poon (wife of Rev. David Poon) on the history of English ministries at Bethel Chinese MB church.
73. Todd, "Port Moody Church."

congregation began with a small class of English junior high students in 1998, where Helen Chia (nee Yueng) was helping with the CBC youth. In the autumn of 1998, I began ministering in the PMPGMBC English ministries. By 1999, there were forty-six in the EM; by 2009, there were 125; and by 2010, there were 130 plus. Back in 1987, at Pacific Grace MB, Enoch Wong, due to health reasons, turned over the executive pastoral leadership of Pacific Grace MB (also known as North Side Pacific Grace) to Rev. David Chan in August 1987.[74] Enoch, however, continued to serve as a volunteer advisor amongst the Chinese MB, with a vision to focus on building up missional churches and church planting. It is notable that much of Enoch's service to the Chinese MB churches (after he left the pastoral position at Pacific Grace MB) was volunteer, or what was called "honorary advisor."[75]

Eventually, Hong Kong immigration numbers declined, and MBCCA churches began determining new directions. On account of the large influx of Mandarin-speaking mainland China immigrants coming to British Columbia, the Port Moody Church would be the first church to initiate a vision to focus their outreach on Mandarin immigrants[76] with Mandarin fellowship and worship services in 1997. The plan to reach Mandarin peoples was put in place in 1997 by Rev. Keynes Kan and his advisor, the honorable Enoch Wong. Oversight was followed through by Rev. Hua. In 1998, Leo Chia would begin a church-planting project, which grew to seventy people in 1999. By 2000, the church was off denominational subsidy and independent under the name of Pacific Grace Mandarin Church. In 2002, it launched from Port Moody to Burnaby under the name Pacific Grace Mandarin Church. Chia would eventually plant two more Mandarin church offshoots in 2006 (Maple Ridge) and in 2009 (Surrey).[77] By "1999 simultaneous translation for Mandarin-speaking Chinese was being added to many worship services."[78] Church-planting in the MBCCA churches would become a passion for the pastoral leaders and MBCCA congregations.[79] In 2016, it was declared there were "nineteen Chinese

---

74. Wong, *Ripples*, 39.

75. Wong, *Ripples*, 39–40.

76. Kwan, "We Are In."

77. Kwan, "We are in," 5. The data here was obtained in a personal interview with Rev. Leo Chia, Burnaby, BC, March 11, 2020.

78. Kwan, "We Are In."

79. This led to the following church plants: Abbotsford Chinese Christian Church, 1989; Vancouver Chinese MB Church, 1989; Tri-City Chinese Christian Church, 1991; South Vancouver Pacific Grace MB Church, 1995; North Shore Pacific Grace MB

congregations . . . exploring the possibility of partnerships between Chinese and Caucasian churches in Richmond and Prince George."[80] By 2018, the British Columbia Mennonite Brethren Chinese MB churches would constitute twenty congregations. The Manitoba Conference would have the Winnipeg Chinese MB Church (developed in the 1980s for refugees and students). The Saskatchewan MB conference would have the Regina Chinese Community Church (registered in 1989). The Alberta MB conference would have Mountain View Grace Church 1995. As Kwan has noted, "Chinese MB churches are especially keen in church planting and overseas missions."[81] The Pacific Grace Chinese Church established a church in Puerto La Cruz, Venezuela, in 1991, and a second mission's church in Caracas, Venezuela, in 1991. A constant theme with the MBCCA churches has been dealing with issues of rapid growth. Johnson has noted that when society generally thinks about people from a Mennonite denomination or Anabaptist tradition, it evokes pictures that date back to the Reformation of the 1500s. However, in Metro Vancouver, "the word ["Mennonite" has] increasingly conjure[d] images of newcomers from China, Hong Kong, and elsewhere in Asia who have discovered an old form of Christianity and made it their own."[82] In the last several decades, there have been "twenty

---

Church, 1997; North Shore Bethel Christian MB Church, 1997; Vancouver Christian Logos Church, 1997; Pacific Grace Mandarin Church, 1998; Richmond Pacific Grace MB Church, 2005; North Shore Pacific Grace Mandarin Church, 2005; and Maple Ridge Pacific Grace Mandarin Church, 2006. Although each of the MBCCA church plants has an exceptional story that can be obtained on the Global Anabaptist Mennonite Encyclopedia Online, the North Shore Pacific Grace MB church growth story is one that was born out of deep hardship for the church planter; For the interested reader, see Hui, *Hot Stream*. The church work was started in September 1, 1997 (154) by To Wang Hui, who interned with Pacific Grace MB Church under David Chan from 1994–97 as an "associate pastor in Cantonese ministry" (6); he was supported by some people from Pacific Grace's north- and south-site mission departments and a "few core families in the [north shore] vicinity" (62). Backing also came from the Board of Church extension in the BC-MBC. In 1998, the church was registered. By 2000, To Wang Hui was ordained (with the late Rev. Enoch Wong present). In 2004, To Wang Hui was diagnosed with Parkinson's disease and later liver cancer; despite these difficulties, the church grew in "quality and quantity" (85). To Wang Hui's legacy is a thriving Cantonese ministry currently led by Rev. Peter Teh and a robust English ministry with the most recent English ministries pastor being Eileen Li.

80. "MB Churches of Canada," 20. These nineteen churches sit in a Mennonite global community of 470,000 members in 3,000 congregations (30). This is a document you can download when you are registered.

81. Kwan, "Building People," 12.

82. Johnson, "Pacific Spirit."

Chinese MB churches [established] in seven cities in three different countries. . . . Fourteen of these churches are in Vancouver's Lower Mainland."[83] Chia has established several Mandarin-speaking congregations, while some of the other Chinese MB churches have provided some form of Mandarin ministries.[84] In 2018, it was reported that the MB denomination was planning a Chinese church plant in the province of Ontario.

C. The Life Cycle of the Church, Assimilation Challenges, and Mission

This section identifies that the life cycle of the church and assimilation factor into the Silent Exodus and contribute to the problem of impacting parents. Chinese parents bring their children to the Chinese church because many see the positive influence the church has on families and children,[85] and the parents are looking for help to raise their children in their own cultural values.[86] It has been noted that "second-generation Asian [North] Americans who grew up as Protestants convert at higher rates . . . than . . . Protestant peers in the general population."[87] Evangelizing second-generation youth is a fruitful field. The challenge has to do with generational assimilation when they become emerging young adults. The intention in this subsection is to make the case that as the church matures and goes through its life cycle, it faces challenges retaining the next generation, which is anecdotally reported to impact the parents and has implications on focusing on the mission of the church. These cultural churches provide holistic sociological and spiritual functions in supporting the Chinese family and cultural heritage.[88] Sociologists acknowledge how the ethnic church has more often promoted youth's resilience.[89] Feedback on the Chinese MB churches

---

83. Kwan, "We Are In."

84. Kwan, "We Are In." Leo Chia, phone interview with Matthew Todd, March 12, 2020. Alice Leung, email interview communication with Matthew Todd, March 11, 2020. Both Chia and Leung noted the MBCCA currently has two Mandarin congregations (NSPGMC and PGMC) and approximately seven Mandarin ministries in its sphere that include Bethel Chinese Christian MB, House for All Nations, Maple Ridge, PGMB, Richmond Chinese MB, Surrey Grace Mandarin, and Willingdon Church.

85. Lu et al., "Chinese Immigrant Families," 121.

86. Lu et al., "Chinese Immigrant Families," 119.

87. Chen and Park, "Pathways of Religious Assimilation," 676.

88. Ebaugh and Chafetz, "Structural," 135–53.

89. Barry and Abo-Zena, "Experience of Meaning-Making," 475.

in Canada informatively indicates that all of the MBCCA churches have had to grapple with generational assimilation and the emerging young adulthood of their English ministries. Kwan once commented on this demographic, "Should these young Christians be members of English-speaking departments in existing churches, or should they form separate churches?"[90] A couple of their English ministry pastors took initiatives in forming separate churches. Pacific Grace MB Church merged a group from their English congregation with Vancouver MB Church, creating South Hill MB Church in November 2007. The merger was classified as a venture into a multicultural church model. PGMBC sent English pastor Mike Nishi to lead the merged congregations, which resulted in a six-year union from 2007 until dissolving in 2013.[91] Another English ministry church planter, who formerly served with Bethel Chinese MB Church, was Nick Suen, who with the blessing of the BCMB planted an English-speaking church called Faithwerks in 2008.[92]

By 2008, the Chinese MB churches in British Columbia and English ministries membership "constituted more than 10 percent of the Mennonite Brethren in the province."[93] The period between 2008 and 2009 represented a high-water mark for the MBCCA English ministries congregations when a survey (conducted between July and October 2008) was executed to profile the English ministries of twelve of the English congregations in the Greater Vancouver area. The findings regarding the state of the English ministries were quite revealing. The twelve Chinese MB churches[94] represented a total group of approximately 3,000 Chinese MB congregants, all from Cantonese-language-based churches (the Mandarin congregation of Rev. Leo Chia was not included in this survey because it was a young church plant). The English ministries represented 21 percent of the total congregants surveyed, of which 20 percent were identified as being in the career and family categories; 28 percent attended college, and 52 percent attended high school.[95] In 2008, the age of the participating churches ranged from three to thirty years

90. Kwan, "We Are In."
91. Southhill Mennonite.
92. Thiessen, "Faithwerks."
93. Guenther, "Ethnicity," 380.
94. The MBCCA churches represented were Bethel CCMB, Burnaby PG, North shore Bethel, North Shore PG, Pacific Grace MB, Port Moody PGMB, Richmond CMB, South Vancouver PGMB, Tricity CC, Vancouver CMB, and Vancouver Christian Logos.
95. Leung, "MBCCA English."

old (in 2025, they are twenty to forty-seven years old). The English ministry congregations in 2008 ranged from two to twenty years old (in 2025, nineteen to thirty-seven years old).[96] With the exception of Port Moody Pacific Grace and Vancouver Chinese MB, which in 2008 had approximately 125 and seventy-five in their English ministries, respectively, all other Chinese MB churches had an average of forty-two in their English ministries. With the exception of Port Moody PG and Vancouver Chinese MB, most of the English ministry (EM) full-time pastors had less than five years' experience with their current churches. Churches like Bethel Chinese MB and Pacific Grace MB had already experienced having multiple EM pastors (EM pastoral attrition was becoming a pattern). When documenting what the participants considered to be their major sources of future growth for English ministries, the majority cited the Awana and children's ministries (nine out of twelve churches had Awana); only two English congregations cited from multicultural outreach. The survey asked questions regarding the church mission, vision, and future goals of the English ministries; nine of them focused on internal development, and three made mention of the Great Commission. That survey cited leadership development and outreach as among the highest needs in the EM. One of my research focuses at the time was "to provide a trajectory of the stages of development of an [sic] English ministries, from adolescence to adulthood."[97] From October 15–16, 2008 a significant MBCCA English pastors' retreat was held at Loon Lake, British Columbia, which represented fourteen English pastors' reflections on the EM profiling survey. The meeting minutes[98] noted that there was a collective interest to explore what could be mutually done amongst them. Concern was expressed about the church model and that none of the Chinese MB churches had a clear vision statement that included the EM regarding where they were going with EM; it was recognized that the vision for the whole church was primarily crafted by executive clergy and boards and not from the English-language pastors. Understandably, there was not one single case where the English pastor could autonomously strategize a vision for what they wanted to look like and where they were going in a Chinese MB church that addressed acculturation and adapting to CBC culture and CBC networks or CBC outreach and mission potential. It was noted that,

---

96. I am referring to how long the English ministry congregation has been servicing EM people, not the age of the EM peoples.
97. Todd, "Development and Transition," 16.
98. MBCCA English Pastors.

for the most part, EM congregations are started in Chinese churches to keep the second generation with their families in the church. It was noted that there was a need for a paradigm (church model) flexible enough for a common vision.[99]

The history and development of the MBCCA churches and the growth of their English ministries can be theologically anchored in texts like Deut 8:2, where it states, "You shall remember all the way which the LORD your God has led you" (NASB). The text is an admonition to remember the things learned along the way, to be journey-oriented and continue to build on the past. The foundational work and examples of Henry and Sara Classen and Enoch and Grace Wong could be viewed as pivotal to the present work. There is a need to look back at the past to gain new inspiration for the present. The past was the path to the present, leaving the challenge to build on the work of the past; this resonates with John 14:12, where it says, "Anyone who believes in me will do the works I have been doing" (NIRV). From 2008–2009, the English chapter of the MBCCA pastors assessed a "profiling [of] what age groups existed in [their lower mainland] churches." It was stated that "all but two of our English language congregations had college, university, career, and family couples in them. Only two were exclusively teen ministry congregations."[100] In 2011, Rev. Yiu Tong Chan of Vancouver Chinese MB Church noted that "we are all experiencing an Exodus of the English-speaking second generation . . . [and a] shortage of second-generation church ministers."[101] Warren Lai sharpens this observation by stating,

> As immigrant families of previous years mature, the Chinese Canadian churches (like many other immigrant churches in North America) experience an increasing, if not massive, loss of their second and third generations; and for those so-called CBC's who stay, they pose questions about the *raison d'être* and the mission of the Chinese Canadian churches.[102]

It is now a good time to reflect on the dynamics of the development and transitioning of assimilating youth, which requires more consideration given the anecdotal recognition of the Silent Exodus of CBC young adults away from their family congregations and the impact it has had on parents.

99. MBCCA English Pastors.
100. Todd, "Development and Transition," 16.
101. Chan, *Looking Back*, viii.
102. Lai, "Is There a Future," 67.

Timothy Tseng has encapsulated the problem by stating, "The Silent Exodus of younger Asian[s] . . . from immigrant Asian churches has continued unabated since the 1970s. . . . Asian Christians in Canada . . . now face a critical 'tipping point' regarding their ministry to emergent adults (late teens, college age to late twenties)."[103] The impact on OBC parents appears to be the most underreported part of the story.

D. The Need to Address the Impact on Parents

In 2015, the assistant conference minister for Chinese churches in the BC Mennonite Brethren Conference published a public book review on my former research on the Silent Exodus from Chinese churches in British Columbia and Alberta,[104] commenting on the scope of the surveys, stating,

> The survey did not include the comparative *perceptions* of the Overseas-born Chinese (OBC) on this topic nor the general reasons for people changing churches. The latter should have been taken into account when considering an optimal English model and vision for change."[105]

This current interdenominational study on OBCs, which includes Mennonite Brethren Chinese Church Association (MBCCA) clergy and parents impacted by the Silent Exodus of emerging adults, is, in part, a response to Leung's critique of the need to "include comparative perceptions" on the reasons for the Silent Exodus.[106] This research focuses on the impact of the Silent Exodus on parents and includes the OBC clergy's anecdotal perception of the impact on parents. The research also includes OBC parents' recommendations on how to support impacted parents.

In summary, anecdotal reporting indicates that the Silent Exodus of youth impacts parents. This chapter contributes to the solution of the problem by helping the reader understand the cultural background and context which the youth exit from and parent impacts occur. Chinese churches share a common history rooted in the immigration experience and founding of congregations that function also as a cultural hub, helping families

---

103. Tseng, "Intergenerational Tension," 50.

104. Todd, *English Ministry Crisis*.

105. Leung, "Research"; emphasis added.

106. Todd, "Empowering." Appendix B, tables A28, B29, B82, B83, B84, and Appendix C pre-focus group questionnaire table C22, "Why the next generation leaves," found in Appendix C raw data.

cope and acculturate. I explored the background of beliefs and practices that have guided attitudes, values, meanings, customs, language, norms, and behaviors. In particular, I took a specific denominational look at the Mennonite Brethren Chinese churches and did a short historical review (roots, development) of foundational personalities who capitalized on Chinese immigration, resulting in rapid church growth. With the development of language congregations come new challenges with a theology of culture and emphasis on ethnicity. The life cycle of the Chinese church, the sociological dynamics of second-generation acculturation, and challenges with a retention of the second generation are all precipitating factors to the Silent Exodus and subsequent impact on parents. Next, I will look at a theological framework that contributes a perspective and possible solution to the problem of impacted parents.

5

A Theology of Family

"What do people mean by quoting the proverb, "The parents eat sour grapes, and the children's teeth are set on edge?" Might it also be said that the children have eaten sour grapes and the parents' teeth are set on edge?

(A RECONSIDERATION OF EZEKIEL 18:2, MATTHEW R. S. TODD)

Theological Issues Related to the Problem

I REMEMBER TAKING A family holiday road trip from British Columbia through Washington, Montana, Idaho, and Utah, all the way down to Arizona and back up the West Coast through California, Oregon, and Washington to British Columbia. It required carefully planning the entire trip and prebooking lodgings and activities, such as visiting the Grand Canyon, Mount Saint Helens, and other locations. In fact, there was only one overnight lodging destination that I forgot to book, so our family spent the night in the middle of a campground surrounded by a tough-looking motorcycle gang suspicious of our presence since I looked like a cop. Who would ever think of traveling by car throughout the North American continent without putting some careful thought into planning and the destination? The same principle applies to parenting. If you ask a parent what the biblical framework is that they are using to navigate the evolving stages of their family, you might get a blank stare. Are you as a parent missing a clear vision for the Christian life, and is that being reflected in your spiritual influence on your child?

The question this book asks is, "What is the impact on Canadian Chinese immigrant Christian parents when their youth separate from the faith and ethnic church?" Chinese Christian parents and Chinese church communities have a theo-cultural framework from which they understand the purpose of the family and a family church.[1] To begin with, theological issues related to the problem seem to be related to a theology of family in the life cycle, a theology of parenting, and a theology for spiritual development that encompasses the developmental stages where individuation interfaces with midlife parenting. This chapter outlines a theological framework that provides one understanding of the purpose of the family by providing a summary on a biblical theology of the family and an overview of divine intention for the family. It constructs a contemporary theological perspective for understanding why youth leave home churches, abandon the faith, or move to other churches that don't share features of their home church. It is intended to advance an expanded understanding of the emerging young adult's life transitions as they interface with social, cultural, and institutional forces. This theological framework is intended to support and inform the experience of parents who have adult children that abandoned their churches and perhaps their faith as well. This discussion takes into consideration that some Christian parents may have possibly embraced incomplete (or false) ideas about biblical promises with regard to the spiritual trajectory of their growing children. They may have been told if they raise their kids in the church that the outcome of CBCs and CRCs will be to embrace the faith carte blanche (a deterministic view), which is not guaranteed biblically. Six key areas will be explored in this chapter:

1. A theological understanding of the family.

---

1. Lu et al., "Chinese Immigrant Families"; Chinese immigrant families understand church as an "extended family" (123), "one family" (124), church as a "Big Family" (123–25), church as a second home (125). ChenFeng notes that the Chinese immigrant Christian community generally sees the Chinese church "as a place of safety and connection." In a North American context where they have often "experience[d] discrimination" (18), the Chinese church is seen as a place that provides "healing," "positive outcomes," "social belonging," (18–19), and "support" for "parenting efforts" (20), as well as support for "the identity of the Chinese [Christian] family" in "reinforcing cultural values . . . in a Chinese Christian way" (20). Six of those core cultural values include collectivism, conformity to norms, emotional self-control, family recognition through achievement, filial piety, and humility: "These values are modeled and reinforced in the Chinese church context" (21).

2. A theological understanding of why young adults leave home and churches.

3. A theological understanding of why Christian parents struggle with children who exit faith communities they were raised in.

4. A theological understanding and review of biblical texts that depict children leaving from their faith-based communities.

5. A theological understanding and overview of how parents from biblical narratives processed the perception of loss of their progeny.

6. An Old and New Testament trajectory focus and purpose for the family of God.

A Theological Understanding of the Family

The goal of this section is to portray a biblical ideal of the purpose for family that provides a foundation to measure discrepancies experienced because of impacts of the fall (Gen 3). This provisional theological framework is not saying only one way is normal, but that God is attributed to providing a purpose for family and the family of God. What was God's original intention for the family? A theological understanding of the family begins with an understanding that family is God's idea, an expression of his sovereignty.[2] The human story begins with God as Father.[3] Paul stated in Eph 3:14, "I kneel to the father from whom every family in heaven and on earth takes its name." Humankind is made for relationships in the image of the Three-in-One God. A theology of family contains the idea that family was intended to "reflect the relationality within the Trinity."[4] Thatcher has noted that "we are invited to visualize the identity of every family past, present, and future as constituted in some way by their relation to God . . . [and] to envisage human parenting as rooted in the being and will of the divine

---

2. Atkinson, *Biblical and Theological Foundations*, 33.

3. Boot, "Theology." For the interested reader, see Balswick and Balswick, *Family*. The Balswicks give a discussion on a Trinitarian perspective of "God as parent in relationship" (1) and cite multiple New Testament texts on "God's intention for the family" in regards to household relationships (3).

4. Balswick and Balswick, *Family*. For example, the Balswicks argue that this includes reflecting the character of God (4), that "distinction and unity coexist" (5), that "family fellowship" is "embraced in love and harmony" (5), and that a healthy relationship is foundational to guiding the child (5).

Parent."⁵ It is clear in "the creation account of Genesis . . . that all people are . . . interconnected and have an originating point in the first personal creation of God, namely, Adam."⁶ Marriage and family are foundational in a Christian worldview. Part of God's good creation included creating man and woman with the potential for family and community, as well as "a need for intimate relationships, a need that draws us to leave the persons from whose bodies we have come—our parents—to form a new 'body' with a new partner (Gen 2:23–24)."⁷ God has created people with the capacity to procreate and replicate the image of God; as such, "the sexual drive [became] . . . a witness to the truth that [people are] not to be alone; [people are] meant for community."⁸ People are made in the imago Dei; fruitfulness and experiencing communion "reach full expression in child and family."⁹ Built into humanity's creation is God's enabling people to procreate and fill the earth with more image bearers. It is "procreation that makes [human] history possible [and helps] . . . perpetuate the initial blessing of God and experience his salvific acts."¹⁰ The purpose of marriage and childbearing is to produce "godly offspring."¹¹ The biblical vision for family is to be image-bearers of God, to glorify God and extend the kingdom. Atkinson argues that the "theological function of the family . . . [begins] . . . with the monotheistic nature of God and the creation that proceeds from this."¹² That is to say, the family potentially is

> a carrier of salvific power . . . [and] it is in and through the events of history God . . . reveal[s] himself to man and bring[s] all things to their destined completion. This includes the family, which . . . becomes the instrument by which God's will for man's salvation is accomplished in history.¹³

---

5. Thatcher, *Theologies and Families*, 3.
6. Atkinson, *Biblical and Theological Foundations*, 203.
7. Garland, *Family*, 92.
8. Atkinson, *Biblical and Theological Foundations*, 57.
9. Atkinson, *Biblical and Theological Foundations*, 62.
10. Atkinson, *Biblical and Theological Foundations*, 65.
11. See Mal 2:15. God is wanting the human family to participate in producing "godly representatives" through their "offspring" (Hebrew *zera*), which refers to "posterity" and family descendants (Baker et al., *Complete Word Study*, 36).
12. Baker et al., *Complete Word Study*, 76.
13. Baker et al., *Complete Word Study*, 77.

A Theology of Family

The Scriptures frequently describe God's love for people using familial images (e.g., "father"); Scripture is intended to deepen human understanding of what God is like.[14] Calvin notes, "God has received [believers] . . . into his family"[15] and takes it upon himself "to nourish us throughout the course of our life."[16] It was and is intended that people "would in many ways represent God."[17] The biblical narratives make it clear that God is concerned about the wellbeing of the generations of the human family. The Old Testament articulates the historical and genealogical connections of the family and their relationship to God, and that family has a purpose for the present and future generations.[18] Understanding "covenant" is "foundational" to "developing a theology of the family" and becomes a "paradigm for the family";[19] "covenant is . . . [God's] . . . unconditional commitment . . . to the creation."[20] Narratives like the flood story are a reminder the Creator has also been at work in preserving the covenant family. God made a covenant to Abraham and spoke to him regarding blessing the present and future members of his family. He also promised to make him a blessing to the families of the nations. God's covenant with Abraham entailed that, in return for his faith and obedience (Gen 15:6; 22:16–18; Gal 3:28–29), God would guide and bless him and the generations after him (Gen 17:7) who followed God in faith and obedience. This covenant promise would extend as an invitation to the families of the nations of the earth (Gen 12:3; 17:4, 7; Gal 3:8). Revealed to Abraham was that the family was "the carrier of the covenant . . . [and] imaged forth the covenant."[21] The "function of [the family is to faithfully] transmit unimpaired the covenant from generation to generation."[22] Children born into the faith family were to be taught the principles of Scripture and "be shaped and formed so that the person would be conformed to God[23] . . . [and] enabled . . . to encounter

---

14. Garland, *Family*, 89.
15. Calvin, *Institutes* 2.1359.
16. Calvin, *Institutes* 2.1360.
17. Grudem, *Systematic Theology*, 443.
18. Joel 1:3.
19. Balswick and Balswick, *Family*, 6.
20. Balswick and Balswick, *Family*, 8.
21. Atkinson, *Biblical and Theological Foundations*, 78.
22. Atkinson, *Biblical and Theological Foundations*, 91.
23. Atkinson, *Biblical and Theological Foundations*, 91.

the reality of God."[24] Calvin argued that parents leave a legacy;[25] however, "family [should be viewed] as a developing system."[26] Kimmel identifies that parents primary goal is to reflect the heart of God, to connect with the heart of the child, and to incline the child to have a heart for God.[27] Families are part of the apex of God's creation. Parents are to instruct and demonstrate living in the faith and life of God; raising children to make a difference in the world is one of a parent's most influential work and acts of stewardship.[28] Psalm 78:3–4 states,

> Things we have heard and known, things our ancestors have told us. We will not hide them from their children; we will tell the next generation the praiseworthy deeds of the Lord, his power, and the wonders he has done.

A theology for the family includes the divine assignment and "obligation [for parents] to care for the next generation."[29] This theme of ensuring instruction for children, grandchildren, and great grandchildren to "tell the generations that follow . . . about God's faithfulness" is found throughout the Scriptures (Deut 4:8–9; Exod 10:2; 13:8, 14).[30] The responsibility of parents is to "provide religious and educational [spiritual] formation for children."[31] Spiritual formation ranges from raising children in the knowledge, nurture, and admonition of God to disciplining, educating, and teaching biblical character.[32] An application of 1 Pet 4:10 for parents would be that parents' lifelong role is to be "faithful stewards of God's grace in various forms." Kimmel argues that this needs to be grace-based, not fear-based or shame-based.[33] Children are on loan to parents who are given the honor of being caretakers of the next generation. Genesis 2:24 states that

---

24. Atkinson, *Biblical and Theological Foundations*, 92.
25. Calvin, *Institutes* 1.385–86.
26. Balswick and Balswick, *Family*, xii.
27. Kimmel, "Theology of Family."
28. Roberts, "Could Family."
29. Freeks, "Pastoral-Theological View," 182.
30. Deut 4:9 (34); 6:1–2; 32:7 (34); Job 8:8–10; Ps 22:30–31; 78:5–7 (35); 102:18; 145:4; 3 John 4 (36). Habecker, *What the Bible Says*.
31. Atkinson, *Biblical and Theological Foundations*, 95.
32. Pollard and Brown, *Theology of the Family*, 276–342.
33. The author argues that grace-based parenting means treating your kids the way God treats you and not limiting grace to salvation by focusing on performance. Kimmel, "Theology of Family."

built into the fabric of the family is the impetus to move beyond its nucleus and expand its influence, for "a man leaves his father and mother and bonds with his wife" (Gen 2:24, CSB). Part of parents' witness to the world can be that they have raised children predisposed to the faith, who embraced faith in Christ for themselves, and become expressions of that faith and witness into their own community contexts. Atkinson notes that "Christianity . . . emerged from within Judaism . . . [where] Christians believed that in Christ the covenant with Abraham had reached its teleological conclusion."[34] Faith in Christ brought one into the family of God and "the family still retains the function of being the carrier of the covenant . . . and everyone within its orbit is affected—even those who are not yet believers (1 Cor 7:12–13, 16)."[35] The "meaning and function of the family" is the same in both the Old and New Testaments.[36] Paul states in Rom 4:16 and Gal 3:29 that if people prioritize faith in God, like Abraham did, then in Christ alone, they are part of the family of God. Therefore, "Paul's use of Abraham . . . is critical to the theology of the family . . . because it points to Abraham as being paradigmatic for all Christians,"[37] which is to say that "in the new covenant in Christ . . . [we] are called into one family of God, which is the Church (Eph 2:19). In its core identity, the Church is not primarily an institution, but . . . is the organic body of Christ."[38] Garland notes that "family is a . . . proving ground for Christian discipleship and a vineyard for the fruits of the Spirit. . . .[39] [Family] provides images . . . Christians are to have with one another in the community of faith."[40] The purpose of Christian families is "to live out the will of the Father. . . . The Church is our new family, bound together . . . by faith in Jesus Christ."[41] Terms for what Christians experience are "adoption"[42] and "inclusion." In the New Testament, many of the authors cite their histories and genealogies in Jewish families of faith, but more significant is the family's relationship to Christ and being a part of the family of God. It is notable that Jesus entered history in the incarnation

---

34. Atkinson, *Biblical and Theological Foundations*, 193.
35. Atkinson, *Biblical and Theological Foundations*, 195.
36. Atkinson, *Biblical and Theological Foundations*, 198.
37. Atkinson, *Biblical and Theological Foundations*, 216.
38. Atkinson, *Biblical and Theological Foundations*, 219.
39. Garland, *Family*, 91.
40. Garland, *Family*, 90.
41. Garland, *Family*, 104.
42. Garland, *Family*, 110.

"in the context of family, becoming the aim and purpose of all the Old Testament genealogies."[43] Perspectives on a biblical understanding of family can be gleaned by making some observations of Jesus with his earthly family. Garland has argued that Mary and Joseph were given a calling and could have declined it, but instead, they took up living faithfully as a family, in the process giving witness to family as a vocation.[44] Jesus's parents were called "to guide him . . . help him learn . . . to suffer for him the pain of birth and then [eventually] let him go."[45] Notably, "the call to live faithfully as family to those we find in our care [and want to help launch] is just as much a response to the call of God as the response to leave everything behind to take up Jesus's cross."[46]

Though there are limited texts on Jesus's formative years, there are notably no references to him dishonoring his parents or diminishing the importance of family. In fact, in Mark 7:9–13, Jesus challenges some of the Pharisees for not doing their familial duty in financially assisting and caring for their elderly parents. Some theologians make a case for Mary being a widow and operating a single-parent home because Joseph is not mentioned in the Gospels after Jesus's temple incident (Luke 2:41–52); by implication, this would have put more responsibility on Jesus, being the eldest, to work (in Mark 6:3 he was called a carpenter—Joseph's profession, noted in Matt 13:55) and care for his mother and younger siblings.[47] Being the oldest, at the time of his death, Jesus took the time to make arrangements for his elderly mother.[48] At the same time, "Jesus affirmed the importance of caring for parents by his own example on the cross and through his teachings on the subject (Matt 15:3–9; Mark 7:9–13)."[49] Jesus understood that the command for those who come of age to honor parents included caring for them when they are elderly practically, both physically and materially.[50] Jesus validated a healthy "attitude [and] sacrificial actions."[51] Yet, Jesus "[did not] . . . permit [family] ties to stand in the way of ones' decision to

---

43. Atkinson, *Biblical and Theological Foundations*, 77.
44. Garland, *Family*, 93–94, 111.
45. Garland, *Family*, 94.
46. Garland, *Family*, 94.
47. Grudem, *Systematic Theology*, 537.
48. John 19:25–27.
49. Houston and Parker, *Vision for the Aging Church*, 127.
50. Tram, "Honor Your Parents," 247–63.
51. Tram, "Honor Your Parents," 262–63.

follow him (Matt 10:35–36)."[52] Furthermore, Jesus also demonstrated that it became necessary to "distance himself from his family" and their expectations on his life in order for him to fulfill the will of God the Father.[53] It has been noted that implicit in Jesus's example with family is that

> Jesus . . . indicated that his relationship to God took priority over family relationships. . . . The point is theological. . . . Those who fail to honor God's will for their lives regardless of cost, even to family, fail to enter the kingdom of God. The Gospels reveal a higher concern than family. The kingdom of God must have top priority. Even family relationships, as important as they are, should not deter one from fulfilling God's plan.[54]

The application of this insight is intergenerational. Both have an obligation to live in the faith and life of God, and both have an obligation to fulfill God's plan with their lives. In Eph 5:22–32 and Col 3:18–22, Paul discusses family relationships and how they are to be God-honoring. Particularly applicable to emerging young adults is Paul's instruction in Eph 6:2 to "honor your father and mother—which is the first commandment with a promise." The word "honor" refers to showing respect and appreciation. The command to "obey," found in Eph 6:1, is only applicable to children (Greek *tekna*, literally referring to a child). Paul's comment to "honor" comes with a promise in Eph 6:3: "that it may go well with you and that you may enjoy long life on the earth." Two aspects of that promise are wellbeing and quality of life. It is referring to the social stability that is produced in a community in which the next generation honors their parents. A healthy society is inconceivable without a strong family life. Part of a healthy community is caring for and respecting the elders of the community. It can be troubling to see societal trends where the culture sees its elders as liabilities. The family was intended to be the context where people could flourish and be nurtured into following God's purposes for their lives. What is clear from the Pauline texts is that God intended there to be a "proper order in the family," and that a "Christian family must take seriously its calling to represent God on earth [which] includes proper. . . function of all family relationships."[55] The transition from being a minor, who are under scriptural instruction to "obey" parents, into being an emerging young adult, where

---

52. Williams, "Family Life and Relations," 245.
53. Anthony, *Theology for Family Ministries*, 98.
54. Anthony, *Theology for Family Ministries*, 98.
55. Anthony, *Theology for Family Ministries*, 105.

the scriptural instruction to "honor" parents, can become an obscure and murky transition—especially when, in many cases, the emerging young adult is still living in the parents' home or dependent on parents for either housing or other benefits. Although legal systems and cultural conventions define a minor as not yet reaching the threshold of adulthood and attach various ages to it (e.g., sixteen, eighteen, nineteen, and twenty-one), individual families' and cultures' perspectives on reaching adulthood do not necessarily line up with these. The transition can also be a bit ambiguous given Asian families generally have a measure of cultural or Confucian-based notions regarding filial piety that come with expectations "to submit to the wishes of parents... well into adulthood."[56]

A theological understanding of the family needs to acknowledge the impact of the fall (Gen 3) and sin on family systems, as well as the problem of pain and suffering for parents in a fallen world. Genesis 3 shows how God responds when his children refuse to accept his influence: he lets them leave and makes redemptive provision, watching to reconcile them. He remains involved, looking for redemptive opportunity to intervene into the family system. God makes provision for the restoration and reconciliation of family relationships and with himself (Mal 4:6; Luke 1:16–17) so that his kingdom purposes can be advanced. Many parents discover that their emerging adults will "have violated [their] values and chosen a different path than [parents] would have chosen for them."[57] When emerging adults are launching, it may not be happening according to the parents' ideal expectations. This can reveal that the "love of... children... commands more [focus] than love of God." Furthermore, "the attitudes about family held by... church members [can reveal that they] are not very different from those of [people outside the church]. One difference is that members of congregations expect the church to help them achieve fulfillment in their family relationships."[58] Parent expectations explain why church clergy can often be blamed for why youth and emerging young adults leave the church. It can be interpreted as a failure of the church in not helping families enough to achieve the fulfillment of their vision of the ideal family. Whether youth and emerging adults have departed the family church because they have strayed from the faith or because they are seeking to live more faithfully, Jesus taught that ideas of family must be brought into a deeper understanding

---

56. Ten Elshof, *Confucius*, 14.
57. Burns, *Doing Life*, 11.
58. Fishburn, *Confronting*, 54–55.

of the eternal family of God.[59] Atkinson notes that in Matt 10:5-7, "Jesus reveals we must love him more than our families."[60] A hard reality in a theology of family is "Jesus dramatically used family relationships in his teachings to illustrate that discipleship costs everything—even one's family and one's own self; [in citing Luke 14:26] "families were not to be preferred over God[61] [and] family relationships are not our first loyalty."[62]

A Deeper Understanding of Why Emerging Young Adults Leave Home and Churches

The goal of this section is to help parents realize that there are multiple reasons for youth leaving their churches, which means the outcome is not in the parents' control; therefore, some pain can come with youths' choices. There are various cultural traditions around various kinds of leaving. Scripture does depict youth transitioning into more independent decision-making that sometimes appears blurred, messy, and impacted by a familial group orientation. Here I want to argue that part of the emotional, social, psychological, and spiritual impact on parents on account of their emerging young adults leaving their Chinese churches could be that an interdisciplinary understanding is missing as to why youths leave home and churches. It has often been said that the functioning of the Chinese church is an extension of how the Chinese family functions.[63] It needs to be acknowledged that there can be multiple sociological, psychological, and theological factors regarding leaving patterns that can contribute to an understanding of why emerging adult CBCs and CRCs leave home, churches, or faith. Uecker et al. point out that some of the sociological factors that funnel into avoiding religious participation or leaving churches can include the "trend of secularization,"[64] "delayed marriage and childbearing," "rising

---

59. Luke 14:25–27. The cost of being a disciple requires prioritizing the call of God first over familial cultural expectations.

60. Atkinson, *Biblical and Theological Foundations*, 201.

61. Garland, *Family*, 99.

62. Garland, *Family*, 111.

63. Lu et al., "Chinese Immigrant Families." The authors note that "the faith community [is] regarded . . . as an 'extended family'" (123; see also 124), and that the "church is a home . . . for family support" (128) and an "important resource . . . for child development and parent child relationships" (123).

64. Uecker et al., "Family Formation."

rates of cohabitation and nonmarital childbearing," "changing gender roles," economic shifts, and seeing the "benefits of congregational life [as] . . . less necessary than in previous generations."[65] Youth leaving churches becomes an issue of concern where the parents experience dissonance and anxiety and "do not support the emerging adult's autonomous" act of leaving.[66] The act of leaving can be a healthy transition or in reaction to parents "exercising psychological control, using manipulative strategies"[67] and experiencing high "conflict levels" that put a strain on family relationships.[68] Although North American studies show that "young adult children from immigrant families are . . . more likely to live with their parents" throughout their twenties,[69] the "acculturation processes may reduce adherence to familyism . . . across generations in Asian . . . families."[70] Researchers have noted that "parents and adult children can have different strong opinions about the right time for leaving home"; in fact, family interdependence is highly valued in "collectivistic-oriented cultures . . . [where] parents and emerging adults in these cultures may disagree more strongly about the criteria for leaving home."[71] It has been noted that young Asian-American males eventually find themselves overrepresented in identifying as nonreligious individuals, and it is debatable whether the exit of some emerging adult males is a move to get away from the hierarchical social position extended to them in the ethnic church context.[72] The *Hemorrhaging Faith* study revealed that, broadly, "more young males are leaving the church than young females."[73] Some research lends itself to the argument that young males in Chinese churches tend to push for a more mainstream form of egalitarianism and empowerment that is present in the broader North American social context.[74] Stecker has commented,

> The question is how can they grow with an adult faith in . . . churches that have never recognized them as adults? The picture comes

65. Uecker et al., "Family Formation," 8–9.
66. Seiffge-Krenke, "Leaving Home," 182.
67. Seiffge-Krenke, "Leaving Home," 183.
68. Seiffge-Krenke, "Leaving Home," 184.
69. Britton, "Race/Ethnicity," 995.
70. Britton, "Race/Ethnicity," 997.
71. Seiffge-Krenke, "Leaving Home," 185.
72. Barry and Abo-Zena, "Experience of Meaning-Making," 474.
73. Penner et al., *Hemorrhaging Faith*, 110.
74. Ho and Wong, "Searching and Manhood," 207–34.

into sharper focus when we realize the only place most of our children are recognized as adults is in the secular world—a world that recognizes them as adults but tells them there is no place or need for their faith. Conversely, in many of our . . . churches we want them to have an adult faith, but we refuse to recognize them as adults.[75]

Categories of Leaving

Dyck has identified six categories of emerging young adult "leavers" from the Christian faith: the postmodernist, the recoiler, the modernist, the neo-pagan, the rebel, and the drifter.[76] He cites that "70 percent of youth leave the church by the time they are twenty-two years old [and that] 80 percent of those reared in the church will be 'disengaged' by the time they are twenty-nine years old."[77] Dyck's research reveals that "many leave the faith for emotional reasons and find intellectual reasons to back it up;[78] [furthermore the] leaving has to do with dealing with 'cognitive dissonance . . . [and] opposing beliefs or behaviors [that] cause psychological distress [and a search] . . . to resolve the tension by dropping or modifying one of those contradictory beliefs or behaviors" to restore harmony in their life.[79] A theological understanding of "leaving" can draw from insights in from the field of ethology. The scientific study of animal behavior demonstrates that in order to fully mature, one must not remain in a dependent parent-child relationship. The parents' primary job is to move their youth from dependence to independence. As emerging adults transition, they go through a "developmental process psychologists call individuation."[80] Tied to this transition is the search for identity and independence.[81]

---

75. Stecker, *Men of Honor*, 181.
76. Dyck, *Generation Ex-Christian*, 15–179.
77. Dyck, *Generation Ex-Christian*, 17.
78. Dyck, *Generation Ex-Christian*, 52.
79. Dyck, *Generation Ex-Christian*, 21.
80. Burns, *Doing Life*, 97.
81. Pang, *Exploration*, 98.

Identity Differentiation

Smith and Snell believe that part of the "social-psychological causal mechanism" behind emerging adults leaving home and faith communities is "identity differentiation."[82] Family development theory holds that "the process of differentiation begins in childhood," intensifying "during late adolescence," and the goal is "to develop a clear sense of self that enables one to ... interact ... in interdependent ways."[83] Identity differentiation is largely achieved "during the twenties, in emerging young adulthood," at a time "when [they] think about 'Who am I and what is my life all about?' They do not want the answer to be defined by their parents anymore. They want space, autonomy, differentiation."[84] Balswick notes that the "process [of differentiation to] establish an identity separate from the family ... socially and psychologically, while remaining connected to the family," involves the "important task of sorting out and determining one's own values and beliefs rather than [just] taking on [those] of one's parents."[85] It can be argued that "achieving a differentiated faith" and "finding" one's "identity and reference in relationship with Christ rather than" being "spiritually enmeshed" with parents is desirable.[86] Smith and Snell note that participating in church

> is one arena that ... emerging adults [have] an opportunity to achieve clear identity differentiation. For most of them, to attend [church] with their families of origin on a regular basis ... feels like being the old dependent child again, a role they feel they have outgrown. For some, even to attend services in another place at a religious congregation that is something like their parents' can feel the same way.... So religion makes a good area in which one can demonstrate that one is different and independent from one's

---

82. Smith and Snell, *Souls*, 79. For the interested reader, Mazor and Enright note that developmental individuation is part of the growth process, and "age increases [developmental] individuation and a decline of the parental view," which is often accompanied by conflict. Mazor and Enright, "Development," 29–47. Alibhai notes that the process of individuation corresponds with the development of the frontal cortex and is about separating identity from parents. This gets manifested as challenging familial values, including religious values and experimentation with religious views. Alibhai, "Process of Individuation."

83. Balswick and Balswick, *Family*, 32.

84. Smith and Snell, *Souls*, 78.

85. Balswick and Balswick, *Family*, 76, 174.

86. Balswick and Balswick, *Family*, 150–51.

parents.... Departing from parents on religious matters... seems to risk few costs.... Not that this differentiation process is typically pursued in a conscious, rational, calculated, deliberate manner—often none of the parties involved recognize what is happening in this identity formation.[87]

One research survey categorizes those who have left the Chinese church as drop-outs.[88] They would represent Smith and Snell's definition of people who view the church they grew up in as a stepping stone to learn morals and then leave after they feel they have learned the basic moral content and "stop attending services."[89] Other CBC emerging young adults may avoid returning to home faith communities and Christian families because they have "grown up out of their former selves... taste[d] [the] freedom of escape and maturity"[90] and want to avoid the rigidity of old ways.[91] Many move-on surveys in research represent this category, those who continue to retain their religious beliefs and are attending and involved with other churches. Cavalcanti and Schleef also noted this pattern of moving on from the family's religion to other churches.[92] For the move-ons, to continue

> going to their [parents'] church or keep practicing their faith in the same old way... [can] feel too much like hanging onto parental oversight.... [They conclude they have] to make a break. Although this does not necessarily involve altering one's basic religious beliefs, it usually does mean making changes to one's involvement in one's family's religious habits and activities and associations.... [This] subtle break from parents' faith contexts manifests as the Silent Exodus.[93]

It can be troubling for parents who get the message from their youth that the family church they were raised in is "not [perceived as] a place of real belonging."[94] Informing this discussion was investigation into Christian life stages and patterns of health. Chapter 6 will explore research on the social sciences perspective and the developmental theories of Arnett,

---

87. Smith and Snell, *Souls*, 78.
88. Todd, *English Ministry Crisis*, 86–101.
89. Smith and Snell, *Souls*, 149.
90. Smith and Snell, *Souls*, 75.
91. Smith and Snell, *Souls*, 74.
92. Cavalcanti and Schleef, "Case for Secular Assimilation?," 478.
93. Smith and Snell, *Souls*, 150.
94. Smith and Snell, *Souls*, 152.

Erickson, and Levinson[95] in their proposals as to what is necessary for emerging young adults to transition to adulthood. Such things might include a measure of separation from family of origin, forming an adult identity, and finding their place in the broader society. Syed notes that "sociologists have used the 'Big Five' markers of adulthood: leaving home, finishing school, getting a job, getting married, and having children."[96] Cognitive development theory helps us understand that faith development happens "as the adolescent transitions into young adulthood . . . [they] examine and question the unexamined conventional, community-referenced faith of the previous stage" to make intentional choices.[97]

Biblical Depictions of Youth Transitions

The goal here in this section is to point out that parents are not in control of the outcome of decisions youth make in the stages of individuation and identity differentiation, and Scripture depicts youth making choices in those stages that can grieve parents. A scriptural look at transitions can help parents be at peace with a normative stage of development. Multiple biblical texts provide the reader with an understanding that a measure of independence was attributed to youth and young adults. For example, Jesus's parable of the prodigal son recognizes a measure of freedom of choice qualitatively different from being a child (Matt 22:28–32), and young people can make independent decisions parents don't approve of (e.g., Rachel stole from her father; Gen 31:19, 30, 32–33). Often, various churches' understanding of adulthood and the age of accountability has been influenced by either culture, Jewish tradition (like the age for bar mitzvah), or church tradition (some preferring the age of twelve as being most appropriate for baptism or confirmation and communion). Burns, an advocate of viewing "emerging adulthood as a rite of passage,"[98] has commented that "the age of accountability in most Western cultures today typically falls somewhere in between the ages of seventeen and twenty-one."[99] However, a review of Scripture seems to give an indication that the age of twenty was a standard

---

95. Levinson's stage theory is cited and taken from Schulz and Ewen, *Adult Development*, 200–02.
96. Syed, "Emerging Adulthood," 15.
97. Balswick and Balswick, *Family*, 148–49.
98. Burns, *Doing Life*, 100.
99. Burns, *Doing Life*, 102.

for things like being able to serve in the army,[100] and the age of thirty was the maturity standard to serve as a priest.[101] Cultural conventions on when an individual was considered to be a responsible adult or serve in the priesthood helps us understand the commencement of Jesus and John the Baptist's ministry around age thirty. It's a reasonable assumption that the "young men" Joshua chose as military spies would be age twenty or over.[102] When God judged the rebellious in the Sinai desert for forty years, those over age twenty would die.[103] When a census was taken, it included "men twenty years old and more."[104] In Num 30:1–5, the reader is given insight into the perception of a "woman" in her "youth," who still lives in her father's house when she makes a vow to Yahweh. The stage of life appears to parallel the twenty-first-century emerging young adult life stage, but under different socioeconomic status and family constructs. If her father "disallows her" vow, then the "Lord shall forgive her, because her father disallowed her." Granted, ancient Near Eastern culture reflected a patriarchal society, but there seems to be a concession for some choices made during this "in-between" life stage: they understood that a person may not be developmentally, authoritatively, or mature enough in their knowledge to understand the gravity of the vow they are making. In the books of Kings, there are multiple depictions of the age of young adults (with a few exceptions) becoming king, the focus being on whether they did good or evil in the eyes of the Lord.[105] Theologically, the focus is on their spiritual disposition for or against God: whether they walked in the ways of the Lord and "did what was right in the eyes of the Lord."[106] In the New Testament, there are frequent general references to transitioning into young adulthood. Paul says in 1 Cor 13:11, "When I was a child, I talked like a child.... When I became a man, I put the ways of childhood behind me." Paul would allude to a qualitative adult transition from being a child by reminding young adults in Eph 6:2 to continue to honor their parents.

100. Num 1:3, 17.
101. Num 4:2.
102. Josh 6:23
103. Num 14:29–33.
104. Num 26:4.
105. 2 Kgs 14:2 (Amaziah: age twenty-five); 2 Kgs 15:32 (Jotham: age twenty-five); 2 Kgs 16:2 (Ahaz: age twenty); 2 Kgs 18:2 (Hezekiahage twenty-five); 2 Kgs 21:19 (Amon: age twenty-two); 2 Kgs 23:31–32 (Jehoahaz: age twenty-three); 2 Kgs 24:8 (Jehoiachin: age eighteen); 2 Kgs 24:18 (Zedekiah: age twenty-one).
106. 2 Kgs 21:22; 22:2; 23:36.

Paul recognized there is a spiritual "transitioning into adulthood" (like that age marker of thirty to serve in the Levitical priesthood) where someone like Timothy was ready to take on the mature weight of leadership.[107] The elderly apostle John also acknowledged that, for young adults, there was this attainment of spiritual maturity, enabling them to be strong and overcome because the Word of God is alive in them.[108] The point in all this discussion is that because the Scriptures legitimately identify a transitional coming of age to be able to make decisions more independently of a young adult's elders, Christian parents should make it their "goal . . . to help your children transition to responsible adulthood"[109] and not allow their emerging young adult's leaving derail them emotionally, socially, or spiritually, nor disrupt their own focus and calling.

A Theological and Developmental Understanding of Midlife Christian Parents' Struggle with the Silent Exodus

My goal here is to help parents appreciate that their struggle with youth leaving can be part of a mix of a possible range of deficits in theological areas, the desire intrinsic to their life stage to guide the next generation, and a generational cultural perspective. Given the anecdotal reporting that parents can struggle over their emerging adults' exiting their faith communities, this section concludes with a theological perspective on why such transitions can be challenging for the parents in their current life stage. As parents reflect on their own life stage and where they need to be equipped as parents going through family transitions, it can empower them to have self-control, manage internal stress, make better decisions, and build on areas where there can be improvement, perseverance, and understanding of their emerging young adults. This section assumes the need for parents to reflect on patriarchy, hierarchy, filial piety, and the Asian preconceptions of adulthood. It also assumes that at the root of parental fears can be generational differences in expectations and understandings of transitioning into

---

107. 1 Tim 4:12; Phil 2:20, 22.
108. 1 John 1:13, 14.
109. Burns, *Doing Life*, 22.

adulthood.[110] Whitehead's resources[111] help explore why midlife parenting is about trying to create a legacy and impart knowledge.[112]

Developmental psychologists tend to agree that one of the important concerns in the adult midyears (roughly between the ages of forty and sixty-five) is that of their teenagers and emerging young adult children.[113] A couple of dominating themes of the midlife years are tied in with personal power, "the desire for responsibility . . . to assume leadership . . . [and] to take control." The second theme is middle-aged parents tend to want to be needed and to provide forms of nurture.[114] This "strong desire to be creative" and "become more nurturing" can be driving forces.[115] Notably, "it is in the mid-years [a parent] is conscious of being a member of the generation now in charge. It is myself and people like me who are in control."[116] In Erikson's developmental theory on midlife adults, "generativity is primarily the concern for establishing and guiding the next generation."[117] The struggle of the midlife adult is "to learn how to 'hold on' appropriately as long as needed and how to 'let go' appropriately as soon as needed."[118] This strain gets felt both in the home and in the English ministry of a Chinese church with young adults because there is a gravitational disposition to transition into a more independent stage of adulthood. There must be a realization that "the challenge of generativity" and the transitioning of emerging young adults can fail; the midlife parent of the home or midlife parents in the church "may be unable to nurture without control."[119] Some may identify the problem rooted in ethno-cultural hierarchical or paternalistic perspectives that can factor into the Silent Exodus. A corrective to hierarchical and paternalistic perspectives is to realize that "to be responsible as an adult means to champion a person . . . without feeling responsible for

---

110. Nelson et al., "If You Want Me," 665–74.

111. Whitehead and Whitehead, *Christian Life Patterns*.

112. To the interested reader: for many Chinese parents, "the Confucian ideal of benevolence or care of the community" can be part of imparting knowledge and passing on a legacy where "the person in the higher position . . . (parent) is expected to care for those in the lower position." Shin and Silzer, *Tapestry*, 151.

113. Whitehead and Whitehead, *Christian Life Patterns*, 113.

114. Whitehead and Whitehead, *Christian Life Patterns*, 114.

115. Balswick and Balswick, *Family*, 165.

116. Balswick and Balswick, *Family*, 118.

117. Balswick and Balswick, *Family*, 120–21.

118. Balswick and Balswick, *Family*, 122.

119. Balswick and Balswick, *Family*, 122.

[their] destiny."[120] It needs to be realized that as a midlife adult parent, there are limitations. For some emerging adults, a midlife parent's disposition to want to be creative and be an influence in a young person's life, or the trajectory of the English Ministry in the church, can be misinterpreted as being controlling rather than encouraging or nurturing. Combining a disposition of some emerging adults towards forms of self-expression and exploration, one can foresee an intergenerational clash where emerging young adults decide to exit the church. Parents do struggle with their youth exiting their faith communities, which may point to a range of theological dimensions and might include the need for the parent to explore the meaning of faith in such a family transition. A parent can be unsure what theologically informs this kind of parent transition and of the parent's role in their child transitioning. A parent can be unsure biblically of the opportunities and risks of the life stage they are temporarily in. They may be ignorant of biblical teaching on spiritual life stages and the spiritual development process these stages go through that can keep them being journey-oriented. It may be debatable as to whether parents struggle more or less because of a lack of spiritual self-care (prayer, Scripture reading) and perspectives they hold on divine faithfulness, love, grace, sovereignty, and their understanding of the church. Struggle may also be attributed to religious and cultural syncretism, cultural myths, and beliefs about parenting. Struggle may also be attributed to the quality of community parents are experiencing that can provide encouragement, support, wisdom, strength, and hope.

A Theological Understanding and Overview of Biblical Texts that Portray the Leaving of Youth from Faith-Based Communities

Not all who wander are lost

J. R. R. TOLKIEN("ALL THAT IS GOLD DOES NOT GLITTER")

The goal here is to help parents realize the topic of youth leaving ethno-religious communities they were raised in is an old issue depicted in Scripture. The outcome was not in the parents' control in many cases; therefore, parents might experience some pain with the choices youth make. Anecdotal reporting indicates that OBC parents are impacted by the exit of their

---

120. Balswick and Balswick, *Family*, 123.

emerging adults from Chinese churches. The argument here is "there is nothing new under the sun"[121] and an overview of biblical texts that portray the leaving of youth from faith-based communities can be informative. A parent can read Scripture and understand that it also depicts families in transitions who also needed to explore the meaning of faith in those transitions. It can be insightful for a parent to recognize God is intimately engaged in the narrative transitions of families. It can be empowering for a parent to biblically discover that their disposition in the family transition is to trust God. I am not equating the quoted narratives as being divine revelation *on the subject of leaving*. The biblical authors, it would seem, are content to accept the cultural dynamics of families (the Jewish way in the OT and the Roman way in the NT) except, at times, to defuse the power hierarchy and advocate for those at the bottom of the power pecking order so that the powerless are given more respect and autonomy than what the culture dictates.[122] I use the term "emerging adults" in this section as an *age parallel* (eighteen to twenty-nine); I am not making an exact Old Testament and New Testament cultural comparison with twenty-first century socioeconomic, institutional, or cultural factors that filter into the contemporary definition of the term "emerging young adult." Many things are different, but leaving one's family, religious community, or faith can be the same. This segment explores an overview of biblical texts that portray the leaving of youth and young adult children from the faith base they were raised in. I will include a broad range of examples like David's family, Eli's family, Joseph's family, Manoah's family (Samson), and the transition from a Joshua generation to a Judges generation. This section provides explicit and implicit theological insights from biblical narratives on the leaving of youth from the faith-based communities they were raised in. It identifies leaving as a recurrent, often normative, portrayal in biblical literature. Because youth leaving ethno-religious communities was a frequent theme in the Bible, it's reasonable to assume that parents were impacted by the exit. The Tower of Babel story in Gen 11 identifies the dispersion and the spread of the human family as a divine intention. It is implicit in the command to

---

121. Eccl 1:9.

122. Wright, *God's People*. Wright identifies that a youth's (young adult's) identity was in their father's house—to break away was countercultural (54). The "legal status" "of children" "was that of property belonging to the father" (222). A youth was considered a "dependent person" (89), and if "a youth . . . place[d] himself outside . . . by disregard for the internal authority of the head of the house," it was problematic (97–98). The "family [was] . . . a vehicle for the faith, history and traditions of Israel" (81).

Adam and Eve to "be fruitful and multiply."[123] The theme of younger family members leaving an ethno-religious community is identified in the call of Abraham when he is told to "leave . . . your father's household."[124] Dispersion is part of divine destiny and purpose, and by implication, leaving an ethno-religious community one was raised in can also be divinely teleological. Luke reminds readers that God determines the times and places people should live,[125] and Gen 12:2 documents that leaving can be part of the predestined directive and sovereign will of God connected to flourishing. Sometimes Scripture depicts the leaving of youth in matrimonial rites of passage. In Gen 24:57, Rebekah exercises her will to leave her family and go marry Isaac. In Ruth 2:11–12, Ruth exercises volition in leaving her "father and mother" to take refuge in God with Naomi; Ruth's choice is a positive portrayal of her as a member of the Moabite diaspora. In 1 Sam 16:18–21, there is a positive depiction of Jesse sending off young David with his blessing and provision to enter into Saul's service.[126] Second Samuel 7:8 tells the reader that David's leaving his family was of the Lord. Yahweh says, "I took you." Acts 13:36 reinforces God's calling associated with leaving by saying "David served God's purpose in his own generation." In 1 Kgs 19:19–21, Elisha leaving his parents to serve in an itinerant ministry with Elijah was associated with the call of God. In Ezra 1:1–2, young "exile families" leaving Babylon was part of God's purposes to rebuild the faith community and temple. Jeremiah's itinerant ministry was part of his call by God to the nations.[127] The Gospel writer Mark, depicted in Mark 14:51 as a "young man," was one who left home as a disciple of Peter in an itinerant ministry to follow God's purposes. Although Paul took issue with some of Mark's youthful immaturity,[128] eventually Mark became helpful to the ministry.[129] Moore has aptly pointed out that "Jesus said bearing

---

123. Gen 1:28.

124. Gen 12:1.

125. Acts 17:26.

126. In 1 Sam 17:56–58, after David kills Goliath, David is referred to as a "young man," and his father is still being inquired of.

127. Jer 1:5–10.

128. Acts 15:36–39 (there was some disagreement over using Mark).

129. 2 Tim 4:11: "Get Mark . . . because he is helpful to me in my ministry."

the cross would mean a willingness to walk away[130] from father or mother, brothers or sisters. . . . The early church was filled with people who had done just that."[131]

In a big picture way, the depiction of the prodigal son in Luke 15:11–32 to a distant country and a life of wasteful living can also be understood as God at work in hidden ways to bring youth back home spiritually.[132] Thematically, the stories of the prodigal son and the parable of the sower (Matt 13:1–23) are about the failure to launch; the focus is on the heart and the idea that "the pure in heart will see God" (Matt 5:8). Sometimes the *leaving* that is portrayed in Scripture is not a matter of proximity but related to freedom in decision-making that doesn't have to defer to the perspective or advisory of parents. In John 2:1–5, Jesus's mother appears to be in charge of some matters at a wedding where the host had run out of wine. Mary speaks to Jesus as if he is still under her parental authority. The dialogue could be viewed as a coming-of-age text where Jesus reminds her that he is emerging out of the young adult stage into a full-fledged adult. At Mary's command, Jesus remarks to her, "Woman, why do you involve me?" Jesus is old enough to make his own decisions. Mary gets the point and then tells the servants, "Do whatever he tells you." Another example of the recognition to make decisions independent of a parent's advice is found in Matt 21:28–31. It is a parable of two types of imperfect sons who refuse to listen to their father. The parable uses a story that presents a common family problem with youth, namely living at home and refusing to help in the work. The language in the parable, "sons" (Greek *tekna*), indicates that they are young people (perhaps implying a certain immaturity in their faith) still living in full reliance financially on the father's family business. Of

---

130. Referring to Jesus's comments in Luke 14:26–27, 33; Matthew 12:50.

131. Moore, *Storm-Tossed Family*, 69.

132. It is argued that in the first century, which was dominated by a Roman cultural perspective, "the most significant feature of the . . . household (*familia*) was that its power was concentrated in the hands of the male head. . . . Members of the household were those persons over whom the *paterfamilias* had . . . power . . . unbroken until his death" (Jeffers, *Greco-Roman World*, 238). A youth couldn't have his own career. This is a key point in the prodigal son story: the youth is going against societal norms by asking for his inheritance before his father's death. Balswick identifies what the prodigal son did was "premature differentiation" (*Family*, 77). It has been suggested that the Roman household code does not allow a young man his own identity while his father is still alive, so he cannot leave his family; that's why he lives off his father's allowance. In the Roman Empire, there is no way for a man to leave his family. Jeffers looks at family structure and parent-child relationships in Jeffers, *Greco-Roman World*, 237–90.

course, first-century societal expectations of how the father-son relationship worked is quite different from twenty-first century ideas of a father-son relationship. In the first century, if a father was the owner of a vineyard, there was an expectation to carry forward the business—"parent-child relationships" involved "imposing structure."[133] But the portrayal given is one of resistance. In Matt 21:29, the son says, "I will not." Matthew 21:30 says that the other son answered "'I will' . . . but he did not go." The point here is that as youth transition, they can and do make choices that can be disappointing in that they may not follow the trajectory of cultural conventions and parental guidance and values. Matthew 19:29 reinforces the fact that youth may leave their families to serve the call of God: "And everyone who has left houses or brothers or sisters or *father or mother* or wife or children or fields for my sake will receive a hundred times as much and will inherit eternal life" (emphasis mine). The bigger picture here in this section is that the biblical portrayal of youth transitioning and disengaging or leaving the faith-based communities they were raised in is depicted in Scripture as one of the optional choices youths make, and it can be connected to things like individuation, differentiation, and their life's calling.

An Overview of How Parents from Biblical Narratives Processed Perceived Loss of Their Next Generation

The goal in this section is to show that parents in many biblical narratives could not control the outcomes of their youths' choices to leave and thus experienced suffering. The study behind this book inquired into what ways parents are impacted when their youth abandon the faith and ethno-religious community. The biblical narratives do depict parents impacted by the loss of their youth when they abandon the faith and ethno-religious community. The question to be explored here is how did parents in these biblical narratives process the perception of their young adults leaving them? Did they pursue emotional health and continue to remain functional, focused and engaged in their own spiritual journey, calling, and testimony? Did they find the resources of prayer, Scripture, and faith community as a source of consolation, love, joy, faith, and hope? Was there an understanding that darkness may try to permeate the life of a family through various family members' movement away from faith? The link to my study can be formulated in the following question: is there an understanding on the part

133. Jeffers, *Greco-Roman World*, 247.

of the parents that because of their relationship with God, they stand in a gap of being a positive influence on their adult child? First Corinthians 7:14 implies children of a Christian parent benefit from being in providential proximity to the influence and testimony of that parent. Was there an understanding that they should remain in focused personal communion with God, looking daily for the good news to permeate their family and church family life? Did they hold firmly to the belief in the sovereignty and love of God?

Genesis 2:24 provides a theological basis for leaving in association with the rite of passage of marriage in stating "for this reason a man will leave his father and mother and be united to his wife." In historic cultures where the survival of the family unit was dependent on the cohesiveness of the extended family, physical leaving may have been more complex than experienced in modern and postmodern societies, where there is a social safety net to help aging and vulnerable family members and parents. Most likely, when a geographical leaving of the family occurred, the parting probably would have been perceived as a loss to the elders of the family. Williams notes that the Old Testament has a lot to say about the family as a sociological unit. He notes that "Israel's social structure was tribal" and the "household" was made up with "extended family . . . [and] every effort was made to preserve the stability of the family."[134] It was in the best interest for the "extended family . . . to provide for its own perpetuation . . . [by] maintain[ing] . . . harmony [and avoiding] strife . . . as destructive to the family's inner cohesiveness."[135] A review of Scripture demonstrates that managing tensions in the family often led to separation of a family member having to leave the family. Examples of this would include Abraham and Lot's separation (Gen 13:5–8), Joseph's separation (Gen 37:12–35), the struggle between the wives of Elkanah (Gen 25:28, 27:15–17), and Jacob and Esau (Gen 27:41). In a review of the Scriptures, more often the perception of loss of young adults is associated with the event of leaving.[136] A variety of themes surface in how parents from biblical narratives processed the perception of loss of their young adults. In some cases, the loss is

---

134. Williams, "Family Life and Relations," 243.
135. Williams, "Family Life and Relations," 244.
136. Note: with some texts it's very difficult to correlate the leaving with an exact age; sometimes the leaving is documented simply as an event.

associated with a sinful event (e.g., Cain)[137] or loss through rebellion,[138] like Samson refusing to submit to his parents' advice to marry someone inside the faith community.[139] Scriptures frequently refer to the loss of the next generation because of the abandonment of the covenant.[140] In some cases, the losses are tied to the spiritual disobedience of the parents.[141] Loss is particularly evident in 1 Sam 3:13 where the priest Eli experienced his sons being judged because he failed to restrain them. It is no wonder that Prov 10:1 says that foolishness brings grief to a mother. The grief brought on by King David's troubled family is often depicted only later after he has failed to discipline his children and they are young adults. There is Absalom's murder and coup (rebellion) against David. David expresses grief over Amnon's death.[142] There is David's mourning and longing for Absalom when his son is banished.[143] There is David's struggle to "bring back the young man Absalom" in trying to restore him.[144] There is the pain of Absalom's conspiracy against David,[145] and ultimately, there is grieving over Absalom's death.[146] It is true that "there is a special kind of agony that comes ... whether a literal parent or a spiritual parent—[to] see a [young person] wandering away from the way he or she was taught and into self-destruction."[147] A parallel here is that many OBC parents viewed Canada as their promised land of milk and maple syrup, and instead, they experienced the loss of their emerging young adult generation leaving (moving on) or going prodigal (dropping out).

Frequently, the Scriptures depict the loss of youth by their engaging in ungodly intermarriages.[148] In a patriarchal period, the book of Ezra particularly depicts ungodly intermarriages as a failure of the parents for condoning this unfaithful practice documented in Israel's historical

---

137. Gen 4:16.
138. Deut 21:18–21.
139. Judg 14:1–3. The parents express grief.
140. Deut 29:22, 25.
141. Deut 28:32, 34.
142. 2 Sam 13:31.
143. 2 Sam 13:37–38.
144. 2 Sam 14:21.
145. 2 Sam 15.
146. 2 Sam 18:33.
147. Moore, *Storm-Tossed Family*, 247.
148. Marrying spouses of other faiths, Judg 3:5; 14:1–3; Ezra 13:23–25.

narratives in association with God's judgment on their communities.[149] We are talking about a culture that practiced arranged marriages. Ezra 10:25–44 elaborates at length about these unholy alliances, and in Ezra 10:3, reform addresses the issue of the young adult men being at risk of becoming a loss to the faith community. Ezra 10:1 indicates the parents were "weeping bitterly" over the matter. In a strange twist, there are two particular intermarriages in the Scriptures that are depicted as being providential and of the Lord. One is of the prophet Hosea's marriage to Gomer.[150] The other is of Esther being taken as a "young"[151] person to be married to a foreign king.[152] The commentary on Esther's uncle's perception of this loss was that he was concerned.[153] In the book of Job, the reader is shown this father's response to the announcement that his "sons and daughters ... [were] dead"[154] on account of spiritual attack. Job laments, "How I long for ... the days ... when my children were around me."[155] In this loss, Job is depicted as grieving and worshiping God.[156]

In Isaiah, the theme of judgment is pervasive on the community because they have turned away from God. The result of that was "the young ... rise against the old," and "youths oppress [God's] people."[157] Jeremiah told the community, "Your children have forsaken me,"[158] and judgment on the "young men"[159] and weeping on behalf of their "daughters"[160] would be the consequence. Associated with losses tied to judgment is the untimely deaths of the young men and young women.[161] The prophetic literature more often expresses the heavenly Father's grief over the loss of young adults. The book of Judges depicts a whole new generation that "did as they saw fit" in their own eyes and represents a low point in Israel's

---

149. Ezra 9:2, 12–14.
150. Hos 1:2.
151. Esth 2:2.
152. Esth 2:8–9.
153. Esth 2:10.
154. Job 1:18–20.
155. Job 29:2, 4–5.
156. Job 1:20–22.
157. Isa 3:5, 12.
158. Jer 5:7.
159. Jer 6:11.
160. Jer 9:20.
161. Lam 1:15; 2:21. See also Ezek 9:6, "slaughter ... young men and maidens."

history.[162] More often, the Scriptures are silent on how the parents perceived the loss of their young adults. One wonders how Daniel and his three friends' parents perceived their lives being taken into exile in Babylon, where unbeknownst to them, God would use them to serve his purposes.[163] A clear impression from the story of the rich young ruler (Matt 19:20) is that God implores young people that he be their spiritual source of life. A rejection of God represents incalculable loss. Although Scripture is often silent on parents' existential experiences with the loss of their youth from the faith and ethno-religious communities, a summary of how parents in various biblical narratives processed the loss of their youth frequently included concern, grief, mourning, desperation, longing, struggle, pain, weeping, bitter tears, and in some cases moved parents to worship.

An Old and New Testament Goal and Purpose for the Family of God

The goal of this section is to help parents realize the aim and purpose for the family of God. The parents are not in control of the outcomes of their children's choices; however, parents are to be faithful in the stewardship of their changing parenting role and influence. My intention is to briefly outline how the Old and New Testaments have provided a trajectory and focus for the family.

Isaiah 43:7 and Eph 1:11–12 indicate that God created the human family for his glory. Early in Gen 1:28, the human family was instructed to "be fruitful" and participate with God to "subdue," "rule over," and be an extension of God's dominion. By Gen 2:15, the idea is expanded to the cultural mandate to partner with, steward, and tend to God's creation. In Gen 12:1–3, the call of Abraham is intended to build the family of God, and through him, "all the families of the earth [would] be blessed." The line of instruction that was to be passed on through Abraham was to "direct [your] children . . . to keep the way of the LORD by doing what is right and just."[164] All who are called into the family of God are given this very same mandate.[165] Every child needs to know that God made them, loves them, and that they have a future; parents are to be committed to cultivate these

---

162. Judg 2:10, 17.
163. Dan 1:4, 6, 17.
164. Gen 18:19.
165. Rom 4:13; 5:17.

things in their children. Each successive generation of youth was to be instructed to "honor [their parents] so that [they] may live long ... that it may go well with [them] in the land."[166] Partnering to build the family of God is reinforced in the Pentateuch with the instruction to the family of God to "fear the LORD your God ... walk in all his ways ... love him ... serve the LORD your God with all your heart and with all your soul."[167] Training is the first obligation in raising children to teach them to love God with their whole heart, mind, soul, and strength, and to "trust in the Lord with all your heart and lean not on [your] own understanding. In all your ways acknowledge him and he will direct your paths" (Prov 3:5-6). As Deut 6:6-7 states, parents are to diligently impress upon and impart a biblical worldview to their children. Joshua aligns his family in this bigger picture by stating "as for me and my household we will serve the LORD."[168] David's charge to Solomon in 1 Kgs 2:2-4 is a strong advisory to adhere to God's purpose for the family:

> "I am about to go the way of all the earth," he said. "So be strong, act like a man, and observe what the LORD your God requires: Walk in obedience to him, and keep his decrees and commands, his laws and regulations, as written in the Law of Moses. Do this so that you may prosper in all you do and wherever you go and that the LORD may keep his promise to me: 'If your descendants watch how they live, and if they walk faithfully before me with all their heart and soul, you will never fail to have a successor on the throne of Israel.'"

The long lists of compressed genealogical history on the godly lineage in books like First and Second Chronicles—which the Gospel of Matthew will later pick up with—show that God has always had a people, and his favor rests on the family of God. There are big-picture purposes for the family of God. Meanwhile, the wisdom literature in the Bible has often addressed the young in focusing on the kind of integrity required to "live according to the word."[169] Chapters in the book of Proverbs often begin with "my son" and then give fatherly, practical advice to youth that to acquire wisdom and live in wisdom is to know the blessing of God in the family of God.[170]

166. Deut 5:16.
167. Deut 10:12 (also repeated in 11:18-22).
168. Josh 24:15.
169. Ps 119:9.
170. Prov 1:4.

Ecclesiastes reminds the family of God to "fear God and keep his commandments, for this is the whole duty of man."[171] The family of God exists to worship God (Mark 11:17), to nurture the intercultural faith family, and to carry out Christ's mission in welcoming others into God's bigger faith family.[172] As part of God's family, Christians are recruited to carry out his mission and purpose (John 20:21, "I am sending you"); God's missional calling and sending also helps form Christian identity. The mission of the faith family is "to be a blessing to the nations"[173] as life-givers and light-bearers. The family of God is intended to announce and reflect the message of God's good news.[174] The culmination for the family of God is ultimately to worship God together[175] in his presence in a new order.[176] Given the fall, the role of godly parents to their offspring is to influence them to turn in faith to Jesus Christ. Because the church is God's family, the work of the church is family work. Parents' love for God and his purposes and their love for their offspring converge into their life purpose. Stokes's research reinforces the finding that transitions, change, and crisis frequently precipitate the need to reevaluate life's purpose.[177] If God is a parent (father), and he has never been able to keep all his children from the beginning in the way of faith, does that make God a bad parent? It does not; nor does it stop God from being a missionary God. By the same token, because things with youth might not go as parents anticipated, it doesn't make one a bad parent, but if parents disengage from serving God's purposes through their lives, parents abdicate living faithfully.

Summary

To summarize, a theological understanding of the family is important to identify divine intention and a biblical ideal of the purpose for family, which provides a foundation to discern cultural conventions and measure discrepancies experienced because of impacts of the fall (Gen 3). A theological framework supports and informs parents' understanding,

171. Eccl 12:13.
172. Matt 28:18–20.
173. Gen 22:18.
174. Mark 16:15.
175. Rev 5:13.
176. Rev 7:9–17; 19:1–9; 22:3–5.
177. Stokes, "Faith," 176.

experiences, and practices. It also addresses a deterministic approach to parenting with a biblical perspective on human free will, which factors into some youth leaving ethno-religious communities. A theological framework provides an understanding of why youth leave faith communities and why parents struggle with those choices. There are multiple reasons for youth leaving their churches, some of which are related to identity differentiation and individuation where the outcome is not in the parents' control; Scripture depicts youth making choices in such life stages that can bring grief to parents. The topic of youth leaving ethno-religious communities they were raised in is an old issue depicted in Scripture. A theological framework provides biblical narratives that depict youth leaving faith communities and a spectrum of how parents processed those experiences. Parents are depicted in many biblical narratives as not being able to control the outcome of the choices their youth make in abandoning the faith and ethno-religious community. The youths choices caused parents to suffer grief. A Scriptural look at family transitions can help parents be at peace with a normative (or unconventional) stage of development. Parents' struggle with youth leaving can be related to a mix of a range of deficits in theological areas, an intrinsic life stage desire to guide the next generation, and a generational cultural perspective. A theological framework factors in divine intention for the creation of the family, provision for fallen human nature in family systems, and redemptive intentions for the family. Despite the fact that parents are not in control of the outcomes of their children's choices, the aim and purpose of parents in the family of God is to be faithful stewards of their influence in a shifting parenting role. A theology of the family life cycle and intergenerational transitions factors into addressing generational disconnect[178] which redirects parents towards emotional health, spiritual growth, and religious engagement. To explore insights, solutions, and theories behind why youth leave the church and the problem of impacted parents, I turn next to insights from the social sciences perspective.

---

178. ChenFeng, "Lived Experience," 6, 65–68.

6

A Social Sciences Framework for Family

Sociological Dynamics

WE NEED INTERDISCIPLINARY PERSPECTIVES because they can create a synthesis and generate innovative ideas to understand or solve a problem. An interdisciplinary approach will look at different points of view and compare them. For example, without insights from the fields of medicine, psychiatry, and psychology, most schoolteachers would be hindered in their understanding of a student with bipolar disorder, ADHD, or autism. Having insights from these different disciplines will affect the way the teacher understands the student, teaches, and conducts the class. The goal of this chapter is to demonstrate that the social sciences provide a multifaceted perspective on life cycle and human development that can be utilized to understand youth transitions and life stage dynamics in which emerging young adults need to take some ownership for the deliberate transitional worldview choices they adopt. The development of transitional life stages like adolescence, emerging young adulthood, and midlife adulthood (parenting) are relatively recent categories (over the last 100–150 years), particularly driven by Western values, urban-industrial development, and longer life spans.[1] Scholars have identified emerging adulthood as a developmental life stage roughly between the ages of eighteen to twenty-nine as being

---

1. Santrock, *Adolescence*, 15; Fasick, "On the Invention," 6–23; Lerner et al., "Human Development," 276–78.

> a distinct period . . . in industrialized societies . . . characterized by change and exploration . . . as they examine the life possibilities open to them and gradually arrive at more enduring choices in love, work and worldviews.[2]

When CBC emerging young adults engage and process the factors of economy, cultural assimilation, relationships, and worldviews, there can be an impact on the preferred relational proximity to OBC parents and their faith communities. In this chapter, I will outline several social forces noted in the social sciences that are push-and-pull factors for youth to leave their ethno-religious communities, which subsequently impacts their parents. These factors include:

- sociological impact of economy and life stage needs;
- sociological impact of cultural assimilation (including redefinitions of family and friendship networks);
- North American and Western individualism;
- sociological impact of secularism (but is there really an impact?);
- a social sciences perspective on the evolving developmental stage of English ministries in Chinese churches;
- developmental psychology;
- neurological factors; and
- generational differences.

Impact of Economy and Life Stage Needs

My goal in this section is to argue that cultural and economic forces and life stage needs (which require geographic mobility—leaving) are factors parents cannot control that may cause youth to leave churches. Parents are impacted by the exit of their children from their churches. Smith and Snell identify that one

> major social transformation contributing to the rise of emerging adulthood as a distinct life phase concerns changes in the [local] and global economy that undermine stable, lifelong careers and replace them . . . with careers with lower security, more frequent

2. Arnett, "Emerging Adulthood," 479.

job changes and an ongoing need for new training and education... that... pushes youth toward... postponing commitments.³

The postponing of commitments includes religious commitments. In Western contexts, there are essentially three criteria recognized in signaling the entrance into adulthood: "accepting responsibility for one's self, making independent decisions, and becoming financially independent."⁴ Historically, sociologists defined "adulthood" by "five traditional markers: leaving home, finishing school, stable employment, marriage, and children."⁵ Researchers are documenting that multiple "economic and social factors . . . lead to a forced emerging adulthood"; the shifts in marketplace have required attaining a higher education if people want to obtain a decent paying career.⁶ Some research cites the challenges of social barriers that can stand in the way of ethnic minority emerging adults in navigating education and job acquisition.⁷ Statistics Canada data of annual interprovincial migration by age group reveals that mobility—either to study or find work out of province—is highest and peaks during the emerging adult years (ages eighteen to twenty-nine).⁸ In the Silent Exodus phenomenon, one of the least studied factors is mobility on account of economic factors that requires the emerging adult to move geographically, which thus destabilizes continuity with their family faith community.⁹ Many youth leave home early¹⁰ and uproot geographically, which "can be symptomatic of a family's emotional system"¹¹ or symptomatic of "poor location relative to the labor market or educational opportunities [which] is [also] related to early home leaving."¹² Syed and Mitchell cited one "residential mobility pattern" study that "26 percent of 18–29-year-old Asian-Americans" moved from

---

3. Smith and Snell, *Souls*, 5.
4. Arnett, "Introduction: Emerging Adulthood," 5.
5. Paulsen et al., "Generational Perspectives," 27.
6. Syed, "Emerging Adulthood," 13.
7. Syed, "Emerging Adulthood," 92.
8. Statistics Canada.
9. In *Listening to Their Voices*, Enoch Wong et al. capture this in their discussion on career adjustment and geographical displacement and how they interfere for some with engagement with regular church attendance; 137–43.
10. Seiffge-Krenke, "Leaving Home," 179.
11. Friedman, *Generation to Generation*, 188.
12. Seiffge-Krenke, "Leaving Home," 179.

their primary residence within one year.[13] Leaving geographic faith families (home and church) more often happens on account of going to university or work and relocating in another geographic area. Smith and Snell note that "religious faith and practice associate with settled lives and tend to be disrupted by social, institutional, and geographic transitions. . . . [Things like] leaving home . . . have been shown by studies to correlate negatively with religious practices."[14] Adding a move to a new geographic place to study, live, and work, followed by the adjustment to the new context, adds plenty of "distraction from religious devotion."[15] Many of the practical "errands, concerns, and activities" associated with university and "recreational life can marginalize a focus on one's spiritual life."[16] Furthermore, it is noted that "repeated life disruptions, transitions, and distractions [discourage putting] . . . down roots [and getting involved] within . . . religious communities that engage in committed faith practices."[17] Another change in this mix is that a new "social network" also "increases the likelihood of reducing former religious practices, if not changing religious beliefs."[18] Census research has found that between the ages of eighteen and twenty-seven, an emerging young adult may change jobs up to eight times.[19] Smith and Snell note, "Many youth today spend five to ten years experimenting with different job and career options before finally deciding on a long-term career direction."[20] It has been noted that "today's emerging adult is less likely to commit to one employer and most likely to have multiple careers."[21] Insufficient and unstable employment factors into delaying entering into adulthood and contributes to mobility. In one study, finding the "summary observation [was] that [the] largest clusters of church transitions correlate with other common life stage transitions such as mobility in regard to employment and study."[22] Unsuitable employment factors into moving away, disengagement, and leaving the church, but leaving also anecdotally is

13. Syed and Mitchell, "How Race and Ethnicity," 90.
14. Smith and Snell, *Souls*, 75.
15. Smith and Snell, *Souls*, 76.
16. Smith and Snell, *Souls*, 77.
17. Smith and Snell, *Souls*, 280.
18. Smith and Snell, *Souls*, 76.
19. Smith and Snell, *Souls*, 90.
20. Smith and Snell, *Souls*, 5.
21. Burns, *Doing Life*, 56.
22. Todd, *English Ministry Crisis*, 92.

interpreted as an exit from the church, especially if the family becomes aware that the emerging young adult has not joined another church in their new geographic location.[23] Hoge et al. have also substantiated that mobility, especially "moving far from home," is a predictor of noninvolvement as well.[24] Although parents may feel a sense of loss or culpability, the ownership for no longer participating in a faith community rests on the emerging adult. Chinese parents may take issue with Dubas and Peterson's identifying that "leaving the parental home [should be] recognized as a normal developmental process of late adolescence and serves as an important marker for the transition into adulthood. . . . [However, expectations and conventions on] the timing . . . of these transitions vary . . . across . . . cultures."[25] The other side of recent economic changes is that they force the emerging adult to prolong their education, thus delaying their independence and needing more parental involvement and support.[26] The delay of independence can be very healthy, except where there is a perception on the part of the emerging adult of overparenting or enmeshment—a sense of being smothered, experiencing a controlling parent, or an unwelcome over-involved parent (perhaps rooted in parental anxiety) that "prevents the [youth] from making independent decisions."[27] A young adult may rebel if they feel a "parent is overstepping normal boundaries,"[28] and pressuring them on matters of religious practice may be one of these areas where "a failure to establish distance between parents and their young adult children [can] result in difficulty in separation."[29] Whitehead has identified that the challenge of young adulthood includes the ability to engage in community, work, and

---

23. Barry and Abo-Zena, "Experience of Meaning-Making," 470. The authors note that "because many emerging adults are immersed in a religious community during their childhood, they are faced with the personal choice of whether and how to remain part of that community, particularly because their geographical location may have made that community more distant." Several drop out and move on; survey cases in my previous research are examples of this leaving the church because of having to relocate (mobility) over employment (Case 14) or study (Cases 12, 14, 21, 29). Todd, *English Ministry Crisis*, 92.

24. Hoge et al., "Determinants," 253. For the interested reader, see also 246 which notes that a main reason for becoming inactive in church for young adults in this study was leaving home and moving away from family either to study or work.

25. Dubas and Peterson, "Geographical Distance," 3.

26. Fingerman and Yahirun, "Emerging Adulthood," 166.

27. Fingerman and Yahirun, "Emerging Adulthood," 170.

28. Fingerman and Yahirun, "Emerging Adulthood," 170.

29. Dubas and Peterson, "Geographical Distance," 3.

a range of relationships in a variety of ways, as well as to be able "to share talents and ambitions."[30] The emerging adult years "involve a willingness to risk one's identity," to be able "to alter the boundaries [of] self," and to "accept the risk of being changed, of coming to a different awareness of who [one] is, as a result of such encounter."[31] If one holds too rigid of an identity—or defends their identity—it can leave very little "room for self-exploration. . . . A stereotyped interpersonal style keeps others at a distance and leaves no room for mutuality,"[32] which is necessary to buffer the impact of the economy and life stage needs.

Impact of Social Forces

My goal for this section is to help parents recognize that the social forces of acculturation and redefinitions of family and friendship networks may be pull factors to leave the church that the parents cannot control and may be impacted by. The implications of the sociological impact of acculturation, which introduces redefinitions of the family and friendship networks, is that they all can contribute to youth leaving their churches and impacting parents. Smith and Snell's national longitudinal research identifies the following:

> Now that [emerging young adults] have grown older . . . met some different people, and maybe seen some of the world, they [become] . . . aware that they were raised in a very particular way that is different from the way others were raised. Sociology and anthropology show that human cultures are . . . significantly socially constructed.[33]

Whether emerging young adults conclude that "all cultures are relative" or come to the conclusion that many "things about the sociocultural world are not fixed . . . but rather human constructions invented,"[34] they are coming to such conclusions through the process of assimilating into the wider North American culture. Research indicates that the emerging adult life stage is one where an improved relationship with their parents is

---

30. Whitehead and Whitehead, *Christian Life Patterns*, 73.
31. Dubas and Peterson, "Geographical Distance," 74.
32. Dubas and Peterson, "Geographical Distance," 75.
33. Smith and Snell, *Souls*, 50–51.
34. Smith and Snell, *Souls*, 50.

desired,[35] but it is also a stage where the youth wants to "loosen [the] grip of [their parents'] authority"[36] and keep "some distance between themselves and their parents."[37] The ages eighteen to twenty-nine should be identified as a developmental period in developed countries that is distinguished as "unsettled time" that impedes "entering marriage and parenthood" until later.[38] Emerging adulthood will involve "many situations that call young adults to risk some part of their self-definition."[39] Friendships and community living intersect with one's life and "challenge it with new information."[40] Emerging adulthood challenges the "capacity for mutual interaction," which is part of the maturing process since "it is only in taking risk ... that [one] can confirm and develop strengths."[41] Emerging adulthood is, in part, growth in one's self-understanding. Growth in navigating relationships is important because maturity requires "the capacity to commit oneself to concrete affiliations and partnerships and to develop the ethical strength to abide by such commitments, even though many call for significant sacrifice and compromise."[42] Smith and Snell's national research has identified that because emerging adults put marriage on hold, their friendship networks become something they "organize their lives around."[43] National research findings demonstrate that many "emerging adults outshine their elders in being open to and usually accepting of people and lifestyles that are different from them. . . . [They] celebrate diversity, [are] . . . inclusive of difference, to overcome racial divides . . . [and] embrace multiculturalism, to avoid being narrowly judgmental toward others who are out of the ordinary."[44] In taking a "more open-minded" posture with people than the more "rigid . . . views they [might have been] raised to hold . . . they report . . . [exposure] to a greater variety of kinds of people and lifestyles and

35. Smith and Snell, *Souls*, 85.
36. Smith and Snell, *Souls*, 43.
37. Smith and Snell, *Souls*, 155.
38. Arnett, "Introduction: Emerging Adulthood," 1.
39. Whitehead and Whitehead, *Christian Life Patterns*, 75.
40. Arnett, "Introduction: Emerging Adulthood," 77.
41. Arnett, "Introduction: Emerging Adulthood," 80–81.
42. Arnett, "Introduction: Emerging Adulthood," 83.
43. Smith and Snell, *Souls*, 154.
44. Smith and Snell, *Souls*, 80. The authors note that "emerging adults can exhibit a very impressive case in associating and getting on with people of different races, ethnicities, appearances, and other attributes that more easily separated people of former generations" (80).

viewpoints... loosening up boundaries... [and] beliefs.⁴⁵ Their "social life" becomes a priority, where they seek contentment in "good relationships with family, friends, and interesting other associates."⁴⁶ National research shows that they "honor diversity"⁴⁷ and "avoid judging whatever is different" to be "socially inclusive," which may have "the unintended consequence of minimizing the importance of religious particularities."⁴⁸ These friendship networks outside the church are often contexts where "religion is a private matter not [brought into] group discussion."⁴⁹ Emerging young adults' relationships have been described as "amorphous" (unstructured) where "the categories and statuses of different kinds of relationships... are more nebulous than in previous generations.... [For example]... old, clear-cut labels, like 'just friends,' dating, courting, and engaged, for instance, are too black-and-white for the way many emerging adults relate today."⁵⁰ Research finds that because emerging young adults "settle down... later,"⁵¹ they "delay... marriage,"⁵² and "postpone family formation and childbearing."⁵³ A segment of this cohort does self-report "other lifestyle options that are higher priorities" like "partying, hooking up, having sex, and cohabiting."⁵⁴ Interviews reveal that "hooking up is common" and has a range of meanings, from "hanging out" to "recreational dating."⁵⁵ Emerging adults report their life stage is a time when "devastating breakups happen... probably on the path to marriage.... Most emerging adults do want to hold off [but]... also yearn for the kind of intimacy, loyalty, and security that only highly committed relationships can deliver."⁵⁶ It can be discouraging for parents who have formerly raised their youth in the Chinese church to realize that temporary forms of cohabitating (taking extended intimate

---

45. Smith and Snell, *Souls*, 50.
46. Smith and Snell, *Souls*, 73.
47. Smith and Snell, *Souls*, 80.
48. Smith and Snell, *Souls*, 81.
49. Smith and Snell, *Souls*, 153.
50. Smith and Snell, *Souls*, 58.
51. Smith and Snell, *Souls*, 56.
52. Smith and Snell, *Souls*, 5.
53. Smith and Snell, *Souls*, 79.
54. Smith and Snell, *Souls*, 83.
55. Smith and Snell, *Souls*, 59, 60.
56. Smith and Snell, *Souls*, 61.

vacations with their boyfriend or girlfriend) or more permanent forms of cohabitation have become options of choice.

Mitchell did a groundbreaking comparison study with emerging adults from four ethno-cultural groups (including Chinese) from the Greater Vancouver area on their attitudes towards cohabitation and whether they viewed it acceptable.[57] Chinese participants made up about one-quarter of the survey sample where "the mean age of the respondents . . . was 26.5."[58] In general, the attitudes of Canadian young adults on cohabitation "have become increasingly liberalized . . . [and] there is a greater proclivity to accept and adopt this behavior."[59] Mitchell's research demonstrated that young adults from "traditional cultures" (e.g., Chinese) "associated with 'collectivist' family values . . . [such as a] strong emphasis on religion, familistic orientations (e.g., extended kinship ties), [and] filial piety . . . [tended to regard] cohabitation outside of legal marriage . . . as unacceptable."[60] Chinese emerging young adults who regularly attended religious services and had "an intact family structure, foreign-born parents . . . [and had] more religious parents," were impacted by these factors in the decreased likelihood of their being in favor of cohabitation.[61] Chinese young adults in Mitchell's study came third in rank order as an ethno-cultural group, giving 19.8 percent "report[ing] . . . that cohabitation is 'very acceptable,'[62] while 58 percent reported it is 'somewhat acceptable.'"[63] Research indicates that choices towards cohabitation are correlated with exiting the church,[64] a dynamic factor that impacts OBC Christian parents emotionally, socially, and spiritually. Smith and Snell's national research (which included youth formally raised in the church) discovered that "forms of cohabitation in non-marital unions among emerging adults are multiple. . . . The vast majority of emerging adults . . . believe that cohabiting is a smart if not absolutely necessary experience and phase for moving toward an eventual successful and happy marriage."[65] Positive beliefs about cohabiting prevail

---

57. Mitchell, "Ethnocultural Reproduction," 391–413.
58. Mitchell, "Ethnocultural Reproduction," 397.
59. Mitchell, "Ethnocultural Reproduction," 392.
60. Mitchell, "Ethnocultural Reproduction," 393.
61. Mitchell, "Ethnocultural Reproduction," 395.
62. Mitchell, "Ethnocultural Reproduction," 400.
63. Mitchell, "Ethnocultural Reproduction," 401.
64. Uecker et al., "Losing My Religion," 1667–92.
65. Smith and Snell, *Souls*, 62.

despite the fact that empirical evidence points out that "cohabiting unions are found to be considerably more fragile than marital relationships,"[66] and "cohabitations . . . have high rates of dissolution, [with] . . . only a relatively small fraction resulting in marriage."[67] Smith and Snell identify that cohabitation practices can be a further reason why an emerging adult may want to "distance themselves from religion" because it "conflicts with [this] lifestyle" choice.[68] In order for them to "reduce [the] . . . cognitive dissonance they feel—arising from the conflict of religious teachings . . . [youth must] . . . mentally discount . . . [those] teachings and socially distance themselves from the source of those teachings."[69] For economic reasons, emerging adults are having to delay and postpone marriage.[70] Fingerman and Yahirun cite the trend that there is "an increase in marital age and a decrease in likelihood of marriage."[71] It is in "the late twenties . . . when young people in . . . highly industrialized countries tend to assume stable adult roles that have historically defined adulthood: marriage, children, [and] stable work."[72] Researchers like Rodney Stark note that young people traditionally register the steepest drop-out rates from faith communities but also note that "later in life when they have married, and especially after children arrive, they become more regular attenders. This happens every generation."[73] Studies on the Silent Exodus and hemorrhaging faith are not in agreement with Stark's speculation on the future "return" given the more recent profound drop-out rates from the church. For example, Dyck cites that historically,

> getting married and having children [might have] been the most powerful draws for young people to come back to church. But with the average age of marriage stretching into the late twenties, and many opting to put off having children . . . some of the most potent motivators to return to church are evaporating.[74]

66. Mitchell, "Ethnocultural Reproduction," 407.
67. Schoen et al., "Family Transitions," 817.
68. Smith and Snell, *Souls*, 83.
69. Smith and Snell, *Souls*, 84.
70. Willoughby and Carroll, "On the Horizon," 280–281.
71. Fingerman and Yahirun, "Emerging Adulthood," 168.
72. Syed, "Emerging Adulthood," 15.
73. Stark, *What Americans Really Believe*, 196.
74. Dyck, *Generation Ex-Christian*, 189.

Smith and Snell also note that "marriage, children and religion tend to go together . . . so the more marriage and children are delayed, the more religious involvement is postponed," and religious postponement "decreases the number of years . . . young people are being actively shaped by public participation in religious traditions."[75] For Generation Y (millennials born between 1980 and 1994), there is a postponement of "marriage until, on average, age twenty-nine for men and twenty-seven for women."[76] It is important to note that research shows that "emerging adults in general have not rejected marriage as an important and hoped for institution [and] . . . relationship goal."[77] Although religious beliefs and religious affiliation do factor into determining readiness and mate selection,[78] research findings have long identified that the tendency of young adults is to assimilate into the broader culture, which contributes to identifying with wider cultural friendship networks, revised definitions of family, and youth moving away from an ethnic church.[79] Longitudinal studies conducted by Uecker et al. concluded that "the majority of young adults who regularly attended religious services as adolescents do not return to religious service attendance, regardless of their family formation."[80] Mullins cites other studies on the pervasive impact of cultural assimilation in the life cycle of an ethnic church.[81] One disturbing finding in the research is "that a low proportion (17 percent) of young emerging adults reported having close friends in the same religious group."[82] Yu has noted the tension that exists in the Chinese family regarding OBCs not being in favor of some

---

75. Smith and Snell, *Souls*, 79.

76. Paulsen et al., "Generational Perspectives," 27.

77. Willoughby and Carroll, "On the Horizon," 292.

78. Willoughby and Carroll, "On the Horizon," 288.

79. Mullins related his study of eleven Japanese Canadian churches to other ethnic churches experiencing leaving during the process of assimilation (322) and identified "membership leakage through mobility and intermarriage" (324). Furthermore, "socialization and education in the institutions of the host society encourages mobility . . . [that] frequently requires geographic mobility" and leaving ethnic faith communities. Mullins, "Life Cycle," 326.

80. Uecker et al., "Family Formation."

81. Uecker et al., "Family Formation," 330. Mullins, in "The Life Cycle of Ethnic Churches," discusses a Canadian history of the impact of cultural assimilation on Dutch churches, Mennonite Brethren churches, Norwegian and Swedish Lutheran churches, and Ukrainian and Polish congregations.

82. Barry and Abo-Zena, "Experience of Meaning-Making," 469.

Canadian liberal views regarding "family [and] marriage,"[83] and how easy it is for CBCs to identify with and "assimilate [into] Western society."[84] Like the father named Tevye in the musical titled *Fiddler on the Roof*, parents can conclude that if their young adult breaks away from the family cultural tradition, that young adult has lost an identity handed to them from their family. One theme in *Fiddler on the Roof* is what it means to be a parent to young adults who make life choices you don't approve of. Sociologists like Mullins have long identified how churches function for ethnic groups in the maintenance and preservation of ethnic culture and identity that tend to segregate from the mainstream majority church culture.[85] Fong argues that "acculturation is much like gravity"[86] in that it is inevitable, and some emerging adults are "more part of the mainstream [and] grow restless and frustrated in [cultural] reservoirs; eventually [they look for ways out]."[87] Some identity exploration is linked to explorations in love, companionship, and friendship networks.[88] This factors into sexual ethics, whether they will marry, definitions of marriage, and intermarriage.[89] The emerging adult who has "responded successfully to the challenges of intimacy is not one who experiences no fear of loss of self in close contact with others but one who has confronted this fear."[90] Evidence of not successfully meeting the challenges of intimacy is that the emerging young adult will "experience strain in many interpersonal situations."[91] The youth has to "come to terms with society's norms, [and] what my culture has to say about how persons are to be together."[92] Studies have documented how immigrant families can "place greater pressure on children to marry someone of the same ethnic or linguistic origin as one way to maintain cultural continuity over

---

83. Yu, "Christianity," 242.

84. Yu, "Christianity," 243.

85. Mullins, "Life Cycle," 322. For the interested reader: the tendency of ethnic churches to segregate from mainstream culture has also been identified in public journalism. See Todd, "Ethnic Churches Flourishing."

86. Fong, *Pursuing the Pearl*, 20.

87. Fong, *Pursuing the Pearl*, 21.

88. Arnett, "Emerging Adulthood," 474.

89. Mullins, "Life Cycle," 324. Leakage through intermarriage.

90. Whitehead and Whitehead, *Christian Life Patterns*, 84.

91. Whitehead and Whitehead, *Christian Life Patterns*, 85.

92. Whitehead and Whitehead, *Christian Life Patterns*, 86.

generations."[93] Furthermore, Smith and Snell's national research cites that "only one in four [emerging adults] thinks it is important to marry someone of his or her own religious faith."[94] An abundance of data is showing CBCs and CRCs marrying out of their ethnic circles[95] and that second generation Asian (North) American "minorities . . . have the highest rates of intermarriage."[96] Intermarriage contributes to some of the dynamics of the Silent Exodus and to many parents' anxiety because it is a factor in emerging adults leaving their ethno-religious communities. Uecker's research provides a ray of hope that though "religious involvement wanes during young adulthood . . . [churches] continue to appeal—for religious, social, practical, and cultural reasons—at least to some young adults as they settle into family life."[97] Furthermore, Smith and Snell's national research interviews revealed that emerging adults do have goals and dreams for their lives to "get a good job, marry, have children . . . [and] raise a family. . . . All spoke as if they still believed in the American middle-class dream and greatly desired to achieve it."[98]

---

93. Fingerman and Yahirun, "Emerging Adulthood," 169–70. For the interested reader, see Di Giacomo, "Identity and Change." The Italian churches resisted assimilation and affiliation with non-Italian churches by maintaining the Italian language and ethnic distinctions, thus limiting their emerging young adults' suitors.

94. Smith and Snell, *Souls*, 141.

95. For the interested reader: based on the 2006 census, Statistics Canada reported that "mixed unions are higher for Canadian-born than foreign-born visible minority groups." In particular, 53.7 percent of Chinese born in Canada were in mixed unions. Statistics Canada, "Portrait of Couples." Fong's data in *Pursuing the Pearl* shows that by the third generation, over 60 percent are in interracial marriages; he notes that interracial dating and marriage are indicators of moving "away from an immigrant outlook" and that LBCs have a concern for the future of their own children in a "multilingual, immigrant-oriented church" (226, 45–46, 195). Rah notes the increase of intercultural and interracial marriages; Rah, *Next Evangelicalism*, 184. Chua anecdotally notes that LBC women "often marry a white person"; *Battle Hymn*, 21. The "high out-marriage rate among Chinese women" is also noted in Kasinitz et al., *Inheriting*, 234, and Todd, *English Ministry Crisis*, 93.

96. Chen and Park, "Pathways of Religious Assimilation," 670.

97. Uecker et al., "Family Formation," 1, 23.

98. Smith and Snell, *Souls*, 69.

North American and Western Individualism

My goal for this section is to help parents realize they may not be able to control their youth acculturating a preference for the values of Western individualism[99] rather than Eastern group-oriented values, which can become a pull factor to leave the ethno-religious community and thus impact the parent. Packard and Ferguson conducted research finding that many young people leave their churches "but not their faith" and identified that there is a connection to the "trend of institutional disaffiliation . . . with the drive toward individualism."[100] Family-systems theory identifies that the impact of "individualism has caused [a heightened] focus on the individual's needs and [view] rather than on . . . groups."[101] Mitchell notes that "individualism is characterized by a quest for self-fulfillment . . . and the emergence of the ideology of materialism. . . . This change erodes old social norms because they are incompatible with values such as freedom and autonomy, companionship and self-gratification."[102] Generally speaking, the Euro-Canadian cultural context is one that has been shaped in valuing "independent selves through the promotion of autonomy, whereas collectivistic cultures [like the Chinese culture, tend to] value interdependent selves through the promotion of relatedness."[103] Syed and Mitchell have argued that "research on family obligation has demonstrated . . . greater frequency of obligatory behaviors among ethnic minorities; [it is thought that] these differences [are] related to differential conceptualizations of adulthood . . . [that] eschew independence in favor of meeting obligations . . . benefiting the family."[104] On account of family obligations, sense of duty, filial piety, and the "lack of access to socioeconomic resources," studies on Asian young adults reveal that they are "more likely [than Caucasian emerging adults] to live at home while attending college and to believe that it is appropriate to live at home until marriage [in many cases] . . . with parents well into adulthood."[105] So the research is showing some variable patterns. Parental anxiety may be

---

99. Arnett and Jensen, "Congregation of One," 451–67. This study identifies the increased cynicism towards religious organizations and how young adults absorb Western individualism in deconstructing a religious upbringing and forging a new belief system.

100. Packard and Ferguson, "Being Done," 515.

101. Balswick and Balswick, *Family*, 23.

102. Mitchell, "Ethnocultural Reproduction," 393.

103. Syed and Mitchell, "How Race and Ethnicity," 89.

104. Syed and Mitchell, "How Race and Ethnicity," 89.

105. Fingerman and Yahirun, "Emerging Adulthood," 172.

linked to the parental recognition that emerging young adults need help longer due to changes primarily in the economy that have a multifaceted impact on the emerging adult to integrate into the adult stage of life. On account of the slow transition into adult life, some have termed this stage of life "adultescence" as emerging adults "look like adults, but still have some latent adolescent traits."[106] One of Hill's sociological research findings is that "many young people return to regular worship during adulthood, particularly when they marry and begin forming their own families."[107] However, with cohabitation being very fashionable and many people choosing the option of not marrying, it means that "the pull of the family formation back into church may be weaker than in the past."[108]

The Presumption of the Impact of Secularism

The goal of this section is to help parents realize youth leaving the church on account of the impact of secularism is an outcome parents may not be able to control but can be impacted by. It is assumed that secularization is one of many factors in why emerging adults leave the church. Is the secularization of emerging adults contributing to them leaving the church and thus having a domino effect impacting OBC parents' emotional, social, and spiritual lives? This section investigates the assumption of a sociological impact of secularism on emerging adults factoring into their decision to leave their faith communities and subsequently impacting OBC parents. Wilson notes that "secularization relates to the diminution in the social significance of religion."[109] Furthermore, "secularization occurs in association with the process in which social organization itself changes from one that is communally-based [sic] to a societally-based [sic] system."[110] Wilson continues: "Things that were once . . . conditioned by religion—are in modern society all organized on practical, empirical, and rational perceptions. Societal organization demands the mobilization of intellectual faculties."[111] That is to say, "Anything that impedes the thrust towards total rationalization

---

106. Burns, *Doing Life*, 59.
107. Hill, *Emerging Adulthood and Faith*, 23.
108. Hill, *Emerging Adulthood and Faith*, 26.
109. Wilson, "Secularization," 149.
110. Wilson, "Secularization," 153.
111. Wilson, "Secularization," 155.

induces pressure for its own elimination or diminution."[112] The argument is that in a secularized "societal system, the supernatural plays no part in the perceived, experienced, and instituted order. The environment is hostile to the super-empirical: it relies on rational, humanly-conceived [sic], planned procedures. . . . There is no room for extra-empirical propositions, or random inspirational intuitions."[113] Based off of "questionnaire studies of disaffiliation" and "why persons drop out" of church, Roozen "concluded that secularization is [a significant] . . . determinant of apostasy."[114] Mitchell has noted that "secularization reduces formalized religious commitment and thus the strength of the moral values derived from religious theology and is accompanied by a shift towards individualistic, self-oriented pursuits."[115] Chen and Park have noted that "all immigrant groups fret about the perilous influence of secular America on their children's faith."[116] Media is rife with news regarding the increasing secularization in Canada.[117] Tse has researched extensively in terms of how the Chinese Canadian churches posture themselves with regard to the secular. For example, he comments that "most Cantonese Protestant conceptions of the public sphere are in fact theologically secular because they reinforce the privacy of religion while leveraging their self-defined ethnicities to make their mark on public space."[118] There is an assumption that secularism means the decline of religion and practice in the public domain; however, secularism may not be impacting a decline of religion and practice in the public domain. Tse asks, for those emerging adults who people claim are secularized, where did they end up?[119] Some of the churches' theories on how immigrant families acculturate into the North American context has been bequeathed to them by the work of Will Herberg and his volume *Protestant, Catholic, Jew*, which implies that immigrants to the North American context will ultimately leave behind aspects of ethnic culture and language "over their religious ones as they integrate into" North American society.[120] Tse argues

112. Wilson, "Secularization," 157.
113. Wilson, "Secularization," 162.
114. Roozen, "Church Dropouts," 430.
115. Mitchell, "Ethnocultural Reproduction," 393.
116. Chen and Park, "Pathways of Religious Assimilation," 666.
117. Van Paassen, "Canada."
118. Tse, "Religious Politics," 10.
119. Personal communication with Justin Tse, January 1, 2020.
120. Tse, "Religious Politics," 21. For the interested reader, see Herberg, *Protestant,*

that "religion [is] not merely confined to religious space"[121] and that people learn to take aspects of religion into "the different social geographies of their own lives."[122] CBC emerging adults have grown up witnessing OBC adults in their churches

> practice democracy in their civil societies . . . [in] the public sphere . . . [in an] attempt to influence the secular state.[123]

In addition,

> when [they] engage their local secular civil societies, they are often drawn into practices of secular contestation that mark their respective public spheres by leveraging their Chinese ethnicity while playing down their theological convictions as private.[124]

It has been noted that in Canada, Chinese OBC Christians are known for their conservativism[125] and "their work in traditional family values, particularly as they revolve around sexuality";[126] their concern over the erosion of family values has initiated "activism [to] defend the private sphere from the intrusion of the state."[127] One frontier of research that Tse has indicated is needed is a study to what extent second-generation Chinese Canadian young adults' views align with their parents' on various issues. Tse comments:

> Research should be conducted to elucidate whether these younger generations' . . . views align with those of their parents, as well as what new issues have captured their imaginations and shaped their practices in the public sphere. . . . [This] might uncover differences in the construction of what it means to be younger generation . . . Asian Canadian and how to practice their faith in secular public contexts.[128]

Catholic, Jew, ix. See also 19, 31.
- 121. Tse, "Religious Politics," 41
- 122. Tse, "Religious Politics," 47.
- 123. Tse, "Religious Politics," 419.
- 124. Tse, "Religious Politics," 519.
- 125. Kong, "Conservatism Persists."
- 126. Tse, "Religious Politics," 218. For the interested reader, see Todd, "Vancouver's."
- 127. Tse, "Religious Politics," 256.
- 128. Tse, "Religious Politics," 538–39.

A Social Sciences Framework for Family

Canadian and American researchers have been trying to get the attention of the church regarding the fact that emerging adults have been disengaging from the church in large numbers.[129] Research identifies that for several decades, secularism has been having an enormous effect on emerging adults leaving their faith-based communities.[130] Some researchers investigating predictors of Chinese Christians' church attendance and religious steadfastness later in life will point to the impact of secularism.[131] Research related to the attempt to try to predict defection includes denominational research examining determinants of church involvement of five hundred young adults who grew up in Presbyterian churches. The survey participants were highly educated, with "90 percent having college to advanced degrees,"[132] which could closely parallel the educational levels today of a CBC emerging young adult cohort. A tiny percentage of Asians were included in this study.[133] The researchers reviewed "religious commitment based off of social learning theory" and "cultural broadening theory."[134] Hoge et al. discovered that young adults who tended to shirk church attendance and religious commitment manifested data results that

---

129. Hiemstra, *Renegotiating*. Hiemstra cites that one in three Christian emerging adults in public universities abandon their faith. For the interested reader, see Penner et al., *Hemorrhaging Faith*. In 2011, the *Hemorrhaging Faith* study broke new ground for Canadian youth and young adult ministry; the study reported that two out of three young adults were leaving the church as they transitioned out of high school. For the interested reader, see Sawler, *Goodbye Generation*; Barna Group, "Most Twentysomethings." The research notes that six out of ten emerging adults disengage from the church after high school. For the interested reader, see Smith and Snell, *Souls*.

130. The secular worldview that dominates the media and educational system has been gauged and measured in the research of Barna Group, *Gen Z*, 25. Kinnaman and Lyons note that "most young people who were involved in church as a teenager disengage from church life and often from Christianity at some point during early adulthood" (*UnChristian*, 26). Many emerging adults process how the church is addressing the multicultural community, the issue of homosexuality, the political environment, real-life dynamics, and whether the church is being accepting, boring, confusing, sensitive, hypocritical, or judgmental.

131. Secularism as defined as "an approach to life divorced from the influence of religion, and thus determined by temporal or worldly concerns"; Reese, "Secularism," 693. Secularism is the offspring of logical positivism that principally embraces the idea that only ideas that can be verified through logical proof are significant.

132. Hoge et al., "Determinants," 245.

133. Hoge et al., "Determinants," 245.

134. Hoge et al., "Determinants," 242, 243.

"showed the influence of early religious socialization to be weak."[135] This deficit compounds "during the college-age years" contributing to a more liberal belief system.[136] However, this study found that the impact of a college education and the impact of secular cultural values were still weak determinants in having an effect on church involvement.[137] Hoge et al. emphasized that early "belief formation [is] most important"[138] and that "recent family experiences [are] second most important";[139] in particular, there is a "moderately strong factor in church involvement" the more children the individual has.[140] Foundational faith formation and practical needs for support with a growing young family are significant determinants effecting religious attendance. The Pew Research Center on Religion and Public Life has identified that young adults around the world are less religious on multiple measures.[141] This finding is supported by a national research study done by Smith and Snell, where they concluded that "emerging adults are, on most sociological measures, the least religious adults" (less likely to pray, to attend church, or to participate in charitable giving and volunteer service) in the North American context, but Smith and Snell saw "little evidence ... of massive secularization among ... emerging adults in the last quarter of the century—the exception being regular church attendance declines among Catholics and mainline Protestants."[142] In contrast, researchers like Chen, Park, and Beyer make the case that religious identity is much higher with first-generation immigrants than with the second generation.[143] Canada is the top country where younger adults are less likely to identify with any religion. Pew research indicates that "there

---

135. Hoge et al., "Determinants," 242, 253.

136. Hoge et al., "Determinants," 242.

137. Hoge et al., "Determinants," The secularizing effect of a college education a weak determinant (243, 253); the impact of counterculture values is also a weak determinant (253).

138. Hoge et al., "Determinants," 242. The researchers note that "early experiences did not prove to be strongly associated with church involvement [at the time of the study], but they did predict religious beliefs, which in turn were strongly associated with church involvement" (253).

139. Hoge et al., "Determinants," 242, 253.

140. Hoge et al., "Determinants," 253.

141. Pew Research Center, "Age Gap in Religion."

142. Smith and Snell, *Souls*, 102.

143. Chen and Park, "Pathways of Religious Assimilation," 678; Beyer, "Religious," 177–99.

is a particularly large gap in religious affiliation—twenty-eight percentage points—in Canada. Younger adults are less likely to attend weekly worship services and pray daily."[144] Smith and Snell's national research identifies that "the importance and practice of religion generally declines between the age period of . . . eighteen to twenty-three. Some or even many . . . go into something of a religious slump during these years."[145] Wong et al. researchers on Chinese Canadian churches, have also noted that faith disengagement of youth and emerging adults is a global phenomenon,[146] and some of the global phenomenon is rooted in how "faith [is being] deconstructed and reshaped by secular and pluralistic influences."[147] Perry argues that statistics are indicating "less than one half of one percent of eighteen- to twenty-three-year-olds hold to a Christian view of the world,"[148] and "more than 80 percent of young adults are spiritually 'disengaged' by age twenty-nine."[149] Furthermore, North American studies indicate 75 to 90 percent or more of second-generation Chinese and Asian emerging adults leave their churches.[150] Chen and Park note this trend, writing that "a slightly higher percentage of second-generation Protestants . . . leave religious affiliation compared to the [North American] average."[151] Not only are many not "religiously assimilating into the [North] American landscape, [many are] bypassing it altogether . . . [and the] disaffiliation rates . . . [outpace] . . . peers in the general population."[152] Sociologist James Penner cited

144. Pew Research Center, "Age Gap in Religion."

145. Smith and Snell, *Souls*, 142.

146. Wong et al., *Listening to Their Voices*, 11–15.

147. Wong et al., *Listening to Their Voices*, 150–51. The authors' conclusion is that only atheist and agnostic interviewees were vocal about this as "the analysis indicates that there is a strong correlation between faith and science as a zero-sum game for this cohort and their abandonment of faith identity" (171).

148. Perry, "That Nones."

149. Perry, "That Nones."

150. Although there doesn't seem to be hard data that can be generalized, Esther Liu provides data that Chinese churches in North America have been consistently losing 80–90 percent of their youth and young adults. Fong notes that "well over 75 percent of the [LBCs] end up leaving the Chinese church. . . . Something is not right." Fong, *Pursuing the Pearl*, 175. For the interested reader, see Cha, *Following*, 146, 148; Wong, "Bridging the Gap," 1–2. In 1986, Law set a precedent in citing longitudinal data on the Silent Exodus, stating, "It has been estimated the dropout rate among [local born Chinese Christians for the past forty years has been as high as 95 percent]"; Law, *Winning*, 131.

151. Chen and Park, "Pathways of Religious Assimilation," 675.

152. Chen and Park, "Pathways of Religious Assimilation," 680.

the *Hemorrhaging Faith* report that included Canadian research findings on young people between the ages of eighteen and thirty-four, and found that "only one in three Canadian young adults who attended church weekly as a child still do so today."[153] Sawler makes the claim that "approximately 90 percent of all the youth will leave the church and faith by the age of twenty five."[154] The point is that this is part of a much larger trend, and the church and families need to come to terms with it. Arnett has pointed out that "research on emerging adults' religious beliefs suggests that regardless of educational background, they consider it important . . . to reexamine the beliefs they have learned in their families and to form a set of beliefs that is the product of their own independent reflections."[155] Sometimes those assessments "lead to rejection of childhood beliefs without the construction of anything more compelling in their place."[156] Further research indicates the tendency for second-generation immigrants to be less religious than first generation immigrants on account of acculturation.[157] Wang identifies that CBC young people are "able to integrate into Canadian society quite easily [on account of] their early exposure to the dominant English language as well as mainstream culture."[158] One of the five pillars of emerging adulthood is an age of instability. Research has shown that on account of acculturation, intergenerational values-based family conflict in immigrant families can be quite prevalent among Asian North Americans.[159]

Here I briefly want to introduce the impact of logical positivism and liberal perspectives that inform the education that emerging young adults receive in the Canadian context. A very high percentage of CBC emerging adults attend college and university and are anecdotally reported to drop out of the ethno-religious community during that period. Should OBC parents be concerned that those educational contexts are corroding religious faith and impacting their children, family, and churches? Smith and

---

153. Penner et al., *Hemorrhaging Faith*. For the interested reader, see Stecker, *Men of Honor*. The author comments that on average, churches "lose approximately 70 to 80 percent of . . . young people who were in the church when they started kindergarten by the time they get to high school graduation. In addition, we will lose in excess of 90 percent of churchgoing high school graduates within five years of their graduation" (87).

154. Sawler, *Goodbye Generation*, 7.

155. Arnett, "Emerging Adulthood," 474.

156. Arnett, "Emerging Adulthood," 474.

157. Van der Bracht et al., "God Bless Our Children?," 33.

158. Wang, "Lived Experiences," 465.

159. Syed and Mitchell, "How Race and Ethnicity," 91.

Snell's national research asked, "Does going to college cause the religious and spiritual lives of [emerging adults] to weaken or decline? The idea that higher education is corrosive to religious faith and practice is widely believed . . . [based off of] . . . an older body of sociological research."[160] Uecker et al. also began with the assumption that higher education contributed to secularizing the emerging adult to walk away from the church and Christian faith.[161] They found instead that emerging adults who did not attend college or university manifested more prevalent forms of religious decline.[162] Multiple studies reinforce the contemporary finding that "it is not those who attend college but in fact those who do not attend college who are the most likely to experience declines in religious service attendance, self-reported importance of religion, and religious affiliation."[163] Going to university does not have a secularizing effect on emerging adults, nor does it "increase the 'risk' of religious decline or apostasy as it did in the not-too-distant past."[164] This view is held by various researchers who argue that simply going to university, studying science, and obtaining a higher education "does not substantially alter the religious trajectories of young people."[165] Hill makes the case that many "students do not come to campus with strong religious commitments in the first place," so if their "religious identity is fragmented and private,"[166] there is a need to look into what has precipitated that. Hill's research has identified that "the patterns [of leaving the church] tell us that the sources of the decline in emerging adulthood faith have been built up over some time."[167] Hill argues that one should be cautious in concluding that university is "a catalyst for total disaffiliation or atheism," as social science data is showing "higher education actually strengthens affiliation and identification with the institutional side of religious life."[168] Hill recognizes that some in the church, as well as some national studies on youth, put forward the idea that emerging adults are leaving because of assumed conflicts between science and religion,

160. Smith and Snell, *Souls*, 248.
161. Uecker, et al., "Losing My Religion," 1667–92.
162. Uecker, et al., "Losing My Religion."
163. Smith and Snell, *Souls*, 248–49.
164. Smith and Snell, *Souls*, 251.
165. Hill, *Emerging Adulthood and Faith*, 32.
166. Hill, *Emerging Adulthood and Faith*, 33.
167. Hill, *Emerging Adulthood and Faith*, 69.
168. Hill, *Emerging Adulthood and Faith*, 36.

but is it true that "youth are being corrupted by the secular agenda of elite scientists?"[169] His findings are that those who are "more religious on a number of measures are less likely to believe there is a conflict,"[170] and that there is "no evidence that they feel pressure to change their beliefs because of science"; in sum, "this is not a widespread challenge for most young people."[171] Smith and Snell point out that there is a general continuity of faith and attendance to religious services from adolescence into emerging adulthood, which is especially correlated with positive parental role models and "socialization, [where] expectations often continue to powerfully shape [them]."[172] They note that "emerging adults who do sustain strong subjective religion in their lives . . . also maintain strong external expressions of faith."[173] Smith and Snell's finding is that "a little more than half of emerging adults remain quite stable in their levels of religious commitment and practice. . . . The primary conclusion . . . is . . . one . . . of . . . continuity."[174] My former research findings with the OBC parents' emerging adults resonated with Smith and Snell's findings that almost half of the CBC emerging adults moved on to another church; the other half dropped out. I want to firmly state my point that the argument of secularism being a source of the Silent Exodus that impacts parents is not compelling. However, the take-home here for parents is to pay attention to the developmental adolescent years and pay attention to those emerging young adults in faith communities in the present. The theological theme behind dropping out of the faith is that "God is dealing with a prodigal cosmos"[175] and it should be recognized, in some measure, that "all of us are prodigals—just at different places in our redemption stories."[176]

169. Hill, *Emerging Adulthood and Faith*, 49.
170. Hill, *Emerging Adulthood and Faith*, 50.
171. Hill, *Emerging Adulthood and Faith*, 57.
172. Smith and Snell, *Souls*, 86.
173. Smith and Snell, *Souls*, 252.
174. Smith and Snell, *Souls*, 282.
175. Moore, *Storm-Tossed Family*, 247.
176. Moore, *Storm-Tossed Family*, 246.

Evolving Developmental Stages of English Ministries in Chinese Churches

Anecdotal reporting indicates OBC parents are impacted emotionally, socially, and spiritually by the exit of their emerging adults. Development psychology offers some insight to the maturing stages and changes an English ministries congregation goes through.

Developmental Psychology

The goal of this section is to help parents realize that they may not be able to control the outcome of choices youth make in evolving, transitional, psychosocial developmental stages; therefore, some pain can come with those choices made. In the field of developmental psychology, various theorists have offered up models of development that have promoted the idea that young people generally move through developmental life stages often somewhat sequentially. My point is that emerging adulthood is a developmental phase parents need to understand and be supportive with. Theorists don't all agree on what that development looks like. For example, Kohlberg assumes that as people move into young adulthood, they "reason differently and make different moral judgements." He proposes "a total of six stages [and that] each level represents a different and higher kind of moral reasoning."[177] Although Kohlberg believes that people progress through stages in an attempt "to reduce tension," many theorists disagree with the hypothesized order of stage theory.[178] Piaget proposes a cognitive theory of development[179] and suggests that stages of cognitive development happen "from the interaction of hereditary and environmental forces."[180] Erickson's psychosocial theory of development[181] "propose[s] that personal growth result[s] from dealing with eight conflicts,"[182] which include addressing identity, roles, and goals in life.[183] It should be noted that with Erickson's

---

177. Plotnik and Mollenauer, *Introduction to Psychology*, 389.
178. Plotnik and Mollenauer, *Introduction to Psychology*, 390.
179. Mussen, "Jean," 703–32.
180. Santrock, *Adolescence*, 53.
181. Erickson, *Identity*.
182. Plotnik and Mollenauer, *Introduction to Psychology*, 373.
183. Plotnik and Mollenauer, *Introduction to Psychology*, 384. Between adolescence and young adulthood, Erickson proposes that stage five of identity versus role confusion

stages, as with many of these stage theories of development, many theorists view the stages as "general descriptions, rather than as challenges everyone confronts in a certain order."[184] Levinson postulates six stages of adult and personality development. Stage one, between the ages of twenty and twenty-four, involves leaving the family. In this "transitional period," the young person "moves out of [the] family home and establishes psychological distance."[185] Stage two, early twenties to late twenties, involves entering the adult world, which is "a time of exploration [for] the young [person] trying out various occupational and interpersonal adult roles."[186] Gould also suggests seven stages of adult and personality development, and of particular interest to this study is his second stage: ages eighteen to twenty-two, where Gould says the "young adult now feels more autonomous and somewhat removed from the family, but worries about being recaptured and made dependent by them, [therefore] the peer group is used as an ally to help cut family ties."[187]

One "new theory of development" in developing and industrialized nations refers to the unique period between the ages of eighteen and twenty-nine termed "emerging adulthood," which is "neither adolescence nor young adulthood."[188] The emerging adulthood period is "not considered to be a universal life stage" but unique to some "industrialized societies due to social and economic changes that have led to delays in marriage, parenthood, and the assumption of other adult roles."[189] The age range of emerging adulthood (ages eighteen to twenty-nine) strongly correlates with the Exodus[190] of CBCs from Chinese churches. Some Chinese Canadian researchers are recognizing that the "characteristics of emerging adults are

---

and stage six, intimacy versus isolation, are progressive stages. Stage five focuses on "a path toward vocation" and, if successful, results in "confidence and purposefulness; if not [feelings of confusion]" (Santrock, *Adolescence*, 63). Stage six focuses on forming "friendship [and] intimate relationships" (Santrock, *Adolescence*, 63). In stage six of young adulthood, resolving the crisis of this phase successfully requires the young adult to "learn to sacrifice some of [their] own wishes in order to form close relationships with other people" (Schulz and Ewen, *Adult Development*, 203).

184. Plotnik and Mollenauer, *Introduction to Psychology*, 385.
185. Schulz and Ewen, *Adult Development*, 200.
186. Schulz and Ewen, *Adult Development*, 200.
187. Schulz and Ewen, *Adult Development*, 201.
188. Syed, "Emerging Adulthood," 11.
189. Syed, "Emerging Adulthood," 11.
190. From this point forward the term "Exodus" is used to refer to the Silent Exodus.

found all over the world," and this new field of emerging adulthood helps provide a framework of understanding for their families.[191] Economic and other institutional and social factors have contributed to a "forced emerging adulthood" phase in the life span. For example, the demands of the marketplace have required higher levels of education to secure gainful employment.[192]

Arnett's research[193] has defined emerging adulthood with five significant features, sometimes called the five pillars of emerging adulthood. In Arnett's model, the first pillar is called "identity exploration," which involves a quest for significance in "work, relationships and ideologies."[194] Identity exploration is a life stage where the emerging adult is learning more about themselves and exploring possibilities. Identity exploration also refers to a time when the individual is discovering to what extent they identify with their own ethnic group.[195] Do they resonate with the perspectives of their religious ethnic group? Do they find those perspectives coherent or confusing? Do those perspectives help integrate purpose in their lives? Do they identify with the religious context their family has raised them in?

The second pillar in Arnett's model is called "instability." Researchers have identified that during the emerging adult phase, there is a higher "tendency to change residences, jobs, and relationships more frequently than at other times of life."[196] It can be stressful for parents to witness the instability of the emerging adult's romantic relationships, changes in jobs, and choices of where they want or need to live (e.g., on campus, off-site, at home, etc.). The second pillar of instability includes changing churches or leaving a church. Arnett's third pillar is called "possibilities," described as the "optimistic spirit of emerging adulthood, [and] refers to the many options that emerging adults see before them."[197] For example, the Chinese church may be viewed as just one option among churches to attend. The fourth pillar in Arnett's model is called "self-focus." Characteristics of this phase are more problematic for parents of emerging adults, and it refers to emerging adults' relative freedom from obligations to parents, spouses,

---

191. Wuji, "Exploration of the Experience," 3.
192. Syed, "Emerging Adulthood," 13.
193. Arnett, "Emerging Adulthood."
194. Syed, "Emerging Adulthood," 12.
195. Syed and Mitchell, "How Race and Ethnicity," 95.
196. Syed, "Emerging Adulthood," 12.
197. Syed, "Emerging Adulthood," 12.

and children, allowing them to pay greater attention to their own lives.[198] What troubles parents and leaders most with this category is what emerging adults prioritize in their eventful lives. Arnett's fifth pillar is called "feeling in-between," which refers to "the subjective experience of emerging adults who acknowledge feeling not quite like adolescents any longer but also not yet fully like adults."[199] Arnett discovered in one survey with Asian-Americans, when asked "Do you think you have reached adulthood?," that a common response was "yes and no."[200]

What theorists have tried to do is "understand the psychological experience of young people as they occupy [this transitional] life space"[201] during the emerging adulthood stage. It can be meaningful for parents and leaders to frame what they are experiencing with their youth in their homes and churches in terms of an evolving developmental life stage. Current cultural, economic, and social forces factor into the evolving developmental stage. Balswick reminds parents that such "developmental theories lack a guiding teleology and understanding of the goal of development" that can only be illuminated by "a theologically informed understanding."[202] In part, a theological understanding of development informs a "goal" to become a "reciprocating self" and "to reflect" the "imago Dei," and that people are "created for community."[203] The theological framework in chapter 5 of this book contains a discussion on a guiding teleology (purpose) and goal of development.

Neurological Factors

Parents and leadership could also benefit from insights on cognitive development that occur during the life stage of emerging adulthood. During this life stage, the development of "complex cognitive abilities enable [young people] to better respond to the demands of adult life."[204] It has been discovered through "developmental [research] studies using structural imaging of the brain . . . emerging young adults [gain] an increased

198. Syed, "Emerging Adulthood," 12.
199. Syed, "Emerging Adulthood," 12.
200. Arnett, "Conceptions," 70.
201. Syed, "Emerging Adulthood," 13.
202. Balswick and Balswick, *Family*, 125.
203. Balswick and Balswick, *Family*, 125, 126, 139.
204. King and Kitchener, "Cognitive Development," 106.

capacity for reasoning and knowledge about the world around them."[205] Neuropsychological studies of electroencephalographic (EEG) activity have shown emerging young adults experience "brain growth, myelin formation [and] predicted spurts of development."[206] With "the use of MRI and other brain-imaging techniques," it's been discovered that "the brain is still undergoing... developmental changes" and does "not engage in higher order brain processing until the mid-twenties."[207] Cognitive development pertains particularly to the areas of divergent thinking[208] in "the capacity to resolve ill-structured problems and make reflective judgments."[209] Cognitive development also applies to moral development. Research has demonstrated that "fully reflective thinking [is] not typically seen until late in the emerging adulthood years."[210] In the emerging adult period, young adults link deeper meaning to life experiences[211] and "develop [their] authority to make choices about others' expectations."[212] It is a stage where there is an "abandonment of absolutistic thinking in favor of more complex thinking,"[213] and a time of cognitive "developmental change that takes place across several judgment domains [that include]... values" and processing truth.[214] One conclusion from the

> literature in developmental and educational psychology as well as in higher education, [is] there is strong evidence that important changes take place in cognition [during this] third decade [like] the speed of processing and the breadth and depth of knowledge.... These [are some of the] data... supported by... structural imaging of the brain.[215]

Knowing that emerging adulthood is a period where neurodevelopment change is "prominent... in association with cortices and the frontolimbic systems involved in executive attention, reward, and social

205. King and Kitchener, "Cognitive Development," 107.
206. King and Kitchener, "Cognitive Development," 118.
207. Balswick and Balswick, *Family*, 31.
208. King and Kitchener, "Cognitive Development," 108.
209. King and Kitchener, "Cognitive Development," 112.
210. King and Kitchener, "Cognitive Development," 113.
211. King and Kitchener, "Cognitive Development," 114.
212. King and Kitchener, "Cognitive Development," 114.
213. King and Kitchener, "Cognitive Development," 115.
214. King and Kitchener, "Cognitive Development," 115.
215. King and Kitchener, "Cognitive Development," 121.

processes"[216] should put parents and leaders at ease in recognizing that part of the behavior they are seeing is cognitive (neural, psychological) growth that "promotes future-oriented decision making."[217] There are parents who see their eighteen-, nineteen-, or twenty-one-year-old and impatiently lament, "You are now an adult, so why aren't you performing (serving) and functioning optimally in the church or marketplace like a fully mature adult?" Research "shows that neural systems supporting core psychological functions [during emerging young adulthood] are under ongoing development throughout this development window."[218] This neural psychological growth is helping the emerging adult to "fine-tune" their adaptive behavior to environmental and cultural pressures.[219] Understanding the developmental and biosocial behavior of youth can help parents and leaders "to be less" condemning of themselves and others and can "liberate parents from feeling overly responsible for" their child's choices and the "undue burden of guilt and shame."[220]

Generational Differences

Many parents tend to express that when they were the age of their emerging young adult, they were more mature, stable, and gainfully employed, serving more in the church and so forth. However, social forces (culture, the economy, and societal institutions) have introduced changes that make this emerging adult life stage different than when their elders were in that same age bracket. There will be generational differences between midlife adult parents who compare their experiences and life progress when they were a similar age to their emerging adults. What is needed is to factor in that the world today has generated differences in social forces (economical and social change) that were not factors in the world twenty to thirty years ago. It could be that parents and leaders were not equipped for changes associated with the emerging young adult life stage, and their assumptions and expectations need to be reconsidered. Whatever the explanation, imposing mid-to-late life adult performance expectations onto emerging young adults can be misinformed and misplaced.

216. Taber-Thomas and Perez-Edgar, "Emerging Adulthood," 126–27.
217. Taber-Thomas and Perez-Edgar, "Emerging Adulthood," 127.
218. Taber-Thomas and Perez-Edgar, "Emerging Adulthood," 129.
219. Taber-Thomas and Perez-Edgar, "Emerging Adulthood," 136–37.
220. Balswick and Balswick, *Family*, 29.

Summary

The social sciences provide a multifaceted perspective on life cycle and human development that can help understand youth transitions and stages. The social sciences identify several social forces that are push-and-pull factors for youth to leave their ethno-religious communities, thus impacting their parents. Collective forces include the sociological impact of cultural and economic forces and life stage needs, which are factors parents cannot control and may cause youth to leave churches. Furthermore, the social forces of cultural assimilation and redefinitions of family and friendship networks may be pull factors to leave the church, which the parents cannot control and which they may be impacted by. Parents may not be able to control their youth acquiring a preference for the values of Western individualism rather than Eastern group-oriented values, which becomes a pull factor to leave the ethno-religious community and thus impacts the parent. Youth leaving the church on account of the impact of secularism is an outcome parents may not be able to control but can be impacted by. Secularism is part of a broad cultural trend; however, determinants on how impactful secularism is are dependent on foundational faith formation, socialization, and positive parenting roles. Consideration of these factors means parents should pay attention to the early childhood, adolescent, and young adult developmental stages in their faith communities. Research findings are not conclusive on the impact of secularism on the worldview trajectories of youth. Developmental psychology offers some insight to the maturing stages and changes an English ministries congregation goes through. Parents may not be able to control the outcome of choices youth make in evolving, transitional, psychosocial developmental stages, and, therefore, some pain can come with their children's choices. The next chapter will turn to breaking research findings on parents' silent suffering when youth dechurch; these findings inform the formation of this book. The study is intended to contribute to a strategy of solutions to the problem of parents being impacted by the Silent Exodus.

7

Breaking Research on Parents' Silent Suffering

MOST OF US KNOW of situations where there is a problem that is like an elephant in the room. Everyone knows it is there, but someone has to initiate breaking the silence on the issue before it can be addressed. We frequently hear about people who break the silence on a difficult topic or a social justice issue in the hope of helping other people (e.g., Asian Lives Matter: Stop Asian Hate, the Hong Kong democracy movement, social policy on drugs, controversy around abortion laws, etc.). When the silence is broken, action can then be taken to help others avoid unnecessary suffering, to address safety issues, or to contribute to an evolving understanding on a subject. Participants in the study represented in this book wanted to break the silence on parents' silent suffering over their youth leaving the faith and church. They wanted to speak out on the issue in the hope that other parents could be equipped to handle the issue, that the church would have the courage to make changes, and that parents could be better supported. In short, the purpose is that new immigrant and local families could learn from other parents' experiences. I want you to consider the findings of this study.

Chinese bicultural churches have separate congregations with two distinct languages and cultures, and for the purposes of this study, tricultural (Cantonese, Mandarin, English) churches are treated as if they were bicultural. Though there is crossover, generally, Chinese-language congregations are highly attended by the parents, while English-language congregations cater to the acculturating Canadian-born. Bicultural church members are predominantly skilled workers, professionals, and businesspeople. My study was originally conceived with a focus on the Mennonite Brethren Chinese Churches Association (MBCCA), a young movement which has grappled with the challenges of immigrant assimilation for the sake of the mission.[1] The issues raised were recognized, however, as readily generalizable to other ethnic churches, and it was judged that including those other churches within the scope of the research would yield more robust conclusions. Thus one-third of the participants in this research, those in phase three, come from an interdenominational background. Participants were drawn predominantly from Metro Vancouver (British Columbia) though a few were from the Prairie Provinces.

Research Questions

In what ways are overseas-born Chinese Canadian Christian parents who have raised their Canadian-born children in an ethnic church impacted when these children leave this church? The study aimed to examine emotional, social, psychological dimensions of this impact, including effects on parents' spiritual journey. It asked what support systems for parents the church now has. The desired outcome of the study was to recommend solutions towards empowerment and spiritual health for parents; towards that end, pastors and parents themselves were invited to share their thoughts about how parents could be better supported. Such proposals, however, are best interpreted through a theological lens, in particular a theology of the family.

To avoid misunderstanding, it is emphasized that this project focuses *not* on the second-generation Exodus itself but rather on the impact of adult children's Exodus upon their parents. Therefore, though data was collected on perceived reasons for the Exodus, this was of secondary interest, that is, to the extent it could illuminate the parents' reactions.

Research Design

This research was executed stepwise in three phases (Table 1). Analysis of findings from each of the earlier phases (i.e., transcribed and coded) informed the design of subsequent phases.

---

1. Todd, "Impact of Generational Assimilation."

Table 1. Overview of the Three Phases of Research

Phase	Procedures	Participant category	Sampling	Denomination	Purpose
1	open-ended survey	former and current clergy	convenience	MB	identify themes in participants' observations of how parents are impacted
2	survey (open-ended questions and Likert scales)	Exodus MB parent, i.e., parent of emerging adult child who has left the Chinese church in which they were raised	snowball	MB	description, in parents' own words, of how they are impacted; obtain suggestions to support impacted parents
3	pre-meeting survey; focus group	clergy; non-Exodus parent; Exodus parent	convenience snowball	various Protestant	obtain further data on impact; obtain suggestions to support impacted parents

Study Participants

Participants in all three phases had been or were still involved in a Chinese church in Canada. There was an attempt to ensure they shared a common Chinese heritage, a similar adult life stage (middle-aged), and familiarity with the Silent Exodus from their families or churches. Despite efforts to balance participants in respect to gender, all but three of the clergy in phases one and three were male, reflecting the overwhelming prevalence of male clergy in the Chinese churches. Parents were invited in phases two and three and encouraged to include spouses. Participants received an invitation to participate and an informed consent document explaining the study's topic, why they were invited, and expected beneficiaries.

Respondents for phase one were current or former clergy drawn from among thirteen churches within the MBCCA. To qualify to participate in phase two, parents must have had one or more CBC children who were no longer attending the English-language congregation of the MBCCA church in which these parents had raised them. Participants in phase three were from interdenominational Chinese church ministerial networks and Chinese church lay networks. They were various clergy; parents whose children were still attending their ethnic Chinese church (hereafter "non-Exodus parents"); or parents who, as in phase two, had one or more children who had left their ethnic Chinese church (hereafter "Exodus parents" [Table 1]).

Phase One Procedures

Using a brief questionnaire in an entirely open-ended format, clergy were asked to list three pastoral observations of the various impacts of the CBC Exodus on parents. All data was coded and analyzed for patterns in the frequency of responses.

Phase Two Procedures

phase two involved a ninety-nine-question survey of parents to describe the various impacts of the Exodus on them. The survey was created using items which the analysis of phase one had identified as being mentioned most frequently. The survey was administered by email with soft-copy attachment. Some surveys were done by phone in Cantonese by an assistant who aided with OBC parents who wanted to participate in the survey in their "mother tongue." The survey had ten sections, described in Appendix Table A8. In Section H of the survey, parents used a Likert scale to rate the applicability of each of the thirty-three parental reactions that clergy had reported in phase one. The other nine sections asked a total of sixty-six free-form questions, which included impacts on themselves and their spouse, their explanation of their own children's Exodus, the impact on their own faith journey, and recommendations to the church in helping to support other Exodus parents. Parents were told there were no right or wrong answers and that they were invited to simply provide their own experience of their CBC's Exodus.

Phase Three Procedures

Upon consent to join the study and before each group was scheduled to meet, participants in phase three were administered a sixteen-item questionnaire. The pre-meeting questionnaire also noted the goal of the study and explained that background information about the participants was being solicited to better understand the context of remarks that they would later make during the focus group discussion. Thus, participants were asked about their Chinese church backgrounds; their perception of the impact of the Exodus on parents and on the Chinese church, particularly regarding its intensity; what they felt was most needed by impacted parents; their interpretation of reasons for the Exodus; and demographic information. The moderator (myself), working with a Chinese language assistant, facilitated three focus groups, each containing between six and ten people. Because of the ongoing COVID-19 pandemic, each group met via a Zoom video conference, which was scheduled for 120 minutes.[2] Members of the focus groups were told that an overview of the goal of the explicit questions was to discover "in what ways, and with what topics, can the church help minister to these parents?" Additional structured questions explored specific aspects of this problem.

Justification of Design Choices

It was determined that a sample of thirty clergy and thirty OBC parents would be informative enough to discover the impacts on parents and the convergences between the clergy and parent reporting. The size of the sample groups afforded the opportunity to find a significant range of intensity of impact. Phase one interviews used a "key informant" approach to gather the observations from current and former serving pastors. Because non-random sampling may limit the transferability or generalizability of findings, it was important to validate the pastors' perceptions of parental impact by asking affected parents themselves about each during phase two. Use of open-ended questions allowed participants to freely express their views and observations. In the context of such a sensitive topic, participants' trust in the researcher, attributable in part to his insider-outsider status, was important in eliciting the sharing of meaningful, in-depth personal perspectives.

---

2. Using Zoom Video Conferencing can be a very effective way of addressing sensitive cross-cultural topics. Archibald et al., "Using Zoom," 1–8.

Ethical Considerations

The topic was sensitive because the Silent Exodus is reported as an issue for which the clergy, church, and parents are often blamed. The research followed the *Belmont Report* with regard to respect for persons (informed consent, respect for privacy), beneficence, and justice (that there would not be a burden of risk). The study did not engage in the use of stipends or money as an incentive to participate. Participants were given confidentiality. They were told how the data would be used, and participants could opt out of the study at any time if they felt uncomfortable. No one withdrew after they signed the consent form, an indicator that participants in this research were highly motivated to contribute to the study.

Analysis

In phase one, coding identified similarities between observations from which categories of impact emerged. The coded observations were ranked by frequency. Frequencies were then compared with regard to several variables: Chinese versus English pastors, associate versus lead pastors, and current versus past MB pastors, as well as years of service and age group.

In phase two, surveys were numbered sequentially in order of receipt. Responses to each question were coded according to a code book. Data was entered in an Excel spreadsheet. Descriptive statistics were compiled on demographics and levels of parents' church participation. Data was examined for patterns, giving particular attention to most frequent responses and outliers. Impacts were categorized as externalized or internalized. Any apparent inconsistencies were flagged for further analysis. Results were compared with findings from phase one.

For the questionnaire in phase three, participants rated the intensity impact on parents within each of the categories on a scale of one to ten. Results were aggregated as low (one to four), medium (five to seven), and high (eight to ten), and the score for each of the three groups of participants was calculated on the basis of midpoints of ranges. For the focus groups, recordings were transcribed, key words and phrases were identified, and occurrences of themes were counted. Intensity and specificity were summarized. Through intercoder negotiation with an assistant, codes and themes were developed. Based on number of mentions, these themes were condensed into categories. Reported impacts and recommendations were compared and contrasted. Data from evaluations administered after conducting the focus group was incorporated into the findings. Questions were analyzed as to the degree they substantiated the key research question. Evidence in support of themes was provided by way of quotes. Comparisons were made across the three groups and with data from the first two phases.

Findings

Table 2. Demographics						
	Phase 1	Phase 2	Phase 3			
Characteristic	MB Clergy	MB Exodus Parents	Overall	Clergy	Non-Exodus Parents	Exodus Parents
Number	30	30	24	9	7	8
Male	27	13	14	9	4	1
Female	3	17	10	0	3	7
Age, range (y)	30–75+	50–72	32–66	44–66	32–50	53–64
Age, mean (y)	52	60	55	55	44a	59a
Duration as a Christian, mean (y)	—	—	32	38	26a	34
Attendance at CC, mean (y)	—	—	24	29	28	19
Still attend CC now	—	—	20	8	6	6
Member of CC	—	—	23	9	7	7
Pastoral experience, range (y)	2–40+	N/A	N/A	—	N/A	N/A
Pastoral experience, mean (y)	21	N/A	N/A	21.9	N/A	N/A
Length of service in CC, mean (y)	2–40	22	27	34	20	31
Denomination						
MB	30	30	3	1	1	1
Other Protestant	N/A	N/A	20	8	6	6
Language of ministry						
Chinese	15	30	11	2	3	6
English	15	0	13	7	4	2
Capacity involved at CC						

Table 2. Demographics						
	Phase 1	Phase 2	Phase 3			
Characteristic	MB Clergy	MB Exodus Parents	Overall	Clergy	Non-Exodus Parents	Exodus Parents
Senior/lead pastor	13	N/A	6	6	0	0
Assoc. pastor/priest	17	N/A	6	3	3d	0
Lay leader	N/A	30	12	0	4	8
CC = Chinese church; N/A = not applicable;—= not asked.						
One respondent in this group did not answer these questions.						
Alliance, Anglican, Baptist, Presbyterian, Evangelical Free Church, Independent, Lutheran, or Pentecostal.						
Lay leadership roles included deacon, lay leader, musician, teacher.						
Participants were recruited on the basis of their parental role. Some respondents in Phases 1 and 3 carried both clergy and parental roles.						

Phase One

Thirty MBCCA clergy from thirteen MBCCA congregational contexts were interviewed. Clergy ranged in age from thirty to over seventy-five, the average being around fifty-two. Twenty-seven were male, three were female. The length of pastoral experience ranged between two and forty years, the average being about eighteen years (Table 2).

Analysis of commonalities in the reported impacts led to identification of four categories: emotional, social, psychological, and spiritual. Among the parental reactions most frequently reported by clergy (Table 3), the top two, namely, anger and blame, are directed outwardly and internally, respectively.

Table 3. Top Eight Clergy Observations of Impacts on Parents

Phase 1				Impact Category	Phase 2		
Rank	Description	Freq.	%		Representative Parent Survey Responses	Case	Survey Question
1	Anger, blame directed toward church pastoral staff	12	40	Spiritual	"No pastoral staff or leaders are able to or interested in answering [my children's] questions about Christian faith.... Church members are objectified as machines to keep the church running, not persons."	7	14
					"If CBC adults feel the church is their home and get nurtured there, they would not leave. Bonding between the pastor and other young adults is a major factor."	12	28
2	Sense of failure in parenting, self-blame, guilt	10	33	Emotional	"I feel upset with myself that I cannot lead him to God."	25	27
					"We blame ourselves for not giving full support to our children's needs."	10	20
					"It feels I am the only bad sheep; I see others doing well, as if nothing happened."	1	20
					"Socially, people do judge, especially when my husband and I are very involved in our ministries at church. They start to wonder why our daughter doesn't come anymore."	26	20
					"Parents who experience their adult child leaving understand you are not to blame."	20	28

Table 3. Top Eight Clergy Observations of Impacts on Parents

Phase 1				Impact Category	Phase 2		
Rank	Description	Freq.	%		Representative Parent Survey Responses	Case	Survey Question
3	At peace if child attends another church	9	30	Spiritual	"The decision to leave our church is not a departure but a transfer only, so it does not bother me."	3	9
					"I do not mind that the adult child joined another church if he still has faith in God. It hurts me only if he abandons God."	5	27
4	Suffer in silence	8	27	Spiritual	"Not much support received."	10	26
					"Church showed concern about the children's leaving but did not show support."	11	26
5	Stress, anxiety, frustration, shock	8	27	Emotional	"Impacted more emotionally."	11	20
					"We went through different stages emotionally but at last we accepted the reality."	17	13
					"I felt sad and frustrated."	1	8
					"We have frustrations and sometimes feel helpless."	26	29
					"It's so hard, and we worry about his spiritual life."	25	20
					"The leaving of my children in fact was a reality check of the state of the church for us."	7	8
6	Disappointment	6	20	Emotional	"We were in disbelief and disappointed."	4	8
					"Feel a bit disappointed, upset, helpless, but need to accept."	29	8

Table 3. Top Eight Clergy Observations of Impacts on Parents							
Phase 1				Impact Category	Phase 2		
Rank	Description	Freq.	%		Representative Parent Survey Responses	Case	Survey Question
7	Feeling shame (withdrawal)	6	20	Social	"I want to leave this church as well. My husband said this was not our problem and we should not leave this church.... It is hard to find another church that fits our age."	28	8
					"Nobody really cares whether my children left church, so I don't feel supported.... Maybe they have judged me."	1	26
8	Hurt, sadness, grief, internal impact	6	20	Emotional	"We were upset for child #2 not going to church. We could not do anything but tell him he is making a mistake."	10	8
					"I cried for child #2 a lot for not attending church anymore. Sometimes seeing other families' children who love and serve God on Sunday can trigger my emotions."	13	13
					"I did experience unhappy feelings because I am worried. It hurt my feelings when she left the church.... She is still not going to any church and that worries me more."	11	13
					"We are sad she no longer attends church with us.... We just miss her when we go to church."	26	8

Phase one established that clergy consistently perceived an impact on parents. Proportions of pastors making observations were very similar regardless of their position as lead or associate or the language of the congregation they served. Some differences in perspective were associated with the pastor's age and length of service.

Phase Two

Of the phase two parents, 59 percent agreed (VAR 44) with the observation that parents are impacted by CBC's Exodus. Each of the perceptions of impact on parents most frequently reported by pastors in phase one were corroborated to a degree by parents in phase two (Table 3; Appendix Table A9). Asked in the phase two survey whether they were impacted emotionally, socially, or spiritually, one parent commented, "All of the above" (Case 28, Survey Question 20 [hereafter SQ]). Another says she has been impacted "emotionally with a feeling of alienation" (Case 30, SQ20). Worry and sadness were frequently expressed (e.g., Cases 24 and 25, SQ8). Sometimes parental disappointment was tempered. Parents blamed pastors for perceived shortcomings with regard to being a role model (Case 4, SQ14); mentoring (Case 13, SQ14); leadership (Case 14, SQ14); caring and sympathy (Case 16, SQ28); leading by example (Case 17, SQ28); and inspiring rather than lecturing (Case 20, SQ28).

The thirty families in phase two had a total of sixty-three young adult children: eight families (27 percent) with one CBC, thirteen families (43 percent) with two CBCs, seven families (23 percent) with three CBCs, and two families (7 percent) with four CBCs. Of these adult children, thirty were classified as having Moved On (MO) to another church, twenty-eight as having Dropped Out (DO) of the church and from the faith, and five as remaining in their parents' church. Parents whose Exodus experience included at least one DO reported significantly greater impact than did parents whose Exodus experience was solely of MO (data not shown). Moreover, stronger impacts were associated with a higher proportion of DOs within a family's Exodus experience (data not shown). Among parents who experienced an Exodus, 27 percent indicated the impact on them is not settled. One parent said, "The disconnect [of their second child] with God hurts and [is] not fading" (Case 10, SQ13) and "we blame ourselves" (Case 10, SQ20). A mother shared that she cried a lot over her child leaving the church and feeling emotionally triggered seeing other families' children in Sunday services (Case 13, SQ13). Another parent noted they are struggling "emotionally with a feeling of alienation" (Case 30, SQ20). One parent expressed the ongoing experience of "feeling upset with "themselves" (Case 25, SQ27). The parent noted identifying with Ps 143:1: "Lord, hear my prayer, listen to my cry for mercy ... come to my relief" (Case 25, SQ30). Some are still dealing with the long-term impact of their youth leaving the church. Significantly, one-third of this convenience sample of OBC parents have been coming to terms for nearly ten years with the Exodus experience and still have not found peace over the Exodus of their child or children; for example, "I am still trying to find peace" (Case 26, SQ27) and "still waiting for God to answer" (Case 28, SQ27). When parents were asked how long the impact on them lasted until it settled, ten parents who were still in pain stated not "until the children come back to faith" (Cases 1, 8, 10, 11, 13, 24, 26, 28–30). However, some parents expressed having come to terms with the painful reality that their children might never return to the church of their upbringing (e.g., Case 17, SQ13). One recognized that "valid reasons of language barrier and identity recognition" explained their child's move to another church (Case 7, SQ17).

Table 4. Phase 2 Parents' Self-Report on How Long the Exodus Impact Took to Settle		
VAR45 In your situation, how long has the impact lasted before it finally settled? __ Years __ Months	Number	%
1 yr. or less	2	12.5
2–4 yrs.	5	31
Never settled	10	62.5
No answer	13a	N/A
a These subjects are excluded from the calculation of percentages.		

Parents expressed the need to be supported and not judged by the church if their child exits. Parents described how the church could support, encourage, and empower OBC parents who experience CBC Exodus in their family. One parent reported reaching out to parents who have withdrawn and commented that the church should support, encourage, and empower parents by being "less judgmental" (Case 7, SQ29). As the questions in phase two probed more sensitive issues, more were left unanswered; this may be linked to shame in saving face.

Phase Three

Pre-Meeting Questionnaire

In each of the four categories of emotional, psychological, spiritual, and social impact as perceived by members of each group (clergy, non-Exodus parents, or Exodus parents), the intensity on a scale of ten was between four and seven, the average being 5.5 (Table 5).

Table 5. Mean Perceived Impacts of CBC Exodus on Exodus Parents as Reported by Phase 3 Participants					
Impact category	N	Overall	Clergy	Non-Exodus Parents	Exodus Parents
		(N = 24)	(n = 9)	(n = 7)	(n = 8)
Yes	24	24	9	7	8
Emotional	23	6.4	6.2	7.0	5.9
Social	24	4.7	4.0	4.3	5.8
Psychological	24	6.1	5.7	6.1	6.4
Spiritual	23	5.4	5.3	6.1	5.7
Impact rating scale ranges from 1 to 10 points.					

Focus Groups

Many of the questions to the focus groups inquired about support for parents (Appendix Table A11), and subsequently, caring ministry was identified as the dominant theme of discussion, which was found to gravitate to three additional major themes (Table 6). The clergy group articulated these themes roughly 30 percent more frequently than did either parent group, and the Exodus parents had less to say about theological equipping than did their non-Exodus counterparts; otherwise, the frequencies of mention were very similar across the groups.

Table 6. Major Themes in Focus Group Discussion		
Theme	Observations	Explanation
Caring ministry	408	concern for helping impacted parents
Christ and culture	146	shame culture, which needs to be addressed
Scope of impact	122	parents are variably impacted
Theological equipping	34	practical biblical parenting principles

Many members of the focus groups articulated criticisms of the theo-cultural model presented in the introduction. One distanced herself from the tacit assumptions that seemed to govern their congregation: "I grew up in Chinese culture. . . . They just assumed once you are baptized . . . you are going to stay in the church forever" (Case 11, SQ4). One Exodus parent expressed that if the child leaves to go to another church, "they [are] actually still in a church . . . still in a family. . . . There's nothing to be concerned about Chinese speaking or English speaking because wherever you can find a home it's a home setting" (Case 21, SQ3). One Exodus parent recalled having asked his church board, "Are you teaching your children to be Christians or are you teaching them to be Chinese?"

Discussion

All three phases of findings in this study validate that parents are impacted by the Exodus of a child. A surprising finding from phase two was the disparity between clergy and parents in ranking of emotional impacts. That is, OBC parents' reporting of negative and positive reactions were unmatched, whereas the clergy's observations converged (see Appendices, Tables A9 and A10). An unsettling question was what to make of the majority of parents who gave very high negative reactions to open-ended questions on the impact intensity (survey sections A–G and I–J) but often downplayed their negative reactions to the CBC Exodus in responses to the closed questions (the Likert scales in Section H). This phenomenon contrasts with the rankings given to all these observables by the English and Chinese clergy who served them, past and present, in the Chinese MB churches. Why was the list of clergy observations and parents self-reporting so unmatched in the order or sequence of mentioned importance?[3] The question to consider was whether the negative effect has been downplayed, suppressed, somewhat forgotten, or is a manifestation of the Chinese cultural practice of "saving face" in disclosing the Exodus (good news versus bad news) and presenting oneself in a "face-saving" way in a public sense (such as in an interview or community conversation at church). Some researchers have identified that objective evidence does not necessarily corroborate how persons present

---

3. Clergy and parent rankings are not directly comparable because the instruments given to phase one and Two (Section H) respondents used different kinds of questions (open and closed).

their lives or family in interviews and on Facebook.[4] Because the parents' self-reporting did not parallel exactly with objective MB clergy observations, it was asked whether the parents might be rationalizing their subjective feelings in dealing with an unpleasant family issue. In consulting with Chinese clergy and researchers, it was suggested that perhaps both a strong personal Christian faith and a strong Chinese traditional family value may influence Exodus parents to "keep the matter in the family," downplaying its negative impact in public view. In Chinese culture, like other shame and honor cultures,[5] it is socially undesirable to expose or casually speak of something shameful in the family to others outside the family. The influence of cultural conventions perhaps explains why 73.3 percent of the parents in this survey reportedly perceived that their CBC Exodus would not affect other people at church (because it is a private matter). Only 62.1 percent reportedly thought people at church would understand what they are going through; 54.2 percent of the parents expressed they were emotionally supported with their child's Exodus (by certain individuals only—but not the church). Furthermore, 33.3 percent reportedly perceived they were neither supported nor judged by the church, meaning they did not think the church was concerned; for example, one parent commented that "church is so normalized with Exodus situation that nobody really cares" (Case 7). Also, 12.5 percent reportedly perceived they were judged by people at church; for example, one commented, "We are very involved in church ministries and leadership; people wondered "where is that perfect family" (VAR92, Case 26). Many of the Exodus parents surveyed in phase two were in leadership positions of some kind. It can be harder for parents (especially those in leadership or serving roles) to come forward with their CBC Exodus issue in such a sociocultural environment. For example, a couple of parents said that "the church was informed of child leaving [sic] but took no action" (parent response category #4 to VAR92). For cultural, personal, and conventional reasons, the tendency to announce the positive and the least hurtful or intense impacts quite possibly could be the most plausible explanation for the discrepancy of positive and negative reactions reported among the parents and clergy in this survey. Regardless, in Section H of the survey findings, the parents collectively have provided

---

4. A cultural lens or a cultural convention (taboo) can be reflected in how the situation is reported. Dey, *Qualitative Data Analysis*, 36; Silverman, "Interpreting Qualitative Data," 97; Gil-Or et al., "'Facebook-Self,'" 1–10.

5. Mayer and Viviers, "Experiences of Shame," 362–66; Cozens, "Shame Cultures," 362–66.

more numerous negative sentiments than the few triumphs reported over the impacts of their CBC's Exodus. The content of the longer list is compatible with the clergy's observations, except that the prioritized order of mentions is different from the parents. There are exceptions among the parents in this survey with respect to their personal comfort in self-disclosing the degree of pain they have experienced from their child's Exodus. The number of "No Answers" and "N/A"s increases with the sensitive nature of deeper trigger questions in the survey. Some people may be more subdued in expressing the intensity of their sentiments and personal reactions than others. Such an interpretation provides more explanation for the parents' survey response behavior and support to the clergy's observations in phase one, regardless of how the parents have listed the intensity of the thirty-three kinds of impacts on them (see Appendices Tables A9 and A10). Key with phase two is the divergence in opinions and parental attitudes that also related to whether their child dropped out or moved on.

The five datasets characterized the impact of CBC Exodus from the perspectives of clergy and parents. Qualitative data from interviews, questionnaires, and focus groups and quantitative data from multiple-choice sections of questionnaires all demonstrated that parents are impacted emotionally, spiritually, socially, and psychologically by the Exodus of a child of theirs. The process by which the primary researcher and assistant reached agreement about observation and interpretation of the focus groups supports their reliability. In the course of cross-checking the answers to overlapping questions in the three phases, some tensions between data that different procedures elicited were investigated, as discussed above. Once this important sociocultural aspect of the Silent Exodus is accounted for, a high level of convergence can be seen in findings corroborating that parents are impacted on a spectrum.

Conclusions

The original contribution to knowledge in this study is that parents are variably impacted emotionally, spiritually, socially, and psychologically when their adult children abandon the faith and ethno-religious community. This impact is exacerbated if multiple children leave. The impact is generally milder if children continue to practice the faith within another church community not necessarily based on Chinese ethnicity. The study showed that parents and clergy alike believe the church needs to improve its support systems for impacted parents. At present, support for CBC Exodus impact is very spotty; there is a need for the church to be better equipped to accompany parents through painful transitions. One interesting finding was the realization that the Silent Exodus and its impact on parents points to a broader effect on the interdenominational mission of the North American Chinese churches. That is, this is not just the problem of individual parents. The Chinese church functions like the Chinese family, and addressing what ails the family reverberates into the family systems of congregational life and affects the mission of the church.

One limitation of this study is that the religious denominations and participants may not be representative of all the Chinese churches. A large-scale national survey using probability sampling of OBC Christian parents would be expected to replicate this study's findings of

- a spectrum of impacts (from moderate to high intensity) on parents that range from emotional, spiritual, social and psychological;
- association of higher emotional impact with DO-type Exodus;
- parents who are still dealing with the long-term impact of their child's Exodus; and
- a deficit in caring ministry.

Given that the impact of CBC Exodus upon parents is a huge problem for the church at large, the current research could be extended by attempting to generalize to the broader North American Chinese churches and to the impact of second-generation Exodus upon immigrant parents of different cultural and religious faiths. This study is part of a much broader problem of dechurching in North America. This study satisfied the objective of investigating how Chinese Canadian immigrant Christian parents were impacted by the Exodus of their children from their ethno-religious community. Qualitative research has confirmed that parents are impacted. The findings empower local and denominational leadership in the religious nonprofit sector to develop preventive strategies to support impacted parents. Recommendations developed from the focus group participants' own suggestions will be presented in chapter 8.

8

Supporting Impacted Parents

A society grows great when old men plant trees in whose shade they shall never sit.

—GREEK PROVERB

IT IS ENCOURAGING TO picture our lives as trees which will benefit our children's and grandchildren's lives. I remember pastoring in a church where one very wealthy and successful couple struggled with a son who had mental health issues and was frequently hospitalized. I admired the fact that various parents in the church were supportive of this couple. There have been times in my own life when I have been fighting the battle for other parents' children at the church but losing the battle at home with my own child. Some of you reading this have been there. I have always treasured times when friends would take time to listen to an area of parenting that I was struggling with, offer some supportive words, or tell me they would include the concern in their prayers.

I think there is support and enormous opportunities for Asian and immigrant churches given the findings and recommendations in this study.

Significance and Implications

The original contribution to knowledge in this study is that parents are variably impacted emotionally, spiritually, socially, and psychologically by the generational assimilation of their second-generation children when youth abandon the faith and ethno-religious community.[1] The ranked mentions across phases one to three place emotional impact the highest, spiritual impact second, and social impact as the lowest ordered. There was no consensus on psychological impact as the groups had different rankings. This qualitative study addressed the gaps in the research on how parents are impacted by the Exodus of their youth.

The study is important because it contributes to the following:

1. The study revealed that the impact on parents is exacerbated by multiple children leaving the ethno-religious community.
2. The study identified a concern for the church to improve their support systems of care for impacted parents.[2]
3. This study attempts to empower church leaders and communities to assist struggling parents with interdisciplinary solutions to integrate faith and parenting during generational assimilation.
4. The study provides strategies to assist leaders with an approach to caring ministry and intervention that can be used to minimize impact and empower parents, thus reversing trends for current and future immigrant families.
5. The study contributes qualitative knowledge and recommendations for best practices in churches for the future of healthier parent and family ministry.

Insights in Previous Research and This Study

Previous research indicated that the process of generational assimilation created tension in the Asian family.[3] Generational assimilation is a dynamic

---

1. For the interested reader, see tables B27, B28, B32, and B34 on how CBC Exodus of the Chinese church affects the OBC parents in Todd, "Empowering."

2. See tables 20, 22, B35, B38, C29 and D9 that all point to improving care in Todd, "Empowering."

3. ChenFeng et al., "Intergenerational Tension," 158, 161; Kwak and Berry,

in tension associated with the Silent Exodus. One of the primary insights in this study was that parents are variably impacted in intensity by a Silent Exodus from ethno-religious communities that is categorically emotional, spiritual, social, and psychological.

Lessons

I discovered that the topic in this study was broadly relevant to interdenominational Chinese churches. With phase two, it was discovered that the research supposition (parents are impacted) was correct; however, the assumption that there might be only two kinds of impact was recalibrated in the discovery of five[4] differentiated impacted parent groups.

Theological Insights Gained

This study identified that it is imperative for parents to be equipped with a theology of parenting and the family, a theology of the family in the life cycle, and a theology of spiritual development that includes maturation and developmental stages. A theology of family, maturation, and changing life stages helps expand an understanding of family transitions and parents' evolving roles, along with aiding them in managing expectations. This prepares parents with an understanding that family is a developing system. A theology of family (combined with a social-sciences perspective on life cycle and human development) helps provide a measure of understanding as to why youth leave ethno-religious communities and why parents struggle with that. A key insight from practical and applied theology is that parents need help in being journey-oriented. A parent's influence needs to evolve as their children age. A theological value on transparency addresses shame culture, the code of silence on impacted parents, embarrassment

---

"Generational Differences," 152–62; Qin, "Our Child," 162–79.

4. This points to a variable scope of impact on parents depending on the type of case the parent is experiencing. The five differentiated impacted parent groups were:
Parents with a single case of drop out (DO)
Parents with a single case of move on (MO)
Parents with multiple cases of drop out (DO)
Parents with multiple cases of move on (MO)
Parents with multiple combined or mixed cases of DO and MO

over youth leaving the church, and cultural avoidance and taboo on sharing about the impact on parents.

Recommendations and Future Action Steps

Participants in phases one to three provided recommended solutions for impacted parents who have experienced a Silent Exodus. Table 7 shows interventions, strategies, and solutions from recommendations to help impacted parents.

Table 7. Interventions, Strategies, and Solutions from Recommendations to Help Impacted Parents		
Phase 1	Phase 2	Phase 3
Equipping keeping a patient commitment to serve God (Case 2)	**Caring Ministry** change the church's approach to caring ministry (Care and Listen)	**Caring Ministry** (laity) support groups prayer community care parent mentors teaching listening (empathy) encouraging comfort visit, fellowship
Equipping being steadfast, praying and trusting God (Case 16)	**Caring Ministry** parent recommendations to the church in a call for more truthful, honest, transparent discussion on impacted parents (VAR97)	**Caring Ministry** (pastor) counsel instruct train parent mentors pastoral diagnostics pray resources (web-based, online, pamphlets in Chinese) care to whole family

Table 7. Interventions, Strategies, and Solutions from Recommendations to Help Impacted Parents

Phase 1	Phase 2	Phase 3
Equipping living in hope (Case 9, 16)	**Caring Ministry** a recommendation to address unawareness, passivity, and indifference towards the suffering of some OBC parents	**Shame Culture** destigmatize shame culture with a grace-based theological perspective break the silence on shame culture
	Equipping recommend informing parents that spiritual disciplines (Scripture and prayer) are core sources of comfort and hope	**Shame Culture** be solution-oriented with shame culture comfort, console, affirm no blaming, condemnation, or guilt (be grace-based) limit the effects of shame and comparison
		Theological Equipping Recommended equipping on the universal church faith, hope God's faithfulness grace being journey-oriented providence, sovereignty
		Recommended Other Equipping equip parents for family transitions and evolving parent roles. equip parents on assimilation trajectories of the Silent Exodus equip parents in preventive measures to live committed to their faith

Table 7. Interventions, Strategies, and Solutions from Recommendations to Help Impacted Parents		
Phase 1	Phase 2	Phase 3
		recommend action step of initiating parent workshops parent mentors preventive measures

Recommendations in Phases One to Three from Clergy and Parents

Phase one clergy recommended pastoral solutions to help support parents. Their equipping recommendations were to keep a patient commitment to serve God, be steadfast in prayer, trust God, and live in hope. An insight here is that prayer can draw people's hearts towards Christ; some youth and adult children do come back to the faith, and parents are encouraged not to give up. Luke 1:50 reminds parents, "His mercy extends to those who fear him, from generation to generation."

Phase two parents equipping recommendations included informing parents' spiritual disciplines (Scripture and prayer) as being core sources of comfort and hope. Parents are urged to go deeper in understanding the Scripture and realize that deterministic biblical interpretations of the spiritual outcomes for youth are based on flawed exegesis. But they should also recognize that God honors free will. If we as parents will commit and follow God each day and influence our kids to do the same, the results are in God's hands. We can be there to listen when our adult children need us, but we also need to give them space to learn. Parents need to debunk cultural myths on parenting and realize we go wrong by trying to do God's part; a parent's part looks different when their children are a minor and when they are an adult. Scripture can be used as prayers for parents' children. Proverbs 20:7 reminds parents that "the righteous lead blameless lives; blessed are their children after them." Parents in phase two made recommendations to the church in a call for more truthful, honest, transparent discussion on impacted parents. They also recommended that the church address unawareness, passivity, and indifference towards the suffering of some parents.

Phase three clergy and parents made four categorical recommendations to the church. In the area of caring ministry to parents, they recommended counsel, instruction, training parent mentors, pastoral diagnostics (a sensitivity in assessing the needs of parents), prayer, developing resources (web-based, online, pamphlets in Chinese and English), and care to the whole family. This can help parents understand their emotions so they stop blaming themselves for a dechurched child. Part of the healing process for parents can be getting in a group or with a friend or friends who will walk with them and pray. Regarding shame culture, participants in the study recommended that shame culture be destigmatized through a grace-based theological perspective, breaking the silence on shame culture. Be solution-oriented with shame culture: comfort, console, affirm, don't blame, don't condemn, and don't guilt. Limit the effects of shame and comparison. The focus groups recommended that the Chinese church could be theologically equipped to see itself as part of the universal big "C" church (there are resources in the mainstream church that can be utilized). Equip the church on faith, hope, grace, God's faithfulness, providence, sovereignty, and being journey-oriented. Equip parents for family transitions and evolving parent roles. Equip parents on assimilation trajectories of the Silent Exodus, and equip parents in preventative measures to live committed to their faith. Earlier in this book I asked, "Are you equipped with a mental map of what you believe about parenting? Do you have a biblical perspective on the family life cycle that includes addressing sin, restoration, grace, and forgiveness?" The parenting call (stewarding) for every life stage should include prioritizing your devotional life, your marriage (if you are married), your wellbeing, and your spiritual influence and spiritual family engagement. Parents are to be a faithful steward of influence in a shifting parent role and put their hope in God. The phase three focus groups finally recommended the step of leaders initiating action-oriented parent workshops with effective content, supportive facilitation, and guidance to help impacted parents adjust and to educate non-impacted younger parents as a preventative measure. I have included a hypothetical workshop in the Appendix of how a leader might organize and conduct such a workshop with various topics.

Insights in the Recommendations

Phase Two Recommendations

- **Recommendations from parents for more care**

    The theme in the recommendations was for the church to change its approach to its care ministries. Parents proposed more demonstrative care, engagement care, transitional care, proactive care, attentive care, empathetic care, equipping care, and relational care.

- **Recommendations to the church in a call for more truthful, honest, and transparent discussion about impact on parents**

    Many parents expressed that the church can help support parents in moving past shame and blaming themselves. The church can help parents listen to their CBCs, to be a learner, to pray (repent, appeal to God for guidance), and facilitate more experienced parents to share their insights and experiences.

- **Recommendations to address unawareness, passivity, and indifference towards the suffering of some OBC parents**

    Two-thirds of the parent participants were requesting that the Chinese churches have more communal discussion on the subject of impacted parents.

- **Recommendations to inform parents that Scripture and prayer are core sources of comfort and hope**

    The strategic opportunity for leadership is to promote 100 percent engagement in spiritual disciplines with parents.

Phase Three Interdenominational Focus Group Recommendations

- **Destigmatize shame culture with a grace-based theological perspective**

    A view represented by two participants was the need for a more grace-based approach to eclipsing shame-based culture.

(Focus group 1—Case 2)
I totally love the answer [to] destigmatize. And that means [parents] hear the message [referring to the impacts of the Silent Exodus on parents] before it happens to them, so they hear the message that this happens, and it is not their fault . . . but they need to hear it before it happens to them as well as afterward.

(Focus group 1—Case 3)
I think what is important is, when caring . . . the answer is to embrace the brokenness because, in our culture, we don't embrace brokenness; once we embrace brokenness, we can have fellowship and we can share. But without that, it's just the cultural thing.

- **Breaking the code of *silence* in shame culture and its impact on parents**

  Various parents recommended breaking the silence on shame culture. The following two "non-Exodus parent focus group two" quotes are exemplary.

  (Case 2)
  Take the silent out of the Exodus. . . . Talk about it. . . . Conversations need to start somewhere so that it is not a taboo, not a stigma to talk about these things.

  (Case 3)
  We have the Silent Exodus, but there is the silent suffering that parents go through too. Because it is agonizing for parents to watch . . . it is painful, it is hurtful, so when it stays silent, then you cannot have healing, because it's never spoken, it's never dealt with.

- **Be solution-oriented within shame culture**

  The following "non-Exodus parent focus group two" cases are examples of being solution-oriented with the impact of shame culture and youth leaving.

  (Case 6)
  Limit the effects of shame or comparison.

  (Case 1)
  There is stigma. . . . Confront some . . . who might be looking at it that way.

(Case 3)
Something to tell the parents . . . I think would be . . . "You did not fail God, you didn't let him down, God still loves you. You didn't fail him or disappoint him in some way." And to have that comfort, that burden taken off their shoulders where they don't have to carry that, can be healthy for them in their spiritual walk and their spiritual life, that they don't carry that guilt unnecessarily.

The following "Exodus parent focus group three" case is an example of recommending the church address shame culture as a community, encouraging and supporting parents.

(Case 11)
If we are going to do church together . . . we have to start being more open about our lives, our struggles. Yes, it's shameful to tell people our kids are going through certain things and we don't know what to do, but I think that's why God put us together.

- **Recommended Action Step of Initiating Parent Workshops**

    Focus groups recommended starting parent solution-based workshops to support and equipping impacted parents.

Recommendations Found in the Literature

Studies identify a range of factors that contribute to passing on the faith, which minimizes impact on parents.[5] Two committed parents in a happy marriage, utilizing a healthy parenting style, are a strong influence on passing on the faith. A study on the range of impact intensities, themes, and categories of the Exodus on Chinese Christian parents was not known before this study. Four fundamental theories combine explanations for why youth leave ethno-religious communities and impact parents. Assimilation theory provides research on why youth leave ethno-religious communities, which creates stress and tension for parents. Social learning theory helps explain how the role modeling of parents has long-term effects on the later choices of youth. Emerging adulthood theory helped explain how cultural forces are factors behind the Silent Exodus phenomenon that dominoes into impact on parents. Religious commitment of parents' theory connected

5. Longitudinal studies predict the general probability of religious influence and the religious outcomes of youth raised with religious families: youth become more likely to be religious.

with my study as to why there is a scope of impact on parents that is tied to their level of spirituality. Each of these theories have elements that could be predictors of probability outcomes of the Silent Exodus phenomenon, and thus predictors of impact on parents. When the elements, factors, and dynamics are aligned in particular directions, the probability trajectories of Exodus can range, and theoretically, so can the impacts on parents' range. It can be predicted if parents and leaders use best practices to minimizing the probability of youth leaving their faith communities (or leaving the faith). Insights from these theories hold the potential to lessen the range of probability of youth leaving and impacting parents. What is new with this study is that it showed that there is a differential range of intensity of impact on parents when youth Exodus their ethno-religious community. Parenting for best probability outcomes with youth should be distinguished from a deterministic view on outcomes. Deterministic and probability parenting perspectives are why it is important that leaders remember the findings in this study and keep the recommendations in their toolbox to support the scope of impacted parents. As was identified earlier in this book, polarized findings with youth leaving or staying with ethno-religious communities can be reconciled by recognizing that parental influence is real, and that parental influence is not a guarantee youth will stay in the faith or church. The background study to this book contributes to knowledge in being an Asian Canadian study that addresses an important gap in research, the connection between the Silent Exodus, and differentiated impacts on parents. Figure 1 shows strategies and solutions recommended on how to support parents.

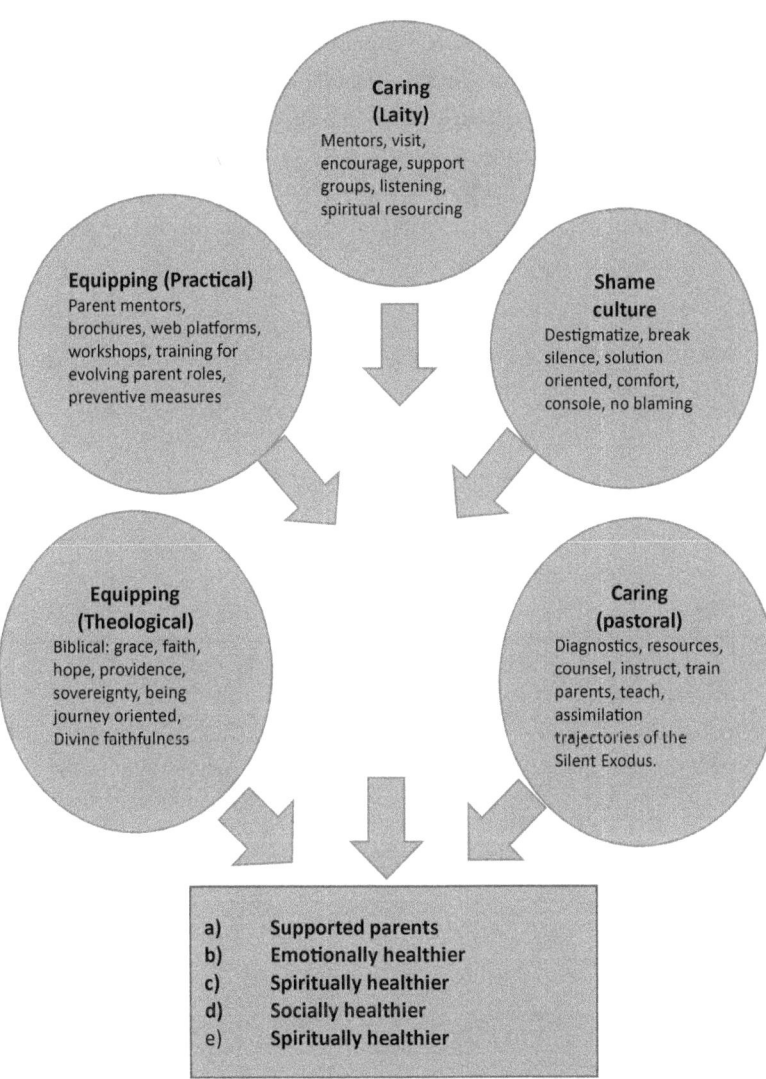

Figure 1. Strategies and solutions recommended on how to support parents.

Summary

In conclusion, the objective of this book has been to investigate what ways Chinese Canadian immigrant Christian parents were impacted by the generational assimilation of their second-generation children when youth abandon the faith and their ethno-religious community. Using the qualitative research method, it was confirmed parents are impacted. The findings empower local and denominational leadership to work on ways to support impacted parents. Recommendations put forth by phases one, two, and three groups provided strategies that contribute to solutions that support parents' wellbeing. The way forward is a call to action in reflective leadership, transparency, and collaborative courage.

> "Speak up for . . . people who have no voice."
>
> (PROVERBS 31:8, THE MESSAGE)

Appendix

Clergy Survey Questionnaire

The survey dispersed to the MBCCA clergy was presented in an email attachment with the following statement:

I am studying to identify OBC (Overseas Born Chinese) parents' perceptions after experiencing their emerging adult CBC (Canadian Born Chinese also known as CRC Canadian Raised Chinese) emerging adults (ages 18–29) exiting Chinese churches they were raised in. This study is an attempt to gauge the psychological and behavioral impact on the parents' faith practices, service and spiritual adjustment. The purpose is to advance some findings and theological solutions towards empowering rekindling, refocusing, recalibrating and restoring a renewed vision for their faith journey and service. The main objective of this research is first to identify the top key sensitivities (understanding, feelings, and emotions) of Chinese Canadian (OBC) parent's perceptions from Chinese Church contexts, regarding the experience of their emerging adults defecting and leaving from Chinese bicultural churches, and assess the emotional and behavioral impact on the parents. My question is:

> A number of people have raised the question as to whether the Overseas born immigrant parents are impacted emotionally, behaviorally or in their interior or exterior faith practices and behaviors by the effects of their emerging adult (18-29) local born leaving/exiting the Chinese church they were raised in. If you agree that the parents are affected, could you provide and list three pastoral observations, in your experience, of ways the parents have been impacted. Feel free to elaborate.

- _____
- _____
- _____

A2 Figure 2. Phase 1: Clergy survey invitation to participate

APPENDIX

A. Start with Some Background

How long have you and your family been attending the specific Chinese church that your adult CBC child(ren) left? Length of time family attending this church: Years _____ Months _____
Name of the Church your family and child(ren) attended: _____
Is your family still attending this church now even without the child(ren) who left? Yes ___ No ___
Are you a baptized (or transfer) member at this church?
Yourself: Yes ___ No ___   The adult child(ren) who left: Yes ___ No ___
Spouse: Yes ___ No ___   Other children (if applicable): Yes ___ No ___
Could you please indicate your Age: _____
Could you please indicate your Gender: Male ___ Female ___
How long have you been a born again Christian? _____ Years _____ Months

B. Talk about People and Relationships in the Church

1. What is your degree of involvement in this church, in what capacity? Participated or served for how many years? For example, just Sunday worship, fellowship–6 yrs, Sunday school teacher –2 yrs, etc.

_____

2. Can you describe the quality of fellowship that you and family received at this Church?

_____

3. Would you say it is (was): Excellent ____ Very good ___ Good ____ So-so _____ Poor _____

4. Did your CBC adult child(ren) involve or serve in the church before s/he decided to leave? For example, participated in what program or served in what ministry or capacity? How many years?

_____

C. About your CBC Adult Child(ren)'s Decision to Leave the Church

5. At what age /life stage did your CBC emerging adult child(ren) decided to leave your church? (If you have more than one CBC adult child left the church, please describe them separately, using Child #1 at university and Child #2 at senior high, etc.)

_____

6. How did it happen? _____

_____

7. What was the reason that your CBC adult child(ren) used or told you about leaving the church?

_____

A3 Figure 3. Phase 2 parent questionnaire

Appendix

8. How has the leaving of your adult CBC child(ren) from the church **affected you (and your spouse)**? What was your (and your spouse's) initial reaction(s)? What was /has been the impact on your relationship with your adult child(ren)?

___

9. How has the leaving of your adult CBC child(ren) **affected other people** in the church? Or would you say there was almost no effect at all?

___

10. Did other people at the church express their care and concern? Yes ____ No ____

11. Did other people at church understand what you and family were experiencing? Yes ____ No ____

12. Did you share your situation with people in church at all? Yes ____ No ____

13. How did you (and spouse) cope with the situation since? Did you go through different stages emotionally till you have come to terms with the reality? What still hurt you (and spouse) the most?

___

D. Your Best Understanding of the Reasons Led to your CBC Adult Child(ren) Leaving the Chinese Church

14. In your honest opinion, the main reason(s) you think that your adult child(ren) leaving the church was because of (there can be more than one reason, write as many as applicable):

1. _____
2. _____
3. _____
4. _____
5. _____

15. Does your child(ren) remain in the faith /attend another church now or have abandoned his/her belief totally? Attend another church now: ____ Abandon belief in God totally: ____

E. Life After your CBC Adult Child(ren) Left the Chinese Church

16. How long ago has it been since your CBC adult child(ren) left the church they were raised in?
How many _____ Years _____ Months ago?

17. Briefly describe **what has changed** in your (and your spouse's) life after your CBC adult child(ren) left the Chinese church?

___

A3 Figure 3. Phase 2 parent questionnaire (cont)

APPENDIX

18. A number of people have debated the issue as to **whether there is an impact (and how long the impact would be)** on OBC Parents when their locally raised adult children left the Chinese church in which they grew up. In your opinion, would you agree with the observation that OBC parents are impacted by this? Yes _____ No _____

19. In your situation, how long the impact has last before it finally settled? __ Years __ Months Or you would say it never settled until the child(ren) comes back to the faith _____

20. If you agree that OBC parents are impacted, could you describe **in what ways** that you or your family are impacted either emotionally, socially in church, psychologically, or spiritually?

_____

21. Can you rate the intensity of the impact on you (and spouse, if applicable) in each aspect using the following scale: (Rate from 1 to 10 - with 1 not being a big deal, 10 being very hurtful) because of the departure of your CBC adult child(ren) from church?

Not a big deal				Mixed feelings			Very hurtful		
1	2	3	4	5	6	7	8	9	10

a) Emotional impact on you: _____ (and spouse): _____
b) Social impact on you: _____ (and spouse): _____
c) Psychological impact on you: _____ (and spouse): _____
d) Spiritual impact on you: _____ (and spouse): _____

22. The following is a list of emotional reactions exhibited by some OBC Parents due to the leaving of their CBC adult child(ren) from the Chinese church. These are observations noted by both English and Chinese pastors (past and present) from over the years in the churches they served. Using the same rating scale of 1 to 10, like above, can you indicate if any of these reactions was present (or still remain) in you (or your spouse) and that how strong they were (are) to both of you when your child(ren) left? **Please write the selected number (1 to 10) in front of the reaction(s) that applied to you.**

A little /Not as strong				Mixed feelings			Very strong feeling		
1	2	3	4	5	6	7	8	9	10

___ Anger and blame pastoral staff /church
___ At peace if CBC adult child(ren) attend other church
___ Consider the leaving a different future for CBC adult children
___ Confusion /feeling lost
___ Disappointment, despair, defeat, discouragement

___ Distrust of pastors
___ Embarrassment / loss of face
___ Feeling disrespected or rejected (by child)
___ Feeling betrayal by child's disobedience
___ Feeling inevitable (fate)

___ Feeling trapped or powerlessness
___ Feeling of loss (abandonment)
___ Feeling numb
___ Focus on improving English ministry
___ Hoping in God
___ Hurt, Sadness, Grief inside but not affecting external practices

A3 Figure 3. Phase 2 parent questionnaire (cont)

Appendix

VAR71 ___ Ignore the problem (denial)	77 ___ Questioned God	___ Stress, anxiety, frustration, fear, shock
VAR72 ___ Indifference	78 ___ Remain steadfast	___ Suffer in silence
VAR73 ___ Lost enthusiasm /withdraw from serving in church	79 ___ Resignation, give-up	___ Undirected anger, resentment, bitterness, anger toward God
VAR74 ___ Passion for God/faith impacted	80 ___ Sense of failure (parenting), Self-blame, Guilt	
VAR75 ___ Patient commitment to serve God	___ Shame	___ Urge to move away to another church /totally leave church
VAR76 ___ Praying and trusting God	___ Skeptical about preachers & preaching	___ Xenophobic

F. Impact on Your Faith Journey

23. Did the leaving of your child(ren) have an impact on your faith and prayer life? Yes ____ No ____

24. Did the leaving have an impact on your willingness to serve in Church ministries? Yes ____ No ____

25. Did the leaving cause you to feel disappointment with God or Bible promises? Yes ____ No ____

26. Did you feel you were emotionally and spiritually supported or judged by the church during your experience of your CBC adult child(ren) leaving? Supported ____ Judged ____ Can you explain?

_____

27. In brief, how have you (and your spouse) adjusted in your spiritual journey since your adult child left the Chinese church? Did you (and spouse) eventually find peace? How?

_____

G. Hindsight Can Be 20/20

28. In hindsight, looking back to what your family experienced, are there any recommendation to the Chinese church that you could offer to clergy and leaders in preventing CBC adults from leaving? What would you want to say to Church leaders that could help other future parents who possibly could experience their adult children leaving the Chinese church?

_____

29. Could you make any recommendation as to how the Church can support, encourage, and empower other parents in the event such an experience actually happens in their family?

_____

30. Has there been any biblical text or stories that have helped you reconcile and grow through this experience of your CBC adult child leaving the Chinese church, or anything that has given you comfort and hope for the future?

A3 Figure 3. Phase 2 parent questionnaire (cont)

Appendix

Table A8. Phase 2 Question Types and Topics			
Section	VR number	Question Type	Topic
A	1–11	Open-ended	Background
B	12–18	Open-ended	People and relationships
C	19–24	Open-ended	About the CBC adult child decision to leave
D	25–35	Open-ended	Impact of child Exodus on parents and church
E	36–41	Open-ended	Best understanding of the reasons that led to their child leaving the Chinese church
F	42–43	Open-ended	Life after their adult child left the Chinese church
G	44–54	Open-ended	Impact on parents—self assessment
H	55–87	Likert scale	Verification of Phase 1 clergy impact observations
I	88–95	Open-ended	Impact on parents' faith journey
J	96–98	Open-ended	Hindsight can be 20/20 recommendations

Table A9. Phase 2 Parents' Rating of 33 Emotional Reactions and Comparison with Clergy Observations				
VAR	Emotional reactions	Number of parent participants	Top parent E.R. rating	Top clergy E.R. rating
55	Anger and blame directed toward pastoral staff and church	23	27	1
56	At peace if CBC adult child(ren) attends other church	23	3	3
57	See leaving as a different future for CBC adult children	22	7	
58	Confusion, feeling lost	21	14	
59	Disappointment, despair, defeat, discouragement	23	11	6
60	Distrust of pastors	20	32	
61	Embarrassment or loss of face	22	23	
62	Feeling disrespected or rejected (by child)	19	30	
63	Feeling betrayal by child's disobedience	19	25	
64	Feeling inevitability (fate)	21	9	
65	Feeling trapped or powerlessness	23	13	
66	Feeling of loss (abandonment)	22	15	

APPENDIX

Table A9. Phase 2 Parents' Rating of 33 Emotional Reactions and Comparison with Clergy Observations

VAR	Emotional reactions	Number of parent participants	Top parent E.R. rating	Top clergy E.R. rating
67	Feeling numb	22	24	
68	Focus on improving English ministry	20	6	
69	Keep hoping in God	25	2	
70	Hurt, sadness, grief inside but not affecting external practices	24	8	8
71	Ignore the problem (denial)	17	19	
72	Indifference	17	21	
73	Loss of enthusiasm, withdraw from serving in church	20	28	
74	Passion for God/faith impacted	20	10	
75	Patience, commitment to serve God	21	4	
76	Praying and trusting God	23	1	
77	Questioned God	21	17	
78	Remain steadfast	23	5	
79	Resignation, given up	20	31	
80	Sense of failure (parenting), self-blame, guilt	20	12	2
81	Shame	19	29	7
82	Skeptical about preachers and preaching	19	18	
83	Stress, anxiety, frustration, fear, shock	19	22	5
84	Suffer in silence	19	16	4
85	Undirected anger, resentment, bitterness, anger toward God	19	26	
86	Urge to move away to another church, totally leave church	19	20	
87	Xenophobic	15	33	

Appendix

Table A10. Emotional Reactions to the Impact of the Silent Exodus: Comparison of Top 8 Phase 1 Clergy Observations and Top 8 Phase 2 Parents Self-Rating

Phase 1 Clergy Top 8 Observations of Parents' Emotional Reactions		Phase 2 OBC Parents' Top 8 Self-Rated Emotional Reactions		
Rank	Description	Rank	Description	Average %
1	Anger and blame directed toward pastors	1	Praying and trusting God	8.2
2	Sense of failure, blame directed toward self, guilt	2	Keeping hope in God	8.1
3	At peace if child attends other church	3	At peace if child attends other church	7.4
4	Suffer in silence	4	Patient, commitment to serve God	6.5
5	Stress, anxiety, frustration, shock	5	Remain steadfast	5.5
6	Disappointment	6	Focus on improving EM	6.0
7	Feeling shame	7	See leaving a different future for CBC adult children	5.5
8	Hurt, sadness, grief, internal impact	8	Hurt, sadness, grief, internal impact, but not affecting external practices	4.6

Table A11. Guide for Moderators of Phase 3 Focus Groups

Route	Q	Time (min)	Question
Opening question	1	5	Introduce yourself and tell us one of your favorite things you experienced while attending a Chinese church.
Introduction question	2	5	Share your prior knowledge and personal observation of the impact on parents of young adults leaving the Chinese church and faith.
Transition question	3	10	What do you think are the most important needs these parents experience after their children leave the church?
Key questions	4	15	What could be done about those needs?
	5	15	What could the church leaders, or the church, put in place to better support parents when their children leave the family church?
	6	15	What might caring for parents look like?
	7	15	How could parents be supported spiritually?
	8	15	What kinds of support could be given to help parents heal?
	9	15	How can the parents group help parents tell their story and share about the broken experiences of their child leaving?

APPENDIX

Table A11. Guide for Moderators of Phase 3 Focus Groups			
Route	Q	Time (min)	Question
Ending	10	10	What final advice would you give regarding ways the impacted parents could be supported?
Total time		120	

Table A12. Phase 2 OBC Parents' Experience of Interaction with People at Church about CBC Exodus							
	N	Yes		No		Not Sure	
		f	%	f	%	f	%
Did other people at church express their care and concern?	24	15	63	6	25	3	13
Did other people at church understand what you were experiencing?	24	12	50	9	39	3	13
Did you share your situation with people in church at all?	24	15	63	6	25	3	13

Table A13. Age and Stage of Life When child Left the church			
Code	Description	#	Percentage
1	at university / college stage	17	30.1%*
2	after university / college	8	14.3%*
3	marriage	4	7.1%
4	career / study relocation other cities / overseas	4	7.1%
5	at jr. /sr. high school stage or just graduated	12	21.4%*
6	at early working career stage	7	12.5%*
7	broken love relationship at church	1	1.8%
8	seek independence lived away from home	3	5.3%

Table A14. Comparisons Between OBCs and CBCs Reasons to Exodus the Church			
Top reasons for leaving	A	B	C
Top 8	Parents assumed reason VAR23	The CBC's reason VAR24	Todd former Western Canada 2015 research
1	Moved from home, independence, business **career** in another city (9)	Boring, no **friends**, not interested in church anymore (8)	Issue: Life stage transition needs unfulfilled within a Chinese church (14)

Appendix

Table A14. Comparisons Between OBCs and CBCs Reasons to Exodus the Church

Top reasons for leaving	A	B	C
Top 8	Parents assumed reason VAR23	The CBC's reason VAR24	Todd former Western Canada 2015 research
2	Did not fit in Chinese church, could not make **friends**, unhappy, see hypocrisy/judging (4)	Reside or **work** in another province or distanced place (5)	Issue: Overemphasis on Chinese cultural identity and ethnocentrism (13)
3	Childhood **friends** left church (3)	Church **leaders** not interested in one as a person but target only for church services. See hypocrisy, upset with people in church, church problems (5)	Issue: church **leadership**, organizational structure, and program issues (13)
4	Unhappy with Chinese church **leaders'** attitudes towards English congregation (3)	Work study excuse, married non-believer and does not want to attend church alone (4)	Issue: Control issues with church power and politics (9)
5	Found church boring, unwilling to go, started with irregular attendance (4)	Needs relevant support with people facing similar challenge in life socially and spiritually and found a more suitable church (2)	Discovered issue: Loneliness and the attempt to seek **friends**, fellowship and relationships (8)
6	No English pastor / left church (at that time) (2)	Faith issue, turned atheist, do not believe anymore, losing and questioning faith (2)	Issue: Perceived choice of a secular lifestyle versus Christianity
7	One young family found a sense of belonging in English speaking church. This was done in consideration for the next generation growing up. Consideration for next generation growing up in environment (1)	Doesn't feel like they fit in church, no friends and no support (1)	Issue: Perceived problems with church beliefs, theology or hypocrisy

Appendix

Table A14. Comparisons Between OBCs and CBCs Reasons to Exodus the Church			
Top reasons for leaving	A	B	C
Top 8	Parents assumed reason VAR23	The CBC's reason VAR24	Todd former Western Canada 2015 research
8		Broken love relationship with someone, parents, church (1)	

Table A15. Main Reason Parents Thought Child Left Church		
1	CBC felt lonely, left out, no friends, lack of supportive peer groups, fellowship	5
2	Boring, discouraged, personal lack of interest in church, laziness	5
3	Accept secular values, no friends are Christians, claimed no need for God	3
4	Felt better use of time socializing or sleeping than attend church	1
5	Church message not meeting CBC needs, not enough or irrelevant programs in EM	5
6	CBC grown-ups know what they need and where they belong, they need to have their own community build up	5
7	CBC have language and cultural concerns, seek where they feel comfortable, want to attend an English church	5
8	Family not paying sufficient attention to CBC's spiritual needs, lack of role model, inconsistent praying for CBC	2
9	CBC more interested in worldly issues of social problems, famine, war than religion	1
10	Busy with work or studies	4
11	Peer pressure to leave when most friends have left	9
12	Do not feel connection with God at church, biblical teachings have no connection to their life, disagree with some Chinese church teachings based on traditions. The child found no love, only rules and service work culture at church but not focusing on God	2
13	Unable to ground personal faith in God's words	4
14	Geographical, relocation or distance reasons for work, career, or studies	5
15	Judgmental attitudes or hypocrisy of other Christians at church, gossip behind people's backs, belittled or made people feel inferior, shame culture	4
16	Lack of pastors or mentors in CBC's early years for spiritual nurturing	2

Table A15. Main Reason Parents Thought Child Left Church		
17	Church too ethnocentric and not welcoming people with other backgrounds	4
18	Church itself lacks care, love, involvement, good leaders, and leadership	4
19	CBC parents want to leave as well, children left with them	2
20	Married to a non-Christian spouse	1

An Example of a Parent Workshop for Impacted Parents

Background

Parents indicated they were impacted on various reaction scales. The parents indicated they wanted some kind of guided support group to be able to share and talk about their experiences. This is an exploratory idea of what could be done in creating a workshop for parents.

The Workshop

This innovation is need focused to help facilitate understanding, healing, connection, a place parents can tell their story, or challenging experiences.

Title: Parents' Peace

Promoted as four workshop sessions for parents who have (or are) experienced a Silent Exodus in the family and church.

The Workshop Plan and Content

Four group sessions that cover the following topic outline:

Appendix

1. Laying down the overview, background, objectives, topics, and benefits

2. The topical terrain of norms, beliefs, experiences, and rethinking theological assumptions

3. Addressing parenting cultural myths on the outcomes of children

4. Exploring the paradigm shift of care to parents of youth that leave the church and faith

The focus is:

"How can our church help impacted parents transition during and after the Exodus of their youth and emerging adults?"

Challenge:

A possible cultural challenge is that parents' support groups might be distasteful in your church. The immigrant view on kinds of support groups needs to be considered. Although the idea of grief, loss, or divorce support groups may be prolific in the mainstream church, consideration needs to be given to the Chinese church perspective experiencing struggles through the lens of an honor and shame culture. Chinese culture is pragmatic and there is the challenge of questioning the value of discussion on topics where it can be thought that there is no solution to bringing CBCs back to the church. In the Western mind, therapeutic forms of support groups, where people can cathartically vent, are common, but they are reported to be less common in the Chinese church context. Hence, designing a careful support experience for parents to process grief and recalibrate can be considered innovative for the Chinese Canadian church context. The recommendations mentioned in this book can improve ministry to parents through workshops with the intention to bring healing, empathy, peace, and spiritual health to suffering parents.

APPENDIX

Assess the Impact of the Silent Exodus Experience on the Parents

This is a time for the group leader to help build the affinity of the group with introductions, sharing their stories and assessing the range of needs in the group. One of the greatest pains, struggles, and feelings of confusion that can fill a parent's heart is experiencing a child abandoning the church and the faith. Some may be struggling to cope with the intense longing to see their youth come back to the faith; others may be deeply depressed or traumatized by their child leaving the faith, and this may be compounded by more than one child leaving the faith and family church.

1. Encourage the parents to be able to express their thoughts, emotions, and experiences associated with the Silent Exodus and be a source of encouragement and affirmation.

Parents need a safe place to talk about the impact of the Silent Exodus on their families and be able to express their feelings on the matter. This is a context in which the group leader can help parents understand that their feelings are normal and acknowledge their perspectives.

2. Determine where specific parents are in the aftermath of the Silent Exodus incident.

It can be helpful to encourage those parents further along in their journey after the Silent Exodus to share how various reactions and feelings progress or diminish over months or years. Parents can also be encouraged to share the range of emotional, spiritual, and social experiences they have gone through. The purpose is to empower parents and equip them for navigating their experience.

3. Review the emotional, spiritual, and social impact on parents ,and watch for maladaptive behaviors or reactions to the experience or suffering.

This would involve paying attention to parents' emotions, words, perceptions, and understandings and watching where they may be stuck or for behaviors that might inhibit the parents' coping, healing, and growing through the difficult experience. Normal behaviors include longing for the prodigal to return to faith or feeling sadness over apostasy. Maladaptive behaviors might be extended depression, embarrassment, shame, avoidance, withdrawal, anger, and anxiety.

4. After the workshop session(s), ensure that the parent(s) are solidly linked to their faith community and resources so they can continue to heal and rebuild.

The workshop experience is temporary, so it's key that the group is retooled and linked to good biblical, interdisciplinary, and faith community resources that can continue to nurture their restoration, healing, and reconciliation process. One of those resources is other parent mentors who have been through the Silent Exodus experience and can listen, share wisdom, and provide an attentive outlet for struggling parents.

5. At the end of the workshop session(s), these parents should be able to experience a healthier emotional, spiritual, and social perspective in their families and faith communities.

When the parents finish your workshop session(s), they should have the tools to help them be less stressed, more at peace, informed, equipped, and spiritually healthy than when they entered. You should move parents to form prayer groups, helping parents to find community and learn to trust sharing with others. It's important to connect with other parent mentors who have been through the process to find support in letting go and carrying the burden of having a prodigal and managing a struggle that has no current closure. It can be helpful to be surrounded with people in the journey who can remind the parent what their responsibility is with adult children and what God's is.

Workshop Outline

Promote the workshop training. A pastor, elder, fellowship leader, or parent mentor can guide the workshop. This would first require time for training group leaders so that they understand the big picture and gain some group leader skills to lead the sessions. Promotion of these groups can be done on the church website, in bulletins, and in announcements.

An outline of the workshop:

> **The context:** *your church*
> **The ideal group size:** *6–12 (smaller is fine)*
> **The recruitment:** *through website*
> **The training:** *train parent mentors, elders, fellowship leaders*
> **The budget:** *Very little budget is needed—just a quiet space. The church can choose to add light refreshments or provide additional resources.*

Future Projections of Workshops for Impacted Parents in the Chinese Church

This workshop contributes a practical method of loving and serving parents to live healthier spiritual lives. I think God takes an interest in innovation that can help future generations in quality of life that shows care, compassion, and "justice."[1] The workshop is based on my study on what is impacting parents. Parents' faith and family futures can be improved; patterns of experience can be changed. This workshop touches on an unmet need to provide a group experience where parents who have similar Silent Exodus experiences can share mutual prayer, encouragement, and hope. I want to contribute to the wellbeing of parents by encouraging parents to care for one another. Providing a supportive workshop experience can be a meaningful care ministry to help make life easier for some parents. It can provide parents an opportunity to voice the loneliness in their journey and to connect, share, and listen to others in similar situations. It creates a community where acts of compassion can be expressed, new understandings reached, and resources for self-care can be gained (dealing with stress, anxiety, sadness, and fear, moving forward emotionally, socially, psychologically, and spiritually). Parishioners will judge this ministry by its fruitfulness. Is it helping parents? What are the testimonies of the parents who have attended your workshop? When churches see that this ministry contributes to the overall health of parents in church and there is a benefit to the overall health of the church, such support group experiences could

---

1. Lanny. *Innovation Theology*, 7.

be recognized as contributing to an enhanced quality of family relationships and contributing to inspiring parents to fulfill their calling to finish well. Pastors are aware that they are often introduced to this kind of challenge in parents' lives during and after it has happened. Ministers want to introduce healing measures to people's brokenness. The conviction behind the workshop experience is it can empower leaders to affect the quality of family life in Chinese churches by removing silence, shame, and confusion. The ideas in your workshop can also be circulated in published form, helping to transform aspects of the Chinese cultural convention on the code of silence around the topic of the Silent Exodus and its impacts on the parents.

Bibliography

Alba, Richard, and Victor Nee. "Rethinking Assimilation theory for a New Era of Immigration." *International Migration Review* 31.4 (1997) 826–74.
Alibhai, Feisal. "The Process of Individuation—Understanding Late Adolescence." YouTube, December 20, 2021. Video. https://www.youtube.com/watch?v=v8G-50Ww924.
Anthony, Michael, and Michelle Anthony. *A Theology for Family Ministries*. Nashville, TN: B & H, 2011.
Archibald, Mandy M., et al. "Using Zoom Video Conferencing for Qualitative Data Collection: Perceptions and Experiences of Researchers and Participants." *International Journal of Qualitative Methods* 18 (2019)1–8.
Arnett, Jeffrey Jensen, and Lene Arnett Jensen. "A Congregation of One: Individualized Religious Beliefs Among Emerging Adults." *Journal of Adolescent Research* 17 (5) (2002) 451–67.
Arnett, Jeffrey Jensen. "Conceptions of the Transition to Adulthood Among Emerging Adults in American Ethnic Groups." *New Directions for Child and Adolescent Development* 100 (2003) 63–75.
———. "Emerging Adulthood: A Theory of Development from the Late Teens Through the Twenties." *American Psychologist* 55.5 (2000) 469–80.
———. "Introduction: Emerging Adulthood Theory and Research: Where We Are and Where We Should Go." In *The Oxford Handbook of Emerging Adulthood*, edited by Jeffrey J. Arnett, 1–7. New York: Oxford University Press, 2016.
Asian and Multicultural Ministries in Canada (AMMIC) Conference Proceedings 2011 and 2012. "Looking Back, Looking Forward: A Dialogue Among North American Asian Christians." Asian and Multicultural Ministries in Canada. Richmond, BC Canada, 2015.
Atkinson, Joseph C. *Biblical and Theological Foundations of the Family*. Washington, DC: Catholic University of American Press, 2014.
Augustine. *The City of God*. Translated by Marcus Dods. Peabody, MA: Hendrickson, 2009.
Baker, Warren, et al., eds. *The Complete Word Study Old Testament*. Word Study Series. Chattanooga, TN: AMG, 1994.
Balswick, Jack O., and Judith K. Balswick. *The Family: A Christian Perspective on the Contemporary Home*. 4th ed. Grand Rapids: Baker Academic, 2014.
Bandura, Albert. *Social Learning Theory*. New York: General Learning, 1971. https://www.decisionskills.com/uploads/5/1/6/0/5160560/bandura_sociallearningtheory.pdf.

Bibliography

Barna Group. *Gen Z: The Culture, Beliefs and Motivations Shaping the Next Generation*, Venture, CA: Barna Group, 2018.

Barry, Carolyn McNamara, et al. "Religiosity and Spirituality During Transition to Adulthood." *International Journal of Behavioral Development* 34.4 (2010) 311–24.

Barry, Carolyn McNamara, and Mona M. Abo-Zena. "The Experience of Meaning-Making: The Role of Religiousness and Spirituality in Emerging Adults Lives." In *The Oxford Handbook of Emerging Adulthood*, edited by Jeffrey J. Arnett, 464–80. New York: Oxford University Press, 2016.

Bedford, Olwen A. "Guilt and Shame in Chinese Culture: A Cross-Cultural Framework from the Perspective of Morality and Identity." *Journal for the Theory of Social Behavior* 33.2 (2003) 127–44.

Bengston, Vern L., et al. *Families and Faith: How Religion Is Passed Down Across Generations*. New York: Oxford University Press, 2013.

Beyer, Peter. "Religious Identity and Educational Attainment Among Recent Immigrants to Canada: Gender, Age, and 2nd Generation." *Journal of International Migration and Integration* 6.2 (2005) 177–99.

Boot, Joe. "A Theology of Family and Culture." *Ezra Institute*, September 7, 2021. https://www.ezrainstitute.ca/resource-library/lectures/a-theology-of-family-and-culture/.

Bremner, Wayne. "Henry G. Classen: City Missionary in Vancouver." *Mennonite Brethren Historical Commission*. Profiles of Mennonite Faith, 2010. http://www.mbhistory.org/profiles/classen.en.html.

Britton, Marcus L. "Race/Ethnicity, Attitudes, and Living with Parents During Young Adulthood." *Journal of Marriage and Family* 75 (2013) 995–1013.

Brown, Susan K., and Frank D. Bean. "Assimilation Models, Old and New: Explaining a Long-Term Process." *Migration Policy Institute*, October 1, 2006. https://www.migrationpolicy.org/article/assimilation-models-old-and-new-explaining-long-term-process.

Bulger, Tara, P. "Bridging the Gap: Effective Strategies to Engage Emerging Adults in the Church." DMin diss., Bethel University, 2024. https://spark.bethel.edu/etd/1057.

Burns, Jim. *Doing Life with Your Adult Children*. Grand Rapids: Zondervan, 2019.

Calvin, John. *Institutes of the Christian Religion*. Edited by John T. McNeill. Translated by Ford Lewis Battles. 2 vols. Philadelphia: Westminster, 1960.

Cavalcanti, H. B., and Debra Schleef, "The Case for Secular Assimilation?: The Latino Experience in Richmond, Virginia." *Journal for the Scientific Study of Religion* 44.4 (2005) 473–83.

Cha, Peter. "Finding a Church Home." In *Following Jesus Without Dishonoring Your Parents*, edited by Jeanette Yep et al., 145–58. Downers Grove, IL: InterVarsity, 1998.

Chan, Joyce, et al., eds. *Looking Back, Looking Forward: A Dialogue Among North American Asian Christians*. Richmond, BC: Asian and Multicultural Ministries in Canada, 2015.

Chen, Carolyn. *Getting Saved in American Immigration and Religious Experience*. Princeton, NJ: Princeton University Press, 2008.

Chen, Carolyn, and Jerry Z. Park. "Pathways of Religious Assimilation: Second-Generation Asian Americans' Religious Retention and Religiosity." *Journal for the Scientific Study of Religion* 58.3 (2019) 666–88.

ChenFeng, Jessica Lynn. "The Lived Experience of Chinese American Christians in Family Life." DPhil diss., Loma Linda University, 2014. https://www.proquest.com/docview/1566477611/fulltextPDF/AEF26852F2EF4E33PQ/6?accountid=35377.

Bibliography

ChenFeng, Jessica Lynn, et al. "Intergenerational Tension, Connectedness, and Separateness in the Lived Experience of First and Second Generational Chinese American Christians." *Contemporary Family Therapy* 37 (2015) 153–64.

Chow, Henry P. H. "Religion, Immigration, and Ethnicity: A Survey of Chinese Evangelical Churches in Canada." *International Journal of Humanities, Social Sciences and Education* 2.6 (2015) 99–107.

Chow, Paul K. "A Survey of Worldview Understanding of Immigrant Chinese Christian Adults in the US: A Case Study of a Cantonese Speaking Sunday School Class at the First Chinese Baptist Church of Walnut." DMin thesis, Biola University, 2013.

Chua, Amy. *Battle Hymn of the Tiger Mother*. New York: Penguin, 2011.

Chuang, D. J. "Silent Exodus: Asian American Christians Leaving Churches" (blog), September 11, 2021. https://djchuang.com/when-asian-american-christian-youth-go-to-college/.

Chung, Ruth H. Gim. "Gender, Ethnicity and Acculturation in Intergenerational Conflict of American College Students." *Cultural Diversity and Ethnic Minority Psychology* 7.4 (2001) 376–86.

Clydesdale, Tim, and Kathleen Garces-Foley. *The Twenty-Something Soul: Understanding the Religious and Secular Lives of American Young Adults*. New York: Oxford University Press, 2019.

Cozens, Simon. "Shame Cultures, Fear Cultures, and Guilt Cultures: Reviewing the Evidence." *The International Bulletin of Mission Research* 42.4 (2018) 362–66.

Davis, Jim, and Michael Graham. *The Great Dechurching: Who's Leaving, Why Are They Going, and What Will It Take to Bring Them Back?* Grand Rapids: Zondervan, 2023.

Dawson, Fabian. "Religious Connections Help New Immigrants with Social Integration." *New Canadian Media*, November 23, 2024. https://newcanadianmedia.ca/religious-connections-help-new-immigrants-with-social-integration/.

DeVries, Larry, et al., eds. *Asian Religions in British Columbia*. Vancouver, BC: UBC, 2010.

Dey, Ian. *Qualitative Data Analysis: A User-Friendly Guide for Social Scientists*. London: Routledge, 1993.

Di Giacomo, Michael. "Identity and Change: The Story of the Italian-Canadian Pentecostal Community." *Canadian Journal of Pentecostal-Charismatic Christianity* 2 (2011) 83–130.

Dubas, Judith Semon, and Anne C. Peterson. "Geographical Distance from Parents and Adjustment During Adolescence and Young Adulthood." *New Directions for Child Development* (1996) 3–19.

Dugdale, Richard. *The Jukes: A Study of Crime, Pauperism, Disease and Heredity*. New York: Putnam's Sons, 1891. https://readingroom.law.gsu.edu/cgi/viewcontent.cgi?article=1000&context=buckvbell.

Drovdahl, Robert, and Jeffrey Keuss. "Emerging Adults and Christian Faith of Emerging Adults in the Pacific Northwest." *Christian Education Journal: Research in Education Ministry* 17.1 (2020) 130–44.

Dyck, Drew. *Generation Ex-Christian: Why Young Adults Are Leaving the Faith and How to Bring Them Back*. Chicago IL: Moody, 2010.

Ebaugh, Helen Rose, and Janet Saltzman Chafetz. "Structural Adaptations in Immigrant Congregations." *Sociology of Religion* 61.2 (2000) 135–53.

Ediger, Gerald C. "Canadian Mennonite Brethren and Language Transition." In *Bridging Troubled Waters: Mennonite Brethren at Mid-Twentieth Century*, edited by Paul Toews, 247–59. Winnipeg: Kindred, 1995.

———. *Crossing the Divide: Language Transition Among Canadian Mennonite Brethren 1940–1970*. Winnipeg: Centre for Mennonite Brethren Studies, 2001.
Ellison, Christopher G., and Darren E. Sherkat. "Obedience and Autonomy: Religion and Parental Values Reconsidered." *Journal for the Scientific Study of Religion* 32.4 (1993) 313–29.
Erickson, Erick. *Identity: Youth and Crisis*. New York: Norton, 1968.
Fasick, Frank A. "On the Invention of Adolescence." *The Journal of Early Adolescence* 14.1 (1994) 6–23.
Fast, Walter E. "Apostle to the City: The Life and Ministry of Henry G. Classen." Prepared for the Culloden MB Church. 1987, 347–70.
Fingerman, Karen L., and Jenjira J. Yahirun. "Emerging Adulthood in the Context of Family." In *The Oxford Handbook of Emerging Adulthood*, edited by Jeffrey J. Arnett, 163–76. New York: Oxford University Press, 2016.
Fishburn, Janet. *Confronting the Idolatry of Family: A New Vision for the Household of God*. Nashville, TN: Abingdon, 1991.
Fong, Kenneth. *Pursuing the Pearl*. Valley Forge, PA: Judson, 2000.
Frank, Harry, et al. "American Responses to Five Categories of Shame in Chinese Culture: A Preliminary Cross-Cultural Construct Validation." *Personality and Individual Differences* 28.5 (2000) 887–96.
Freeks, Fazel Ebrihiam. "A Pastoral-Theological View on the Fundamental Role of the Father in Variance with Contemporary Family Structures and Its Adverse Challenges for Fatherhood." *Journal for Christian Scholarship* (2017) 177–92.
Friedman, Edwin H. *Generation to Generation: Family Process in Church and Synagogue*. New York: Guilford, 1985.
Garland, Diana R. *Family Ministry: A Comprehensive Guide*. 2nd ed. Downers Grove, IL: InterVarsity, 2012.
Gil-Or, Oren, et al. "The 'Facebook-Self': Characteristics and Psychological Predictors of False Self-Presentation on Facebook." *Frontiers in Psychology* 6.99 (2015) 1–10.
Gordon, Milton M. *Assimilation in American Life: The Role of Race, Religion, and National Origins*. New York: Oxford University Press, 1964.
———. "The Nature of Assimilation." In *Incorporating Diversity: Rethinking Assimilation in a Multicultural Age*, edited by Peter Kivisto, 95–110. London: Routledge, 2005.
Grudem, Wayne. *Systematic Theology*. Grand Rapids: Zondervan, 1994.
Guenther, Bruce L. "Ethnicity and Evangelical Protestants in Canada." In *Christianity and Ethnicity in Canada*, edited by Paul Bramadat and David Seljak, 365–414. Toronto: University of Toronto, 2008.
Gunnoe, Marjorie Lindner, and Kristin A. Moore. "Predictors of Religiosity Among Youth Aged 17–22: A Longitudinal Study of the National Survey of Children." *Journal for the Scientific Study of Religion* 41 (2002) 613–22.
Habecker, Hal. *What the Bible Says About Growing Older: The Exciting Potential of This Season of Life*. Plano, TX: Finishing Well, 2019.
Heimstra, Rick. *Competition for Character Education: What Emerging Adulthood Means for Christian Higher Education in Canada*. Toronto: Faith Today, 2018. https://p2c.com/wp-content/themes/avada-corp/files/Competition-for-Character-Education.pdf.
———. "Not Christian Anymore." *Faith Today*, January 8, 2020. https://www.faithtoday.ca/Magazines/2020-Jan-Feb/Not-Christian-anymore.

Bibliography

Herberg, Will. *Protestant, Catholic, Jew: An Essay in American Religious Sociology.* Chicago: University of Chicago Press, 1983.

Hill, Jonathan P. *Emerging Adulthood and Faith.* Grand Rapids: Calvin College Press, 2015.

———. "Faith and Understanding: Specifying the Impact of Higher Education on Religious Belief." *Journal for the Scientific Study of Religion* 50.3 (2011) 533–51.

Hirschman, Charles. "The Role of Religion in the Origins and Adaptation of Immigrant Groups in the United States." *International Migration Review* 38.3 (2004) 1206–33.

Ho, Koon-Ming, and Yuk-Shuen Wong. "Searching for Manhood: Reflecting Growing Up in a Chinese Way." *Asian Journal of Counseling* 13.2 (2006) 207–34.

Hoge, Dean R., et al. "Determinants of Church Involvement of Young Adults Who Grew Up in Presbyterian Churches." *Journal for the Scientific Study of Religion* 32.3 (1993) 242–55.

Houston, James M., and Michael Parker. *A Vision for the Aging Church.* Downers Grove, IL: InterVarsity, 2011.

Hui, To Wang. *A Hot Stream Beneath the Frozen Man.* Translated by Priscilla Yuk Kit Yung. Vancouver, BC: Eternal, 2009.

Hunsberger, Bruce E. "Apostasy: A Social Learning Perspective." *Review of Religious Research* 25.1 (1983) 21–38.

Jantz, Harold. "Created a Road We Are Still Upon." In *Canadian Mennonite Brethren: 1910–2010: Leaders Who Shaped Us,* edited by Harold Jantz, 109–20. Winnipeg, MB: Kindred, 2010.

Jantz, Harold, ed. *Canadian Mennonite Brethren: 1910–2010: Leaders Who Shaped Us.* Winnipeg, MB: Kindred, 2010.

Janzen, Rich, et al. "Integrating Immigrants into the Life of Canadian Urban Christian Congregations: Findings from a National Survey." *Review of Religious Research* 53.4 (2012) 441–70.

Jeffers, James S. *The Greco-Roman World of the New Testament Era: Exploring the Background of Early Christianity.* Downers Grove, IL: InterVarsity, 1999.

Johnson, Pat. "Pacific Spirit: Chinese Mennonites Reflect West Coast Mix." *Vancouver Courier,* May 16, 2014. https://www.vancourier.com/news/pacific-spirit-chinese-mennonites-reflect-west-coast-mix-1.1064330.

Jost, Lynn, and Connie Faber. *Family Matters: Discovering the Mennonite Brethren.* Winnipeg, MB: Kindred, 2002.

Kasinitz, Philip, et al. *Inheriting the City: The Children of Immigrants Come of Age.* New York: Russell Sage Foundation, 2008.

Kimmel, Tim. "A Theology of Family." *Family Matters,* May 25, 2014. https://foclonline.org/talk/theology-family.

King, Patricia M., and Karen Strohm Kitchener. "Cognitive Development in the Emerging Adult: The Emergence of Complex Cognitive Skills." *The Oxford Handbook of Emerging Adulthood,* edited by Jeffrey J. Arnett, 105–25. New York: Oxford University Press, 2016.

Kinnaman, David, and Gabe Lyons. *UnChristian: What a New Generation Really Thinks About Christianity . . . and Why it Matters.* Grand Rapids: Baker, 2007.

Kong, Justin. "Conservatism Persists in Chinese Canadian Churches." *New Canadian Media,* October 30, 2015. https://newcanadianmedia.ca/conservatism-in-chinese-canadian-churches/.

Kraybill, Donald B. *Concise Encyclopedia of Amish, Brethren, Hutterites, and Mennonites.* Baltimore, MD: Johns Hopkins University Press, 2010.

Bibliography

Kwak, Kyunghwa, and John W. Berry. "Generational Differences in Acculturation Among Asian Families in Canada: A Comparison of Vietnamese, Korean, and East-Indian Groups." *International Journal of Psychology* 36 (2001) 152–62.

Kwan, Joseph. "Building People Takes a Hundred Years?" *MB Chinese Herald* (2010) 11–12.

Kwan, Joseph, ed. "Study Conference Reports, From Cultural Isolation to Multicultural Diversity." *Mennonite Brethren Herald* 46.12 (2007) 16–17.

———. "We Are in the Same Family." *Mennonite Brethren Herald*, November 9, 2001. Translated by Ed Leung. https://mbherald.com/we-are-in-the-same-family/.

Lai, Warren. "Is There a Future for the Chinese Canadian Churches?: Challenges, Opportunities and Responses." In *Looking Back, Looking Forward: A Dialogue Among North American Asian Christians*, edited by Joyce Chan et al., 67–76. Richmond, BC: Asian and Multicultural Ministries in Canada, 2015.

Lanny, Vincent. *Innovation Theology: A Biblical Inquiry and Exploration*. Kindle. Eugene, OR: Wipf & Stock, 2017.

Law, Gail. "A Model for the American Ethnic Churches." In *A Winning Combination: ABC/OBC: Understanding the Cultural Tensions in Chinese Churches*, edited by Cecelia Yau, 131–41. Petaluma, CA: Chinese Christian Mission, 1986.

———. "A Model for the American Ethnic Chinese Churches." *Theology, News and Notes* (1984) 21–26.

Lee, Helen. "Silent Exodus: Can the East Asian Church in America Reverse the Flight of Its Next Generation?" *Christianity Today* 40.12 (1996) 50–53.

Lerner, Richard M., et al. "Human Development, Theories of." In Vol. 11 of *International Encyclopedia of the Social and Behavioral Sciences*, edited by James D. Wright, 276–78. 2nd ed. Amsterdam: Elseveier, 2015. https://www.researchgate.net/publication/304183737_Human_Development_Theories_of.

Leung, David H. MBCCA English ministry profile document "English Ministry at a Glance as of 2008/9." Abbotsford, BC: unpublished, 2009.

———. "Not I, but Christ." In *Leaders who Shaped Us; Canadian Mennonite Brethren: 1910–2010*, edited by Harold Jantz, 273–83. Winnipeg, MB: Kindred, 2010.

———. "Research Addresses 'Silent Exodus.'" *MB Herald*, November 20, 2015. https://mbherald.com/english-ministry-crisis-chinese-churches/.

Leung, Stephen. "Prologue." In *Looking Back, Looking Forward: A Dialogue Among North American Asian Christians*, edited by Joyce Chan et al., xi–xiv. Richmond, BC: Asian and Multicultural Ministries in Canada, 2015.

Li, Jin, et al. "The Organization of Chinese Shame Concepts." *Cognition and Emotion* 18.6 (2004) 767–97.

Lu, Yaxin, et al. "Chinese Immigrant Families and Christian Faith Community: A Qualitative Study." *Family and Consumer Sciences Research Journal* 41.2 (2012) 118–30.

Lui, Esther. "Cultural Tensions Within Chinese American Families and Churches." *Fullness in Christ Fellowship* (blog). https://behold.oc.org/?p=32212.

Mayer, Claude-Hélène, and Rian Viviers. "Experiences of Shame by Race and Culture: An Exploratory Study." *Journal of Psychology in Africa* 27.4 (2017) 362–66. https://www.tandfonline.com/doi/full/10.1080/14330237.2017.1347759.

Mazor, Aviva, and Robert D. Enright. "The Development of the Individuation Process from a Social-Cognitive Perspective." *Journal of Adolescence* 11.1 (1988) 29–47.

"MB Churches of Canada 2016 National MB Report," 20.

Bibliography

MBCCA English Pastors (2008). MBCCA English Chapter pastors meeting minutes, October 16, 2008, Loon Lake, BC, MBCCA English pastors retreat, October 15–16, 2008.

Mitchell, Barbara A. "Ethnocultural Reproduction and Attitudes Towards Cohabiting Relationships." *Canadian Review of Sociology* 38.4 (2001) 391–413.

Moore, Russell D. *The Storm-Tossed Family: How the Cross Reshapes the Home*. Nashville, TN: B & H, 2018.

Mullins, Mark. "The Life Cycle of Ethnic Churches in Sociological Perspective." *Japanese Journal of Religious Studies* 14.4 (1987) 321–34.

Mussen, Paul Henry. "Jean Piaget Piaget's Theory." In vol. 1 of *Carmichael's Manual of Child Psychology*, edited by Paul Henry Mussen, 703–32. New York: Wiley, 1970.

Myers, Scott M. "An Interactive Model of Religiosity Inheritance: The Importance of Family Context." *American Sociological Review* 61.5 (1996) 858–66.

Nelson, Larry J., et al. "If You Want Me to Treat You Like an Adult, Start Acting Like One!: Comparing the Criteria that Emerging Adults and Their Parents Have for Adulthood." *Journal of Family Psychology* 21.4 (2007) 665–74. http://dx.doi.org/10.1037/0893-3200.21.4.665.

O'Conner, Tim, et al. "The Relative Influence of Youth and Adult Experiences on Personal Spirituality and Church Involvement." *Journal for the Scientific Study of Religion* 41.4 (2002) 723–32. https://www.researchgate.net/publication/229642677_The_Relative_Influence_of_Youth_and_Adult_Experiences_on_Personal_Spirituality_and_Church_Involvement.

Ong, Andrew. "7 Issues in the Chinese American Church." *Reformed Margins* (blog), August 3, 2017. http://reformedmargins.com/7-issues-in-the-chinese-american-church/).

Osei-Owusu, Yaw. *The African Elephant: Why Millennials Are Leaving the African Diaspora Church*. Maryland, PA: n.p., 2020.

Packard Josh, and Todd W. Ferguson. "Being Done: Why People Leave the Church, But Not Their Faith." *Sociological Perspectives* 62.4 (2019) 499–517.

Pang, Wuji. *An Exploration of the Experience of Chinese Emerging Adults—University Students Transitioning to Mature Adulthood*. Master's thesis, University of Ottawa, November 4, 2011. https://ruor.uottawa.ca/bitstream/10393/20432/3/Pang_Wuji_2011_Thesis.pdf.

Paulsen, Jacob A., et al. "Generational Perspectives on Emerging Adulthood: A Focus on Narcissism." In *The Oxford Handbook of Emerging Adulthood*, edited by Jeffrey J. Arnett, 26–44. New York: Oxford University Press, 2016.

Penner, J., et al. *Hemorrhaging Faith: Why and When Canadian Young Adults are Leaving, Staying and Returning to the Church*. Ottawa, ON: Evangelical Fellowship of Canada, 2011. https://faithformationlearningexchange.net/uploads/5/2/4/6/5246709/hemorrhaging-faith-april-4-2013.pdf.

Perry, Bob. "That 'Nones' May Not Perish." *Christian Research Journal* 40.4 (2017). https://www.equip.org/article/that-nones-may-not-perish/?fbclid=IwAR1JmzC5qNKEqKOtbSukjrArp6hrcsjojYi88tsZC_Eo_XLTzCf_j8VD580.

Petts, Richard J. "Parental Religiosity and Youth Religiosity: Variations by Family Structure." *Sociology of Religion* (2014) 1–26.

Pew Research Center. "Young Adults Around the World Are Less Religious by Several Measures." *Pew Research*, June 13, 2018. https://www.pewforum.org/2018/06/13/young-adults-around-the-world-are-less-religious-by-several-measures/.

Bibliography

Pew Research Center: Religion and Public Life. "The Age Gap in Religion Around the World." 2018. https://www.pewresearch.org/religion/2018/06/13/the-age-gap-in-religion-around-the-world/#:~:text=Overall%2C%20adults%20ages%2018%20to,older%20adults%20on%20this%20question.

Plett, Cornelius F. "Hindrances to Growth." In *Krimmer Mennonite Brethren Church*, 331–35. Winnipeg, MB: Kindred, 1985.

Plotnik, Rod, and Sandra Mollenauer. *Introduction to Psychology*. New York: Newbery Award Records, 1986.

Pollard, Jeff, and Scott T. Brown. *A Theology of the Family*. Wake Forest, NC: The National Center for Family-Integrated Churches, 2014.

Port Moody Pacific Grace MB Church, 20th Anniversary Album: In Prayer we multiply 1995–2015. Port Moody, BC, n.p., 2015.

Qin, Desiree Baolian. "Our Child Doesn't Talk to Us Anymore: Alienation in Immigrant Chinese Families." *Anthropology and Education Quarterly* 37.2 (2006) 162–79.

Rah, Soong-Cha Rah. *The Next Evangelicalism: Freeing the Church from Western Cultural Captivity*. Downers Grover, IL: InterVarsity, 2009.

Redekop, John H. "Ethnicity as a Problem in Church Ministries." In *A People Apart*, 131–39. Winnipeg, MB: Kindred, 1987.

———. "Mennonites and Ethnicity: Some Religious and Historical Considerations." In *A People Apart*, 131–41. Winnipeg, MB: Kindred, 1987.

Reese, William L. "Secularism." In *Dictionary of Philosophy and Religion*, 693. Amherst, NY: Humanity, 1999.

Reimer, Willy. "Executive Director: Looking Back—Looking Forward." CCMBC Ministry Book, July 5, 2016. 4–6. https://issuu.com/mbherald/docs/ministry_booklet_-_issuu_-_smaller.

Roberts, Mark. "Could Family Be Part of a Calling?" *Theology of Work Project*. https://www.theologyofwork.org/resources/could-family-be-part-of-a-calling.

Roozen, David A. "Church Dropouts: Changing Patterns of Disengagement and Re-entry." *Review of Religious Research* 21.4 (1980) 427–50.

Santrock, John W. *Adolescence*. Dubuque, IA: William C. Brown, 1987.

Sawler, David. *Goodbye Generation: A Conversation About Why Youth and Young Adults Leave the Church*. Winnipeg, MB: Ponder, 2008.

Schoen, Robert, et al. "Family Transitions in Young Adulthood." *Demography* 44.4 (2007) 807–20.

Schulz, Richard, and Robert B. Ewen. *Adult Development and Aging: Myths and Emerging Realities*. New York: MacMillan, 1988.

Seiffge-Krenke, Inge. "Leaving Home: Antecedents, Consequences, and Cultural Patterns." In *The Oxford Handbook of Emerging Adulthood*, edited by Jeffrey J. Arnett, 179–89. New York: Oxford University Press, 2016.

Shin, Benjamin C., and Sheryl Takagi Silzer. *Tapestry of Grace: Untangling the Cultural Complexities in Asian American Life and Ministry*. Eugene, OR: Wipf & Stock, 2016.

Silverman, David. "Interpreting Qualitative Data: Methods for Analyzing Talk, Text and Interaction." London: SAGE, 1993. https://www.researchgate.net/publication/31718316_Interpreting_Qualitative_Data_Methods_for_Analyzing_Talk_Text_and_Interaction_D_Silverman.

Smith, Christian, and Amy Adamczyk. *Handing Down the Faith: How Parents Pass their Religion on to the Next Generation*. New York: Oxford University Press, 2021.

Bibliography

Smith, Christian, and Patricia Snell. *Souls in Transition: The Religious and Spiritual Lives of Emerging Adults*. New York: Oxford University Press, 2009.

Sohn, Ezra. "Attitudes of Asian American Christians Towards the Ethnic Churches They Left." DMin diss., Alliance Theological Seminary, 2017.

"Southhill Mennonite Brethren Church (Vancouver, British Columbia, Canada)." https://www.gameo.org/index.php?title=South_Hill_Mennonite_Brethren_Church_(Vancouver,_British_Columbia,_Canada).

Stark, Rodney. *What Americans Really Believe*. Waco, TX: Baylor University Press, 2008.

Statistics Canada. "Estimates of the Components of Interprovincial Migration, by Age and Gender, Annual." https://www150.statcan.gc.ca/t1/tbl1/en/tv.action?pid=1710001501.

———. "A Portrait of Couples in Mixed Unions by Place of Birth and Visible Minority Group." https://www150.statcan.gc.ca/n1/pub/11-008-x/2010001/article/11143-eng.htm.

Stecker, Chuck. *Men of Honor Women of Virtue: The Power of Rites of Passage into Godly Adulthood*. Denver, CO: Seismic, 2015.

Stokes, Kenneth. "Faith Development in the Adult Life Cycle." *Journal of Religious Gerontology* 7 (1990) 167–84.

Study Conference Reports. "From Cultural Isolation to Multicultural Diversity." *Mennonite Brethren Herald* 46.12 (2007) 16–17.

Syed, Moin. "Emerging Adulthood: Developmental Stage, Theory or Nonsense." *The Oxford Handbook of Emerging Adulthood*, edited by Jeffrey J. Arnett, 11–25. New York: Oxford University Press, 2016.

Syed, Moin, and Lauren L. Mitchell. "How Race and Ethnicity Shape Emerging Adulthood." In *The Oxford Book of Emerging Adulthood*, edited by Jeffrey J. Arnett, 87–101. New York: Oxford University Press, 2016.

Taber-Thomas, Bradley, and Koraly Perez-Edgar. "Emerging Adulthood Brain Development." In *The Oxford Handbook of Emerging Adulthood*, edited by Jeffrey J. Arnett, 126–41. New York, Oxford University Press, 2016.

Ten Elshof, Gregg A. *Confucius for Christians: What an Ancient Chinese Worldview Can Teach Us About Life in Christ*. Grand Rapids: Eerdmans, 2015.

Thatcher, Adrian. *Theologies and Families*. Oxford: Blackwell, 2007.

Thiessen, Richard D. "Faithwerks (Vancouver, British Columbia Canada)." *Global Anabaptist Mennonite Encyclopedia Online*, October 2017. https://gameo.org/index.php?title=Faithwerks_(Vancouver,_British_Columbia,_Canada)&oldid=155557.

Todd, Douglas. "Ethnic Churches Flourishing: But Some Vancouver Christians Worry the Various Ethnic Groups Still Tend to Stick to Themselves Instead of Mingling with Others." *Vancouver Sun*, February 5, 2011. https://vancouversun.com/news/staff-blogs/ethnic-churches-flourishing.

———. "Vancouver's 100,000 Chinese Christians 'Fraught' Over Gay Debate." *Vancouver Sun*, November 1, 2016. https://vancouversun.com/life/vancouvers-100000-chinese-christians-fraught-over-gays.

Todd, Matthew R. S. "The Close of a Chapter: Celebrating the Ministry of Enoch Wong, Senior Servant of God." *Mennonite Brethren Herald* (2005), 26–27.

———. "The Development and Transition of English Ministry in the Chinese Canadian Church." *MB Chinese Herald* (2009), 16–18.

———. *Developing a Transformational English Ministry in Chinese Churches*. Victoria, BC: Friesen, 2016.

———. "Empowering Chinese Canadian Parents in Ethno-Religious Communities Who Have Been Impacted by Generational Assimilation." PhD diss., Bakke Graduate University, 2023.

———. *English Ministry Crisis in Chinese Canadian Churches*. Eugene, OR: Wipf & Stock, 2015.

———. "The Impact of Generational Assimilation upon Chinese Canadian Mennonite Brethren Immigrant Churches." *Anabaptist Witness* 10.2 (2023) 65–88.

———. "Port Moody Church Celebrates and Looks Back." *Mennonite Brethren Herald*, July 1, 2005. https://mbherald.com/port-moody-church-celebrates-and-looks-back/.

Toews, John A. "Facing Cultural Change." *A History of the Mennonite Brethren Church*, edited by A. J. Klassen. Hillsboro, KS: Mennonite Brethren, 1975.

Tram, Charlie. "Honor Your Parents: A Command for Adults." *Journal of the Evangelical Theological Society* 60.2 (2017) 247–63.

Tsai-Chae, A. H., and D. K. Nagata. "Asian Values and Perceptions of Intergenerational Family Conflict Among Asian American Students." *Cultural Diversity and Ethnic Minority Psychology* 14.3 (2008) 205–14.

Tse, Justin K. H. "Making a Cantonese-Christian Family: Quotidian Habits of Language and Background in a Transnational Hong-Konger Church." *Population, Space and Place* (2011) 756–68.

———. "Religious Politics in Pacific Space: Grounding Cantonese Protestant Theologies in Secular Civil Societies." PhD diss., University of British Columbia, December 5, 2013.

Tseng, Timothy. "Intergenerational Mission: The Tipping Point of Asian North American Churches." In *Looking Back, Looking Forward: A Dialogue Among North American Asian Christians*, edited by Joyce Chan et al., 49–64. Richmond, BC: Asian and Multicultural Ministries in Canada, 2015.

Uecker, Jeremy E., et al. "Family Formation and Returning to Institutional Religion by Young Adults." *Journal for the Scientific Study of Religion* 55.2 (2016). https://www.researchgate.net/publication/306054604_Family_Formation_and_Returning_to_Institutional_Religion_in_Young_Adulthood.

Uecker, Jeremy E., et al. "Losing My Religion: The Social Sources of Religious Decline in Early Adulthood." *Social Forces* 85.4 (2007) 1667–92.

Van der Bracht, K., et al. "God Bless Our Children?: The Role of Generation, Discrimination and Religious Context for Migrants in Europe." *International Migration* 51.3 (2013) 23–37.

Van Paassen, Kevin. "Canada Marching from Religion to Secularization." *The Globe and Mail*, December 15, 2017. https://www.theglobeandmail.com/news/national/canada-marching-from-religion-to-secularization/article1320108/.

Vincent, Lanny. *Innovation Theology: A Biblical Inquiry and Exploration*. Kindle ed. Eugene, OR: Wipf & Stock, 2017.

Wang, Fei. "The Lived Experiences of Canadian-Born and Foreign-Born Chinese Canadian Post-Secondary Students in Northern Ontario." *Journal of International Students* 6.2 (2016) 451–77.

Wang, Peter Wei-Kung. "Moving Beyond the Tension and Conflict Between First and Second Generation Within the Chinese Immigrant Church in America." DMin diss., Gordon-Conwell Theological Seminary, 2010.

Bibliography

Wenkel, David H. "Jesus at Age 30: Further Evidence for Luke's Portrait of a Priestly Jesus?" *Biblical Theology Bulletin: Journal of Bible and Culture* 44.4 (2014) 195–201. https://static1.squarespace.com/static/533ad320e4b0061876d9dd15/t/561beacbe4b042ca cd2ecb25/1444670155245/Jesus+at+Age+Thirty+-+BTB+-+2014+-++Wenkel.pdf.

Whitehead, Evelyn Eaton, and James D. Whitehead. *Christian Life Patterns: The Psychological Challenges and Religious Invitations of Adult Life*. New York: Crossroad, 2003.

Williams, J. Allen Jr., and Susan T. Ortega. "Dimensions of Ethnic Assimilation: An Empirical Appraisal of Gordon's Typology." *Social Science Quarterly* 71.4 (1990) 697–710.

Williams, William C. "Family Life and Relations." In *Baker Theological Dictionary of the Bible*, edited by Walter A. Elwell, 243–45. Grand Rapids: Baker, 1996.

Willoughby, Brian J., and Jason S. Carroll. "On the Horizon: Marriage Timing, Beliefs, and Consequences in Emerging Adults." In *The Oxford Handbook of Emerging Adulthood*, edited by Jeffrey J. Arnett, 280–95. New York: Oxford University Press, 2016.

Wilson, Bryan. "Secularization and its Discontents." In *Religion in Sociological Perspective*, edited by Bryan Wilson, 148–79. New York: Oxford University Press, 1989.

Winship, Albert Edward. *Jukes-Edwards: A Study in Education and Heredity (1900)*. Harrisburg, PA: R. L. Myers, 2010.

Wong, Enoch Kin On. "How Am I Going to Grow Up?: An Exploration of Congregational Transition Among Second-Generation Chinese Canadian Evangelicals and Servant-Leadership." PhD diss., Gonzaga University, 2015. https://search.proquest.com/docview/1681561062

Wong, Enoch Kin On, et al. "Listening to Their Voices: An Exploration of Faith Journeys of Canadian-Born Chinese Christians." *CCCOWE Canada*, July 11, 2018.

Wong, Grace. "Ripples: Eight Decades of God's Grace." Unpublished manuscript, 2005.

Wong, Joseph. "Bridging the Gap." *About Face* (1990) 1–2.

Wright, Christopher J. H. *God's People in God's Land: Family, Land and Property in the Old Testament*. Grand Rapids: Eerdmans, 2003.

Wuji, Paul. "An Exploration of the Experience of Chinese Emerging Adults— University Students Transitioning to Mature Adulthood." Master's thesis, University of Ottawa, 2011, 1–142. https://pdfs.semanticscholar.org/1cb0/f0b4af621374d68637c8f3b99fda66b5881f.pdf.

Xu, Xiao. "Immigrants Providing a Boost to Declining Church Attendance in Canada." *The Globe and Mail*, December 22, 2017. https://www.theglobeandmail.com/news/british-columbia/immigrants-providing-a-boost-to-declining-church-attendance-in-canada/article37423409/.

Yu, Li. "Christianity as a Chinese Belief." *Asian Religions in British Columbia*, edited by Larry DeVries et al., 233–48. Vancouver, BC: University of British Columbia, 2010.

Zhang, Jing. "Understanding the Concept of Shame in the Chinese Culture." *NYS Child Welfare/Child Protective Services Training Institute* 4, October 29, 2015. https://digitalcommons.buffalostate.edu/cgi/viewcontent.cgi?article=1006&context=cwcps triaininginstitute.

Index

Note: Page numbers in *italics* indicate figures, and page numbers in **bold** indicate tables in the text, and references following "n" refer notes.

Abo-Zena, Mona M., 88n23
Abraham, 57, 59, 80
acculturation, 12–14, 21, 29, 34–35
    Fong on, 95
    sociological impact, 89–96
Adamczyk, Amy, 11
adaptability, 8
adultescence, 98
adulthood, emerging
    age range, 108
    Arnett's model, 109–10
    cognitive development, 110–12
    developmental psychology, 107–10
    friendships, 89, 90–91, 94–95
    generational differences, 112
    leaving home (*See* faith abandonment, youth)
    as life stage, 84–85
    marriages and, 90–96, 96n95
    mobility, 85–88
    secularization, 5, 98–106
    transition to, 61–62, 68–70, 86
adulthood theory, emerging, 19, 21–22, 28–30, 86, 141
age of accountability, 68–69
Arnett, Jeffrey Jensen, 67–68, 97n99, 104, 109–10
Asian parents, 32–33
assimilation, 94, 115, 133
    theory, 18, 19, 30–31, 141
    trajectories, 29, 138
    See also generational assimilation
Atkinson, Joseph C., 56, 59, 63
authoritative parenting, 9

Balswick, Jack O., 13n12, 55n3–4, 66, 75n132, 110
Balswick, Judith K., 13n12, 55n3–4, 66, 75n132, 110
Barry, Carolyn McNamara, 88n23
Belmont Report, 119
Bethel Chinese MB Church, 44
Bible, 3, 4, 7, 57, 59, 80–82
    youth departure examples, 73–76
    See also Scripture(s)
bicultural churches, 114–15
brain imaging of young adults, 110–11.
    See also cognitive development
Bremner, Wayne, 41
Burnaby Pacific Grace, 44, 45
Burns, Jim, 68
Burr, Aaron, Jr., 7

Calvin, John, 57, 58
Canadian-Born Chinese (CBC), 9, 12–14, 49–50, 104–6. *See also* Silent Exodus
Canadian Chinese churches. *See* Chinese church(es)
Cantonese congregations, 18, 18n32, 37–38, 41
care/caring, 58, 60–61, 138, 139, *143*, 160

175

Index

career options. *See* job and career options
caring ministry, 127, 133, *135–136*, 138, 160
Cavalcanti, H. B., 35, 67
Chan, David, 45
Chan, Yiu Tong, 50
Chang, Isaac, 39–40
Chen, Carolyn, 14n16, 15, 99, 102, 103
ChenFeng, Jessica Lynn, 14n15, 54n1
Chia, Helen, 45
Chia, Leo, 45, 47, 47n84
childbearing, 56, 63–64
Chinese Christians, 17–18, 54n1. *See also* dechurching; parents
Chinese church(es), 11, 16–17, 18, 54n1
    cultural values and, 14n15
    history, 34, 35–37
    Mennonite Brethren (*See* Mennonite Brethren Chinese churches)
    recommendations to, 138–39
    theological and cultural understanding, 14n15
Chinese culture, 17–18, 33
Chinese immigrants/immigration, 11–19, 32–37
Chow, Henry P. H., 16
Chow, Paul K., 17
Christ, 8–9
    faith in, 4, 59
    family relationships, 59–63
    prodigal son, 68
Chu, Eddie, 41–42
Chua, Amy, 96n95
Classen, Henry G., 40–42, 50
Classen, Sara, 40–42, 50
cognitive development, 68, 110–12
cohabitation, 64, 91–93, 98
Confucian values, 17–18, 33
cultural myths, 24, 25–31

Davis, Jim, 11
dechurching, 1, 24
    impact on parents, 10–22, 70–72
    parenting styles and, 13
    reasons, 13–14, 63–68
    widespread issue, 11, 25
    See also faith abandonment, youth; research on Silent Exodus impact

developmental psychology, 107–10
developmental theory, 18–19, 28–30, 71
DGR (Dutch, German, Russian) ethnicity, 39–40
Dubas, Judith Semon, 88
Dyck, David, 38–39n31
Dyck, Drew, 65, 93

economic factors, 85–89
education, 86, 88
    secularism and, 101–2, 104–5
Edwards, Jonathan, 6–7
Edwards, Timothy, 6
egalitarianism, 64
emerging adulthood. *See* adulthood, emerging
employment factors. *See* job and career options
empowerment, 64
English ministries, 44–45, 48–50, 107–12
Enright, Robert D., 66n82
Erickson, Erick, 68, 107–8
ethnic churches, 15n18, 29, 35–36. *See also* Chinese church(es)
evil, 7, 69

faith, 1–2
    community, 4
    transmission, 4–5, 9, 23–24, 30
    and parenting, 3–8
    See also dechurching; faith abandonment, youth
faith abandonment, youth, 63–68
    biblical examples, 72–80
    economic factors, 85–89
    identity differentiation, 66–68, 83
    individualism, 97–98
    push-and-pull factors, 85
    secularism/secularization, 98–106
    social factors, 89–96
    See also dechurching; research on Silent Exodus impact
family, 138
    family tree studies 6–7
    of God, 55, 80–82
    theological understanding, 55–63, 134–35
feeling in-between, 110

Index

Ferguson, Todd W., 97
Fong, Kenneth, 95, 96n95, 103n150
forgiveness, 8, 24
friendships, 7, 89, 90–91, 94–95

gardening metaphor, 2–3
Garland, Diana R., 14n14, 59, 60
generational assimilation, 12, 21, 22, 28
    research findings, 133–34
Generation Y, 94
geographic mobility. *See* mobility
God, 1–9, 27, 61, 74
    covenant with Abraham, 57
    and family, 6, 55–58, 80–82
    godly offspring, 6, 26
godly parents, 6, 25–26
Gordon, Milton, 19
grace
    in parenting, 8, 58
    honor and shame culture
        destigmatizing, 139–40
Graham, Michael, 11
Guenther, Bruce L., 39

Hemorrhaging Faith (Penner), 64, 101n29, 104
Herberg, Will, 19, 29, 35–36, 99
Hill, Jonathan P., 98, 105–6
Hirschman, Charles, 15n18, 36
Hoge, Dean R., 88, 88n24, 101–2, 102nn137–38
home environment, 9
honor and shame culture, 13n8, 18, 33, 129, 138, 139–41, 157
honoring parents, 18, 33, 60–62, 69, 81
Hui, To Wang, 45–46n79

identity, 1, 33, 36, 89, 95
    differentiation, 66–68, 83
    exploration, 109
    religious, 102–3
individualism, 33, 97–98, 113
individuation, 68, 83
instability, 109
intentional parenting, 10
intermarriage, 4, 78–79, 94n79, 95, 96. *See also* marriages

Jefferson, Thomas, 7
Jensen, Lene Arnett, 97n99
job and career options, 87–88
Johnson, Pat, 46
Jukes, Max, 6

Kan, Keynes, 43, 45
Kimmel, Tim, 58
Kinnaman, David, 101n130
Kohlberg, Lawrence, 107
Kwan, Joseph, 37, 44, 46, 48

Lai, Warren, 50
Leung, Alice, 47n84
Leung, David H., 51
Levinson, Daniel, 68, 108
Lewis, C. S., 3
Li, Great, 41
Li, Paul, 41
life cycle theory, 18–19, 28, 30–31
life stage needs, 85–89
love in parenting, 7
Lu, Yaxin, 35
Lyons, Gabe, 101n130

Mandarin congregations, 18, 18n32, 38, 42, 45, 47, 47n84, 48
Manitoba Conference, 46
marriages, 9, 29, 33, 35, 77
    arranged, 79
    Christian view, 4, 9, 56
    emerging adults and, 90–96, 96n95
    See also intermarriage
Mazor, Aviva, 66n82
Mennonite Brethren Chinese churches, 18
    branches, 44–47
    challenges, 47–51
    history, 37–44
    and Silent Exodus, 51–52
    structure, 37–38
    vision statement, 49
Mennonite Brethren Chinese Churches Association (MBCCA), 34, 115
midlife parents, 70–72
Mitchell, Barbara A., 92, 97, 99
Mitchell, Lauren L., 86–87, 97
mobility, 85–88

Index

Moore, Russell D., 74–75
morality, 5, 7–8
motivational issues, 8
Mullins, Mark, 40, 94, 94n79, 95
multicultural church model, 48

Neufeld, Sue, 41
New Testament, 7, 59, 80–82
Nishi, Mike, 48

obedience, 17, 17n27, 33, 57
Old Testament, 7, 57, 59, 80–82

Pacific Grace Mandarin Church, 45
Pacific Grace Mennonite Brethren Church (PGMBC), 42–47
Pacific Grace Mission Chapel, 41–42
Packard, Josh, 97
parenting
    authoritative, 9
    boundaries, 7–8
    faithful, 7–8
    grace-based, 8, 58
    intentional, 10
    religious commitment, 30
    training, 4–5
parents
    Asian, 32–33
    as caretakers, 58
    committment to faith, 9
    godly, 6, 25–26
    home environment, 9
    honoring, 60–62, 69, 81
    midlife, 70–72
    recommendations for impacted, 139–44
    self-reporting on Silent Exodus, 117, 125–26, **126**, 128–30
    support to, 132–45
    workshops, 138, 141, 156–61
    See also adulthood, emerging theory; dechurching; faith abandonment; youth
parents, recommendations for, 135–44
    focus groups, 139–41
    interventions, strategies, and solutions, **135–37**, *143*

literature and, 141–42
honor and shame culture (*See* honor and shame culture)
Park, Jerry Z., 15, 99, 102, 103
Paul, 4, 74, 55, 59, 61, 69–70
Penner, James, 103–4
Hemorrhaging Faith, 64, 101n29, 104
Peters, George, 39
Peterson, Anne C., 88
Pew Research Center on Religion and Public Life, 102–3
Poon, David, 44
Port Moody Pacific Grace Chinese Church, 44–45, 49
prayers, 132, 137, 139
Protestant, Catholic, Jew (Herberg), 99
Protestants, 43–44, 47, 99, 102, 103. *See also* Chinese church(es)
Pursuing the Pearl (Fong), 96n95

Rah, Soong-Cha Rah, 96n95
reflective thinking, 111
religious commitment, 19, 22, 28, 30, 86, 141–42
religious engagement, 21
religious identity, 102–3
research on Silent Exodus impact, 114–19
    analysis, 119–20
    design, 115, **116**
    ethics, 119
    findings, **120–21**
    focus groups, **127**, 127–28
    parental reactions reports, 117, 121, **122–24**, 125, 128–30
    participants, 116–17
    questionnaire, 118, 127, **127**
respect, 119
    faithful parenting, 7
    to parents, 18, 33, 60–62, 69, 81
Roozen, David A., 99

salvation, 2, 4, 24, 56, 58n33
Schleef, Debra, 35, 67
Scripture(s), 4, 137, 139
    children, 72–80, 83
    families, 26–27, 57–58
    transitioning to adulthood, 63, 68–70

Index

Scripture Union Canada, 43
secularism/secularization, 5, 98–106
    education and, 101–2, 104–5
self-focus model, 109–10
shame. *See* honor and shame culture
Silent Exodus, 12, 22, 50–52
    impact, 33–34 (*See also* research on Silent Exodus impact)
    and intermarriage, 4, 78–79, 94n79, 95, 96
    and midlife parents, 70–72
    and mobility, 85–88
    recommendations for parents, 135–44
    and secularism, 106
    See also dechurching; faith abandonment, youth
Smith, Christian, 66–67, 85–86, 87, 89–96, 102–6
    faith transmission, 11
Snell, Patricia, 66–67, 85–86, 87, 89–94, 96, 102–6
social learning theory, 18, 19, 20–21, 28–29, 30–31, 141
South Hill MB Church, 48
Stark, Rodney, 93
Statistics Canada, 86, 96n95
Stecker, Chuck, 64–65, 104n153
Stoddard, Esther, 6
Suen, Nick, 48
Sunday school, 41
Syed, Moin, 68, 86–87, 97

thankfulness, 8
Thatcher, Adrian, 55–56
theology on
    children 57–58, 80–82
    Chinese church, 14n15
    family 55–63, 134–35
    parents' and Silent Exodus, 70–72, 76–80
    youth leaving faith, 72–76
Tiananmen Square massacre, 43
Todd, Matthew R. S., xin4, 53
Tolkien, J. R. R., 72
Tse, Justin K. H., 17, 99–100
Tseng, Timothy, 51

Uecker, Jeremy E., 63–64, 94, 96, 105

Vancouver Chinese MB Church, 49
Voth, Heinrich, 38–39n31

Whitehead, Evelyn Eaton, 71, 88–89
Whitehead, James D., 71, 88–89
Williams, William C., 77
Wilson, Bryan, 98
Winship, A. E., 6–7
wisdom, 7, 81
Wong, Enoch, 42–43, 45, 50
Wong, Grace, 42, 43, 50
Wong, Rose, 41
workshops, 138, 141, 156–61
Wright, Christopher J. H., 73n122

Xu, Xiao, 16–17

Yiu, Valerie, 43
Yu, Li, 36–37, 38, 43–44

Zhuang, Miller, 43

www.ingramcontent.com/pod-product-compliance
Lightning Source LLC
Chambersburg PA
CBHW062044220426
43662CB00010B/1649